Expert Systems
PRINCIPLES and PRACTICE

Expert Systems
PRINCIPLES and PRACTICE

A BONNET
J-P HATON
J-M TRUONG-NGOC

Translated by
JACK HOWLETT

PRENTICE HALL
New York • London • Toronto • Sydney • Tokyo

The original edition of this work was published
in France by InterEditions, Paris,
under the title
Systèmes-Experts: Vers la maîtrise technique,
© 1986 by InterEditions.

First published 1988 by
Prentice Hall International (UK) Ltd,
66 Wood Lane End, Hemel Hempstead,
Hertfordshire, HP2 4RG
A division of
Simon & Schuster International Group

Printed and bound in Great Britain by
A. Wheaton & Co. Ltd, Exeter

British Library Cataloguing in Publication Data

Bonnet, Alain
    Expert systems: principles and practice.
    1. Expert systems (Computer science)
    I. Title   II. Haton, Jean-Paul
    III. Truong-Ngoc, Jean-Michel   IV. Systèmes
    experts. *English*
    006.3'3   QA76.76.E95
    ISBN 0-13-295635-7

1 2 3 4 5   92 91 90 89 88

ISBN 0-13-295635-7

Contents

v

Acknowledgements

It has been the authors' aim throughout this book to illustrate their proposals with real-life examples drawn from their daily experience with expert systems. They would not have been able to achieve this aim without the full understanding of a number of their clients and colleauges who have been more than willing for their achievements to be presented here – something rather uncommon in a field in which secrecy is often the rule. Thanks are due first, therefore, to:

– MM. Garrido and Guerin, of the European Space Agency,
– Mme Recoque, Compagnie des Machines Bull,
– M. de Lapparent, French Atomic Energy Commission,
– Mme Guérard, French telecommunication authority,
– MM. Baudot and Edelman, Dumez-Bâtiment construction company,
– MM. Coleno, Le Renard and Millier, French national institute for research in agronomy,
– MM. Bordenave, Plagne and Richard, Paris urban transport authority.

The book has benefitted equally from the contributions of two knowledge engineers with the Cognitch company:

– Christophe Assemat, on hybrid architectures for expert systems,
– Pierre Vesoul, on applications in space research and technology.

The book as a whole expresses the experience built up by the authors and their colleagues in Cognitech and owes much to the time and effort made available for this presentation.
On particular points thanks are due to:

– Bernard Burtschy, of the Ecole Nationale Supérieure des Télécommunications, who read and contributed to the chapter on validation of expert systems,
– Michel Gondran, who provided information concerning developments in Electricité de France,
– Jean Saulais, for information concerning applications made by Avions Marcel Dassault.

And, finally, there are thanks to the following for their critical review of the contents and their verbal and written comments:

– Michel Clerget, Thierry Marois and Liliane Stéhelin, of Cognitech,
– Marie-Christine Haton, of the University of Nancy,
– Jean-Claude Rault, of the Agence de l'Informatique.

INTRODUCTION

Aims and structure of the book

EXPERT SYSTEMS FOR THE ENTERPRISE

This book aims to serve the needs of one of the major role-players in the development of expert systems: the *enterprise* – a term we shall use to mean some large, active and important body such as a commercial or industrial company, a public utility or a government laboratory or other institution. Our motivation for setting such an aim has come from our experience in activities related to artificial intelligence (AI) and expert systems, especially those concerned with weaving the use of these techniques into the fabric of European industry.

There is no paradox in saying that whilst many expert systems are developed *in* an enterprise, these are for the most part not developed *by* that enterprise; this is only another way of saying that too often a system is produced simply as an intellectual exercise – or perhaps a status symbol – by a group of enlightened individuals, often working unknown to or even in opposition to their management. Because of this, the expert system has taken on something of the nature of a work of art, bringing to its creator the admiration of a select group of initiates and then relegated to the museum to be revered along with those classics Dendral, Prospector and Mycin.

Faced with the need to make some decision on such art-objects, the enterprise tends to oscillate between flat rejection – accompanied by comments on the seriousness with which such decisions have to be made, the apparent immaturity of AI, the need to postpone any decision ('let's wait and see what the Japanese do' was the agreed recent strategy of a large French national enterprise) – and giving limited support as a sort of sporting gesture or enlightened patronage. There are few enterprises that, having recognized the expert system as a major tool for their future competitiveness, lay down a firm strategy, allocate adequate resources and set up a proper organization for development. Pioneers in this way in France are CIMSA (Compagnie Informatique Militaire, Spatiale et Aéronautique), Commissariat à l'Energie Atomique, CGE, (Compag-

1

nie Générale d'Electricité) Compagnie Bancaire, Dumez, Elf-Aquitaine, Electronique Serge Dassaut, Institut National de la Recherche Agronomique and Schlumberger; but none of these can compare in resources with the 300 AI specialists recruited by the American Boeing company. Much of this temporizing is due to ignorance of the potential of this new technology and of the answers to: What should we do? Why should we do it? How should we do it? In the absence of satisfactory answers, many prefer, quite reasonably, to abstain. This book has been written to help understand the importance of expert systems as industrial products or aids to industrial production, and to show how they can be produced industrially.

Thus the book is not addressed primarily to builders of expert systems – there is already a plentiful supply of literature here; in contrast, it sets out to guide those who, whilst not having to construct such systems, have to formulate and manage an enterprise's policy for expert systems. This entails identifying needs, specifying the problems to be solved and what will be regarded as a solution, allocating resources, choosing suppliers, recruiting and training staff, planning implementations, evaluating results and, above all, creating a climate in which this work can flourish. The artist-creator usually has little taste for, even disdains, such tasks; but an organization that has any regard for its productivity and for the quality of its products neglects them at its peril. We take the viewpoint, therefore, of an organization that both produces and uses expert systems, not of the individual writer or implementer. Accordingly, we do not restrict ourselves to the purely technical aspects of the subject but emphasize the strategic, tactical and logistic considerations. It seems to us that 'getting something done' is a more difficult matter, and less well documented, than 'doing'.

The reader will notice that we speak of implementation, operation, penetration and even acclimatization of expert systems in and to their intended environment, rather than of development, construction and production. This characterizes our view of expert systems as essential subsystems embedded in more general systems whose performance they enhance but without which they are of no interest. Strictly, one should speak of *expert subsystems* that interact with clearly specified main systems, for example for production, information retrieval or processing, and decision making. An essential condition for the success of the expert subsystem is that the main system is totally understood and that possible interactions between the two are taken into account at an early stage in the project.

STRUCTURE OF THE BOOK

Putting an expert system into operation in an enterprise requires the coordinated actions of a large number of participants in a process that moves along the same lines whatever the context. At each stage in this process every participant has a clear objective, plays a defined role and uses methods that are precisely specified. This book aims to describe such methods. Before going into more detail it may be helpful if we say who these participants are and indicate the main ways in which they collaborate.

The participants in the implementation of an expert system

The collaborative functions

There are seven collaborative functions or activities involved in implementing any AI application, in particular an expert system; these are shown diagrammatically in Figure I.1.

(1) Use in service: this states the need for the aid that the system is to provide and uses the expertise that it provides when implemented.
(2) Field expertise: this holds and keeps up-to-date the knowledge and methods of reasoning that the proposed system is intended to provide, it spreads this among the users by means of advisory sessions, consultations and formal teaching.
(3) Strategy: this identifies and specifies the importance of AI for the enterprise, in terms of future competitive advantage and/or increased quality or economic value of existing products or processes.
(4) Project management: this identifies the potential applications, decides on the resources needed, plans and initiates the development, evaluates the results, and prepares for the introduction of the expert system into its intended user environment.
(5) Knowledge engineering: this gathers the required knowledge from the field experts and represents it as a computer model.
(6) Tool-making: this provides the knowledge engineers with the hardware and software tools they will need for their activities.
(7) AI expertise: this provides the basic concepts and methods needed by the two previous groups.

Pathology of expert system projects

Experience has shown that the absence of any of the above functions is

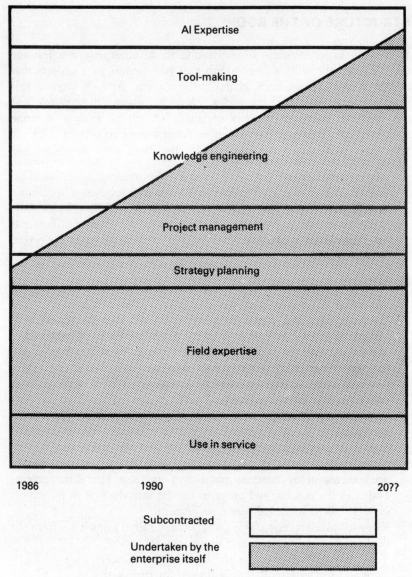

Figure I.1   The seven activities in an expert system project, with the progressive
undertaking by the enterprise concerned

fatal to the progress of the project; the death of many such projects, because of failure to observe the functions, has occurred.

Inadequacies in the strategy can result in:

(1) the enterprise taking no account of AI;
(2) a proliferation of clandestine projects initiated and pursued by staff who are more aware than their management; these will often duplicate work already done or will be only a partial attack on a problem and will dissipate resources without any hope that a product will be used;
(3) systems being produced that are ill-adapted to the real needs because of over-emphasis on the wrong criteria – for example, on technicalities rather than economic considerations – when the choice of application was made;
(4) stillborn systems, obsolete as soon as produced, because of failure to take into account likely technological developments when the project was launched.

Similarly, inadequacies in the project lead to:

(1) the usual symptoms of lack of discipline in the development teams, dates slipping and targets not being met, with the consequent withdrawal of interest and support by the management and by the experts associated with the projects, who see nothing useful being produced;
(2) no proper validation or evaluation of the product;
(3) the indifferent, cynical or even hostile reaction of the user organization when presented for the first time with the system that is supposed to solve their problems but which was developed without any account being taken of the ergonomic, psychological or social conditions in which it is to be used. It is fruitless to describe the advantages the system will bring if the user has not been consulted, preferably at an early stage, on the decisions made to produce it and put it into service.

It may seem hard to believe, but expert systems have been produced without the participation of any expert in the field of application. There are many known cases where it has been thought possible to economize by giving the responsibility for gathering the facts and the methods of reasoning to bright young workers who, whilst they may have the best academic qualifications, do not have the qualities that distinguish the true expert: the intuition that, combined with a grasp of high-level strategies for problem solving and the wisdom that only years of patient and careful work can give, enables him to go straight from the statement of a problem to its solution. The commonest tell-tale sign of a system so produced is that it closely resembles decision trees used to teach the rudiments of some subject – such trees being the only ones with which these inexperienced workers have had contact. It should never be forgotten that an expert system is a computer program that reproduces some human intellectual activities, so if it imitates those of a novice it will be no more than a novice system.

A mistake that has been made frequently during the past years, particularly in France, is to confuse the programming techniques appropriate to expert systems with the systems themselves: thus programs have been called expert which are not the result of any collaboration with a human expert but simply give a separation of certain knowledge items from means for their interpretation. Modularity has never been a necessary condition for an expert system; it is simply a way of constructing programs. It has proved valuable and effective because knowledge of the particular field is built up incrementally. This eases the problems of program construction and of providing explanations of conclusions reached, but is not indispensible. Explanations can be provided by procedural systems, but the participation of a field expert, who conveys knowledge to a knowledge engineer, is an absolute necessity if a successful expert system is to be achieved; even if the system is built up by a learning process the expert is needed as a guide.

Expert system pathology is equally rich in examples of systems developed without a knowledge engineer. The task of the engineer is to help the expert to express his knowledge and his way of thinking, a Socratic question-and-answer process that, because it may require the expert to bring deeply hidden, perhaps even repressed, knowledge to the surface of his mind, could be considered almost Freudian. This is left to the expert himself if there is no knowledge engineer.

Even when knowledge engineers have participated, projects have suffered because the engineers have not been competent. Knowledge engineers have to be highly skilled with a very broad scientific culture, able to listen intelligently to what the expert is saying, detect gaps and even logical inconsistencies and have enough social and psychological *savoir faire* to hear what he is *not* saying explicitly. In addition they must be able to formalize what is probably a rather shapeless discussion so as to make it possible for the machine to reproduce the knowledge conveyed, and thus must have at their fingertips a wide range of methods for representing knowledge. A knowledge engineer who knows only about, say, production rules is in the same position as a fisherman who has only a wide-mesh net. The performance and reliability of any expert system depends directly on the engineer's general scientific culture, ability to listen and knowledge of AI techniques.

Inadequacies in the tool-making function result in:

(1) Serious loss in productivity because of the choice of inappropriate techniques. This is especially the case when underpowered hardware is used for the development, or software tools of too-narrow scope.

(2) Erratic, expensive and in the end fruitless developments because the team, having been unable or unwilling to find suitable tools (should any exist) in the marketplace, and having under-estimated the skills and resources needed to produce these, has set out to design and build its own. This 'do-it-yourself' tendency is often the result of misunderstanding, or having only a poor grasp of, the strategic priorities of the enterprise; and is often found in teams left without clear directives. The team then concentrates on an enjoyable activity that becomes an end in itself – the production of a tool – with the consequence that the development of a simple model of an expert system that was to have taken at most three man-months is preceded by the development of one of the tools which takes very much longer.

Finally, there is the AI expertise function. Failures here can result in false expectations of the program because the aims have been set too high. A famous example is the history of automatic translation of natural languages in the USA in the 1960s: the severe holdups that this work encountered were a consequence of the fact that there were no known methods for representing the meaning of a sentence in a computer. The lesson that translation without understanding is impossible was learned only some 25 years later; there are now several projects for computer-*aided* translation – the change of wording is revealing – that take note of this.

How the enterprise learns to work with expert systems

The introduction of AI

Four routes for the introduction of AI can be distinguished:

(1) buying in a complete AI product;
(2) buying in a product that has AI components;
(3) subcontracting to an external organization for an AI application, to be integrated into one of the enterprise's own products or production processes;
(4) building up technical skills within the enterprise with a view to developing its own systems.

AI as a consumable product

We shall not give much space to consideration of the first two of these methods, which are more a matter of consumption than of acquisition of AI. An enterprise that buys in a complete AI product, or a product with AI components, may very well add a non-negligible value to its own production but derives no benefit where knowledge of this technique is concerned – just as a company that buys electrical or mechanical components to build television sets or trucks acquires no expertise in electronics or mechanical science.

Consider here a future, hypothetical stage in the AI industry: the stage at which the industry can design and deliver reliable products, well adapted to the needs of many and varied users, produced in large numbers and at low cost. In short, the stage at which it will have become part of the world of everyday objects as common as transistors and integrated circuits today: no manufacturer of washing machines, for example, now puts in his publicity material anything about his use of transistors in the control. In the long term this mass market will probably be the most remunerative for the enterprises that make AI products or components. Like the hermit crab, AI will slide into the shell of existing products which it will make more effective – expert systems for diagnosing breakdowns integrated into the onboard computer of an automobile, in phonology for locks controlled by voice recognition, and so on. But it will also create new products and services that would be unimaginable without it, such as advisory or counseling services of all kinds – legal, medical, financial – for personal or professional use, available everywhere and at all times in natural languages over the future telephone system.

AI as an integrated activity in an enterprise

In contrast to the first two routes, the second two are characterized by:

(1) requiring the enterprise to become genuinely involved in the development of an intelligent system;
(2) corresponding more closely to the present state of AI's penetration into industry.

Subcontracting and developing one's own expertise are not necessarily mutually exclusive, and in fact frequently form two stages in the process of acquiring technical skill: often a company will decide to have a specialist service organization develop its first application, to assess the suitability and feasibility of this application, with the hope that the outcome will make the importance of integrating AI into the company clear enough to embark on the route to self-sufficiency.

However, the route to mastery of AI techniques will be taken only by enterprises that are for the most part:

(1) very large and/or very rich; or
(2) have important and varied potential applications of AI, which justify the investment required; or
(3) are engaged in very special and therefore sensitive technical developments which exclude on security grounds the possibility of subcontracting.

It is with such enterprises in mind that we, the authors, have planned and written this book. We are convinced that the natural course for the most important and competitive enterprises is to take charge progressively of the different functions described on p. 3, in the manner shown in Figure I.1.

The assimilation or expert systems

There are four stages in assimilating expert systems into the enterprise (Figure I.2) These, possibly overlapping, are:

(1) alerting the organization;
(2) study of the impact;
(3) development of the first expert system;
(4) acquisition of technical mastery.

The remainder of the book is concerned with this progression. After the summary that follows, each stage is the subject of a separate chapter.

Stage 1: alerting the organization (Chapter 1)
The aim here is to arouse the interest of the top management of the enterprise by drawing attention to a potential source of profit or progress; and so to set in motion the rest of the process. A number of methods are employed, which combine to overcome the scepticism of the decision makers:

(1) publication of papers and books;
(2) seminars, demonstrations, exhibitions;
(3) successful activities of specialist AI consulting organizations;
(4) Two-way movement of specially trained staff between the enterprise and centers for advanced AI researches.

A danger here is that this activity may have the unwanted effect of raising expectations to an unattainable level, and the opinion formers should be aware of their responsibility in this regard. We take up this point in Chapter 1 where we discuss the type of information that is likely to lead to a reasonable appreciation of the basic concepts, methods, achievements and potentials of expert systems, and also of their limitations.

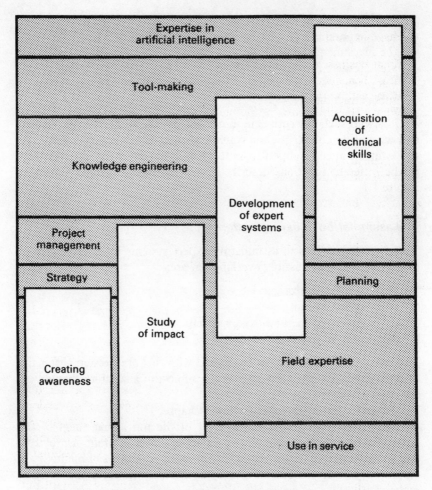

Figure I.2   The four stages of incorporation of AI into an enterprise

Stage 2: study of the impact (Chapter 2)

This will follow if Stage 1 is successful. It concerns the first four activities of p. 3: use in service, field expertise, strategy and project management respectively. Ideally it is a matter of assessing the value and both the medium- and long-term consequences of introducing the new techniques, for the external relations of the enterprise – markets, competition, prices – and for its internal conditions – human and technical resources; and then of drawing up a strategic plan for future aims, methods and resources.

This stage must provide the decision makers with documented answers to questions such as:

What business is the enterprise in?
What benefits can be expected from investment in AI?
What will be the consequences of *not* making this investment?
What is feasible: now, in the medium term, in the long term? What should we start with? What aims should we have?
Does the enterprise have the human, technical and financial means to embark on this?
What difficulties can be foreseen?

In reality, this essential stage is either:

(1) implicit (in other activities) to the point of nonexistence; this is especially the case when the previous stage (that of creating awareness) has been too successful and raised enthusiasm to a level that is unwarranted and soon proves fatal; or
(2) conducted without method or competence; or
(3) at the opposite extreme, conducted with an abundance of methodological precautions and overloaded with expertise, with the result that the study becomes an end in itself and no concrete decision ever emerges. This is typical of the situation when the work has been subcontracted, so requiring the external consultant to combine great expertise in AI with a good knowledge of the enterprise in question and the ability to acquire information accurately in discussion, together with an effective investigative technique. In fact, because AI is a very sensitive technique that should be introduced into the inner workings of an enterprise with great caution, what is really required is that its proponents, and especially consultants and service organizations, should demonstrate not only their competence in AI itself but also their more general mastery of managing change.

The second chapter describes the authors' recommendation for the way this stage should be conducted, a method that has been validated by several important organizations.

Stage 3: development of the first expert system (Chapter 3)
The successful production of an expert system depends, ultimately, on two individuals or groups of individuals; the expert in the field and the knowledge engineer who translates the expert's knowledge into computer software. The relations that develop between these participants must be founded on mutual understanding, mutual confidence and complete

absence of withholding of information. The success of the project depends very largely on the quality of these relations.

It also depends on the discipline with which the project is managed; Chapter 3 describes the methods taught and used by the Cognitech company, which again have been validated in actual developments, in the construction of some tens of expert systems. The company recommends four stages;

(1) quick production of a *demonstrator*, a working system developed to check the feasibility and timeliness of the project and to establish the conditions for the development of the final product;
(2) production of a *prototype*, for testing;
(3) if necessary or desirable, production of an *advanced demonstrator*;
(4) production and putting into operation of the final product.

Stage 4: acquisition of technical mastery (Chapter 4)
As we have already said, we are convinced that self-sufficiency in the design, construction, operation and maintenance of expert systems is an end to which all large organizations should be working; and in Europe some 800 enterprises are now interested in this. The acquisition of a novel technology, its incorporation into the enterprise's products and production processes, and, more broadly, the infiltration into its culture, have required much effort by the proponents of the change. The very speed with which expert systems have been taken up in industry has in fact caught even the most optimistic person unprepared.

A number of organizations have already embarked on the road from a simple intellectual interest in AI to the complete assimilation into their activities, either into their production processes or as a product or component of a product. We felt is best to start this fourth chapter with some accounts of their experiences, and then to attempt a synthesis of the main things that have to be attended to in order to achieve the desired end: recruitment and training of staff, building up of material and intellectual resources, ensuring industrial cooperation.

1

Understanding what is at stake: the awareness-creating stage

1.1 CONSULATIONS WITH EXPERTS

1.1.1 Tom

TOM: Are you there? Can you hear me better? I was asking what age are your tomatoes?

GROWER: . . . ?

TOM: I mean, are they seedlings, in the nursery, just planted out, mature?

GROWER: Mature.

TOM: What variety?

GROWER: They're Montfauvet.

TOM: Montfavet 83–4 or 84–4?

GROWER: 83–4, I think.

TOM: How do you cultivate them? Under cover or in the open?

GROWER: Under cover.

TOM: In earth, or earth-free?

GROWER: In earth.

TOM: Hmmm . . . and how do you water them, these tomatoes?

GROWER: . . .

TOM: Along the rows? With a sprinkler? Individually?

GROWER: Oh, individually, rather!

TOM: Where are you calling from? I mean, the south east, the south west . . . ?

GROWER: Pyrénées Orientales, sir.

TOM: Just call me Tom. Tell me, how are the sick plants distributed – in rows, scattered, in clumps . . . ?

GROWER: Scattered.

TOM: Have you noticed any withering of the leaves, perhaps with yellowing and then drying out completely? But careful! Don't confuse this with simple spots on the leaves.

GROWER: No, I don't think there has been any of that.

TOM: Are there spots on the leaves?

GROWER: Oh, yes!

TOM: These leaves, are they odd shaped? You see what I mean? Too short, spindly ...?

GROWER: I don't quite know how to answer. Some are like you say, some are normal ....

TOM: Never mind .... According to you, there's some anomaly in the leaf coloring, a mosaic perhaps, or yellowing without withering, or even yellowing and drying out?

GROWER: No, that's not it.

TOM: Is there any change at the neck – you know, the part of the stem that's just at earth level?

GROWER: No, I haven't seen any.

TOM: And the roots, do they seem normal?

GROWER: Yes, quite.

TOM: Take a careful look at the stem. Both the outside and inside – for the inside, get a knife and slit the stem across at different thicknesses and look carefully at the channels and the pith. OK? Do you notice anything?

GROWER: No, nothing special.

TOM: Good! Let's move on to something else. Anything unusual or changes in the fruit?

GROWER: No.

TOM: Have you seen any insects on the plants?

GROWER: No.

TOM: Have you noticed any spots with rings like little target cards on the leaves?

GROWER: Yes.

TOM: Aha!

GROWER: Are you on to something, Tom?

TOM: Perhaps .... Actually, this suggests to me a *Botrytis* but I'm still not sure, it could as well be *Alternaria dauci*. Let's see .... Take a careful look at the top surface of the leaves: do you see any brown spots with a yellow halo?

GROWER: No.

TOM: Hmmm .... Well, any gray-beige spots scattered over the top surface?

GROWER: Yes.

TOM: In that case, it's more likely to be a *Botrytis*. On these gray-beige spots, is there a gray felt?

GROWER: Yes, there is!

TOM: Then it's certainly a *Botrytis*! Are there little brown spots on the leaves?

GROWER: Why, is that important?

TOM: Not very, but that might suggest things like *Xanthomonas* or *Pseudomonas* or an X or Y potato virus or even tobacco mosaic . . . .

GROWER: Anyhow, there aren't any of those spots.

TOM: Nor any oily spots?

GROWER: No, really!

TOM: Good, you can relax now, I've no more questions. There's no doubt that it's a *Botrytis cinerea* – a kind of fungus, if you like. Would you like to know how to treat it?

GROWER: Rather, if possible!

TOM: This is what you must do. Grind up some fungicide of the cyclic imide type and in your cultivation alternate this with thiram, dichlorfluanide and chlorothalonil. Ventilate your cloches well, OK? Try not to knock against the plants, and try to get rid of any vegetable refuse as completely as possible. That's all – goodbye!

GROWER: Just a minute, Tom! How do I . . . . Oh, he's hung up. These experts are really busy.

Consider this dialogue for a moment. On one side we have a market gardener, growing tomatoes in the East Pyrenees, probably on a small scale. He is rather overpowered by the vocabulary of his questioner whom, one feels, he does not contact very often. Worried, perhaps a little touchy; for some time he has been noticing something amiss with his plants – light stains on the leaves; he had not paid much attention to this but now he is getting quite worried: if his crop is spoiled he is in serious trouble, for with debts outstanding he cannot afford to cut his margins. And with all this competition from the Italians and the Spaniards, selling gets harder – nowadays to make a living you have to be in the market early and with the best quality . . . . And he has no idea what to make of these spots.

On the other side – the story does not tell us where – is this expert, Tom. How did our grower find him? That is something of a mystery. By a miracle, the cynic would say: just try to find an expert in tomato diseases by searching the telephone directory. What do you call such a person? If a cow is ill you send for the vet; if your wife, for the doctor. But for spots on tomato plants? One has to be in the know, to realize that there is a good chance of getting useful information from a French body called the National Institute for Research in Agronomy; and in fact the appropriate part of the Institute is one of the Regional Groups for Plant Health, and for tomatoes the Avignon group is the one to contact.

This expert is not very talkative; he prefers to be the one who puts the questions, for then he can cut short any lengthy replies. He likes to go straight to the point; first a few pieces of general information about the variety in question, the stage of growth it has reached, the style of cultivation, something to give an idea of the environment. He is not held up by mistakes on the other hand – for example, 'Montfauvet' when it should be 'Montfavet', but there is no need to make a mountain of that. He can see what is meant – he would not be an expert otherwise. Then a few well-posed questions to direct the inquiry and suggest lines to be followed: withering of leaves; spots on the leaves, suggesting problems with the vascular tissue; or anomalous coloration, suggesting a viral infection. This is routine, perhaps, but the expert proceeds very methodically, telling his client exactly how to examine his plant: 'slit the stem across', and how to distinguish between similar symptoms: 'don't confuse this with simple spots'. Lack of precision in the replies does not worry him: 'I don't quite know how to answer' – he can get along without it, he is the expert. As it is now certain that the trouble is shown only in the leaves he concentrates on that symptom. The fact that the spots are concentric rings is interesting (Aha!) and means that the infection could be either *Botrytis* or *Alternaria*. A few more questions and it is settled: the gray-beige coloring of the spots and the gray felting remove the last doubts. To be quite sure he quickly eliminates a few minor possibilities, explaining his reasoning – 'that might suggest things like *Xanthomonas*' – to the client who is getting more and more impatient to know the verdict, and above all the treatment.

The reader will doubtless have guessed that this expert Tom, as easily accessible to tomato growers in the East Pyrenees as to those in Brittany, to the large and to the small, available day and night, every day (including Sundays), laconic but precise, tolerant of the client's mistakes or imprecisions, rigorous but taking time to explain what is to be done – this expert is actually a computer program. It is one of 25 expert systems developed in France by the National Institute for Research in Agronomy (INRA) with the collaboration with the company Cognitech, to achieve better protection of crops by improving diognosis of plant diseases.

INRA is an organization for both fundamental and applied research in agronomy; its purpose is to distribute the results of its research to relevant agriculturalists so that good value is obtained from them. AI was seen originally as a means of deriving benefit from INRA's knowledge in the particular case of vegetable pathology; the need is particularly acute here, because in the industrialized countries between 12% and 15% of the harvest is lost each year before gathering, because of delayed diagnosis of diseases, a proportion that can rise to 33% when the weather is particularly bad; and in third world countries the loss can average 60%. In France responsibility for providing diagnosis has rested with the various services concerned with protection of vegetable crops and some half-dozen regional centers, the Groupements Regionaux d'Interet Scientifique Phyto-Sanitaire, or GRISPs (regional groups for the scientific study of plant health), in which are found the 200 or so French experts in this subject. This dispersion of knowledge between a large number of highly specialized experts is one of the reasons for the problem: a specimen of a sick plant could in some cases go from center to center before the right expert was found. Thus expert systems were seen as a means for making all such dispersed, specialized knowledge equally available at many places; in fact directly to the agriculturalist himself via the Teletel network, for example.

The first step was to develop a demonstrator system to evaluate the feasibility of the proposal. This system – Tom – was found to perform as well as the combined group of experts whose knowledge it reproduced – that is, better than any one taken individually. Further, Tom gave a diagnosis within about 15 minutes, against the 48 hours to 3 weeks needed with the traditional organization. Given this success, INRA decided to initiate a general program of developing expert systems for consultations concerning vegetable pathology and to make available to growers, from 1987 onwards, a network of such systems dealing with the greater part of European vegetable production. This project constitutes one of the world's most important developments of expert systems.

This project can act an example in a second way: it illustrates perfectly the process of assimilation of AI by an organization – just what this book aims to describe and to promote. INRA entered this field around 1984 under pressure of a real need and with a few elementary but sound ideas, and is now one of the organizations closest to mastering the technique. The eight knowledge engineers on its staff were trained by Cognitech and in this process had the experience, perhaps unique so far, of developing a *series* of expert systems intended for widespread use, with all the constraints of quality that that implies. Most important, the effort was not that of a single laboratory or department but of the entire organization, and headed by the top management.

The dialogue with which we started this chapter helps us comment straight away on the possibilities and limitations of AI. The reader will doubtless have found it difficult to believe that such a dialogue between a human and a machine was actually possible, and his skepticism is justified in some ways – but not all. It scarcely needs to be said that an *oral* dialogue of this quality is far beyond the bounds of present possibilities: Tom and his clients communicate by means of written or displayed messages, and will do so for a long time to come. But in other respects the dialogue is quite faithful to present achievements. The correcting of mis-spellings, Montfauvet understood as the correct Montfavet, for example, which makes Tom so tolerant of such errors, is thoroughly operational as is the request for more precision – Montfavet 83–4 or 84–4? – and also the ability to explain how a conclusion is reached.

However, one can have two views about Tom's propensity for little linguistic touches intended to given an impression of real humanity to what is an automaton, such as 'Hmm', 'Aha!', 'Good! Let's move on . . .'. There is no difficulty in making the program produce these, but it depends on tricks that the user soon sees through and finds boring. It would be possible to defeat this objection by introducing rules for the conduct of the conversation into the program, which would produce expressions that were perfectly adapted to the situation at that moment and varied enough so as not to seem automatic; but the result would not be worth the considerable work required, especially when one recalls the work still to be done if we are to solve even the basic problems of knowledge representation. Tom's recognition of expressions such as 'Not at all' and 'Oh, no!' is well within the bounds of possibility, as has been shown by certain computer-aided teaching systems which accept such responses from the students; but the writer of the program is not likely to foresee all the possible ways of saying 'No'.

To sum up, it would require an enormous effort of syntactic and semantic analysis and generation of the language to achieve a natural-sounding dialogue between a computer and a human user; and this is not a matter with which designers of expert systems are concerned at present. We now give, as a second example, something that is closer to an actual dialogue with an expert system. This is with Rufus [Cognitech, 1985c], developed for the Paris urban railway system RATP, to enable the value of expert systems in engineering maintenance and in training maintenance engineers to be assessed.

1.1.2 Rufus

This dialogue concerns the diagnosis of a train breakdown. The questions are put by Rufus and are numbered in order; the user's replies are always Yes, No or a number giving either a measure read on the test equipment or the choice from a set of possible responses displayed by the system.

1. What failure is shown? The possibilities are:
   0. Unknown
   1. Dead motor

      2. Tractive effort low
      3. Rheostat inactive
      4. Door failure
      5. General failure to close
      6. General failure to open
      7. Local failure to close
      8. Failure to stay closed
      9. Local failure to open
    10. Failure of start warning
1 (i.e. response 1 equals 'dead motor')

2. How many units in the train? Reply can be a number from 1 to 3
1

Set driver's key to Normal
Set direction Forward or Reverse
Close the circuit-breakers
Set the speed selector to Neutral
Set key TE to HS

3. Does the inactive motor's warning light show?
YES

Do isolation tests on the leading motor and look at the Qmeter

4. What is the Qmeter position? Reply can be any number
1

The dead motor is the leading motor
Set test mode
Set the TEST/CHECK key to CHECK
Set the speed selector to TS

5. Does the inactive motor's warning light still show?
NO

Set the TEST/CHECK key to HS
Set the speed selector to Neutral
Close the circuit-breakers
Select direction Forward

6. Have the circuit-breakers opened?
NO

7. Select direction Reverse
Have the circuit-breakers opened?
NO

8. Select test mode
   Note the JH carefully: has it moved?
   YES

9. Has the JH gone through its full cycle $0 \to -1$, $-1 \to 0$?
   YES

10. Close the circuit-breakers.
    Note the JH carefully: has it moved?
    YES

11. Has the JH gone through its full cycle $0 \to -1$, $-1 \to 0$?
    YES

    Check the following:
       Speed selector in Neutral
       Direction selected
       Circuit breakers closed
       Isolater in normal position
    THERE IS A CONTROL FAILURE IN THE CIRCUIT-BREAKERS

12. Is fuse 88A OK?
    YES

13. Is fuse 103E-108a OK?
    YES

14. Are the RCD relays OK?
    YES

    Finish.
    There is a control failure in the circuit-breakers
    Check circuit 108B.

Having given these two dialogues as examples, we now continue with a more systematic account of expert systems, with the aim of increasing awareness both of their possibilities and of their limitations. We start (Section 1.2) with an elementary review of the basic principles, with apologies to the reader to whom this is already familiar, and inviting the reader who would like to go deeper to consult some of the general works given in the bibliography. Then in Section 1.3, making as much use as possible of actual examples, we attempt to show what ends can expert systems serve and what ends are they already serving; and finally in Section 1.4 we look briefly at the market for expert systems, considered as products that can bring profits to their constructors.

1.2 WHAT IS AN EXPERT SYSTEM?

1.2.1 Some history

Initial research into expert systems coincided with a loss of interest by researchers into the representation of 'universal' methods – the universality of which was equaled only by their inability to solve any particular problems [Nilsson, 1980]: a reflection of the well-known compromise between generality and efficiency. Edward Feigenbaum in the early 1960s became interested in inductive and empirical methods of reasoning, a typical problem here being that of constructing the most acceptable hypothesis that gives a good interpretation of a given set of data. The wish to model this type of scientific behavior led to the setting up of a project, Dendral [Feigenbaum *et al.*, 1971], a collaboration between information scientists and experts in other fields, among whom was the chemist and geneticist Joshua Lederberg. The particular field chosen for experimentation was chemical analysis by mass spectrometry. A mass spectrometer determines the chemical composition of a substance by bombarding a small sample with high-energy electrons, so breaking the molecule into a number of simpler fragments which can then be identified. The structure of the original molecule can be deduced from the information obtained about these fragments.

For several years this work was treated with much reserve by the AI establishment, because it lay outside the fields then dominant. However, AI researchers soon found themselves again facing the central problem of how to represent and structure knowledge, since they were not simply concerned with mere 'toy' problems in which the number of parameters to be considered was very small.

Research into mechanisms for reasoning in particular fields made considerable progress in, for example, medical diagnosis with Mycin [Shortliffe, 1976] and interpretation of geological data with Prospector [Duda *et al.*, 1979]. New enthusiasm grew for developing general tools for representing knowledge, that would apply equally in all fields; expert system research could then be considered as truly forming a part of AI. Meanwhile great progress had been made in automatic proof of theorems and solution of general problems, laying the theoretical foundations for the methodology of *knowledge-based systems*.

The first lesson drawn from the development of programs such as Dendral – which contained a huge amout of specialized chemical knowledge – was that the cost of making even the smallest change was prohibitive, because the special knowledge was closely integrated into the reasoning mechanisms. A fundamentally important idea gradually emerged that the mass of knowledge and the reasoning mechanisms should be kept completely separate; another way of saying that there should be 'universal' reasoning mechanisms that could be applied in any field. Thus there developed the concept of the 'inference engine', a sort of empty shell that could be filled with the special knowledge relating to any particular field.

There is of course no truly universal engine, just as there is no universal syntax, but there are regularities or structures that are common to many fields, and advantage can be taken of these by basing different expert systems on the same general principles.

It is important to realize that there are many types of problem for which the expert system approach is not appropriate. For example, if all potential solutions to a problem can be examined in an acceptable time, using available computer power, there is no point in looking for any other method: one can be certain that the machine has not overlooked any crucial parameter values, in contrast to the human solver who may have great reasoning powers and the ability to short-circuit any number of paths that would lead nowhere, but is equally capable of astonishing blunders and forgetfulness that may result in missing an obvious solution.

For many problems, however, this method of exhaustive search is ruled out because of the time it would take. This is the case for chess, for example: to decide a move by examining all the situations that could ressult would involve assessing some 10^{120} possibilities. Other cases arise in industry, for example in the laying out of integrated circuits on cards and in the generation of test sequences. And, of course, there are problems for which no algorithm is known. In such cases, therefore, we have to use methods which do not guarantee success but which may enable spectacular short cuts to be made, and which, at present at least, can be devised only by humans. These are what are called *heuristic* methods and are those that underlie the representation of knowledge in expert systems.

1.2.2 What is an expert system?

The first definition that comes to mind is 'a program that contains a large body of knowledge concerning one special field, this having been provided by one or more human experts in that field, and able to achieve the same performance in problem-solving as those experts.' This is not to be understood as excluding knowledge taken from books or other written material originating with the experts when this is available, but experience has shown that experts rarely put their deep knowledge on paper; there seem always to be layers of subliminal knowledge which do not emerge into consciousness spontaneously, and which it is the aim of expert systems to capture and express formally.

This suggested definition is consistent with the historical development of the subject but does not take account of the methodological aspects. From the very nature of the task of representing human expertise in the computer – that is, of the collection of informal methods (the heuristic methods just defined) that comprise human intuition – it is virtually impossible to obtain all the reasoning rules used by the expert at any one time. Methods for constructing the system have therefore to be found that allow this to be done in an evolutionary way, with additions and improvements being made continuously as the human expert gradually reveals his knowledge to the knowledge engineer. We shall have much to say about the knowledge engineer, an information scientist of a very special type, whose task is to bring about this revelation and formalization.

The method that has gradually developed has led to the principle of separating the representation of the knowledge of the particular field from that of the logical mechanisms for processing and interpreting this knowledge. This allows the store of knowledge to be modified easily, because the statements that contain this knowledge can then be written in declarative form and therefore do not have to be in any particular order, and also are more easily accessible than if they were incorporated into a program. Thus any of the rules, for example of the type A & B $\Rightarrow$ C, can be changed or deleted or a rule added without the risk of introducing a bug into the program, something that cannot be done with a program of the classical procedural type.

1.2.2.1 The anatomy of expert systems

Figure 1.1 shows what has become the standard architecture for expert systems; more details can be found in Laurière, 1982, Cordier, 1984 and Bonnet, 1984.

The formalism for knowledge representation that we describe first is known as *production rules*; this formalism is not the only possibility but is the one most used and the easiest to explain.

After a simplified account, intended to give a basic understanding of the structure and process, we describe some more advanced architectures that correspond to real-life developments.

The facts base. This comprises the permanent facts of the field to which the problem belongs, together with the special facts concerning

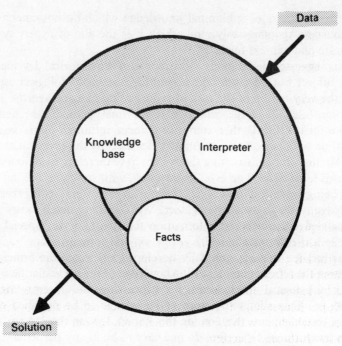

Figure 1.1 Basic architecture of an expert system

the particular problem that has to be solved – these latter form what is also called a database. The facts base is the working memory of the system; consider some examples from the system Tom that we have already described:

Permanent facts (relevant to all tomato diseases):

the Marquise variety is resistant to tobacco mosaic virus
oidium is a fungus
yellowing or violet are anomalies of leaf coloration

Facts that are special to the particular problem:

the tomato plant examined has yellow spots on the leaves
there is browning of the rootlets of the tomato plant examined
the affected plants are distributed along single rows

The knowledge base. This consists of rules – production rules, as we have said – which usually enable deductions to be made from the given facts, so adding new facts to the base. From Tom again we have this example:

>   **if**   the stalk shows some variation from the normal
> **and**   this variation is black and wet
> **then**   there is a possibility of Dydimella lycopersici (0.5)
>   **or**   Phytophthora nicotianae (0.5)

A rule consists of a left part beginning with **if**, stating conditions, and a right part beginning **then**, stating what follows if those conditions hold. The numbers in parentheses (e.g. 0.5) are indicators of the degree of confidence with which the various conclusions can be held; these can range from +1 (perfect certainty) to −1 (certainty that the conclusion does not hold): thus they are not probabilities.

The inference engine. This has to use the knowledge base so as to reason about the problem, given the contents of the facts base. It consists mainly of an algorithm for *pattern-matching* or *filtering* that examines the *premise* of a rule [the left or **if** part] to find whether or not this holds, according to the contents of the facts base. Regarding a premise as a set of logical clauses linked by logical connectives AND, OR it can be given a value TRUE or FALSE; but here it can be given a 'relative' truth value by assigning to it a coefficient which, as with the rules, indicates the degree of confidence with which its truth can be accepted.

This process is very simple to implement if the rules contain only constants – the case of propositional logic – and more complex if they contain variables – the case of predicate logic. In the latter case the algorithm is said to be one of *unification*; here a given rule can be brought into action by different instantiations of the variables and therefore several times, whereas in the former case any rule can be brought into action at most once.

1.2.2.2 Physiology of expert systems

To show how an expert system actually works we shall first simplify what is done in many existing systems; this makes the basic principles, which are not affected, easier to understand. First we assume that all the facts are certainly true, certainly false or completely unknown, so there is no concept of probability or plausibility. Next, that there is no possibility of asking the user of the system, in the course of the reasoning, if a fact is true: all the facts from which the process has to start are known at the beginning. Finally, a fact given at the start cannot be questioned subsequently.

There are two main methods for triggering (i.e. putting into operation) the rules. The first, called *forward chaining*, is a process of examining the left part of each rule in turn and applying the rule whenever the conditions for this part are found to hold; the process ends when it ceases to give any new facts. This may be called *fact-directed reasoning* since the course is guided by the data of the problem. The second method is called *backward chaining*; here the goal to be attained is given and the right parts of the rules are examined to find which of these include this goal; this sets up new goals (verification of the conditions given in the left parts of the relevant rules) which are subgoals for the original goal, and so on until a known fact is reached. The process fails when a necessary fact cannot be established. This is called *goal-directed reasoning*.

The choice between the two methods can depend on the problem; for some problems the goal cannot be fixed in advance and therefore only forward chaining is feasible. Many systems use both methods in a complementary manner.

Consider the following very simple example. The knowledge base consists of seven rules (the numbering has no significance):

    R5 if Z and L then S
    R1 if A and N then E
    R3 if D or M then Z
    R2 if A then M
    R4 if Q and (not W) and (not Z) then N
    R6 if L and M then E
    R7 if B and C then Q
    Known facts (facts base) = (A, L)
    Goal to be established = E

The clauses (i.e. facts) A, D, E, M, N, Q, Z that appear in the rules can be of any form or nature, such as 'cholesterol level > 40' or 'at least one resistor in the circuit is burnt out'.

We study the applications of backward and forward chaining respectively in the next two sections.

Backward chaining

This is represented diagrammatically in Figure 1.2. the attempt to establish E can be made by two different routes, via either R1 or R6. Starting with R1 requires the system to prove A and N, and since A is given this sets up N as a new sub-goal; N follows from R4 if Q and (not W) and (not Z) can be proved. To prove Q we have to prove B and C then (R7), but B cannot be deduced from the given rules and therefore this route leads to a check.

Having failed in this attempt, the inference engine then looks for other possible routes, and the only one is via R6. This requires L and M to be

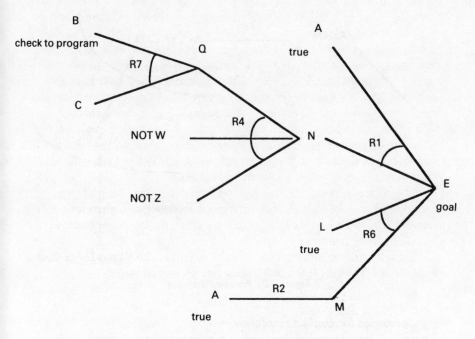

Figure 1.2   Backward chaining, with goal E

proved; L is given so the system looks for ways to prove M, the new sub-goal. R2 will give M as A if A can be proved, and A is given; so M follows and hence E.

Forward chaining
This is shown in Figure 1.3. In this process the engine examines the left part of each rule to see which, if any, are satisfied by the hypotheses and which therefore provide new facts. In its crudest form it looks at the whole set of rules *en bloc*, but alternatively it can take them in order according to some strategy; we shall discuss some possible strategies below. Here, regarding the process as a sequence of iterations through the rules:

first iteration: R2 and R6 are triggered
second iteration: R3 (could not have been triggered at the first iteration, because M was not established at that stage)
third iteration: R5 (not possible until Z was established)

The goal E is reached at this stage; as it happens, not further iteration is possible and the process stops here.

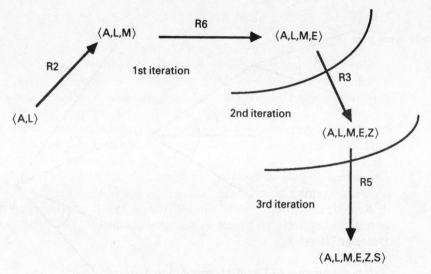

Figure 1.3   Forward chaining

Strategies for conflict resolution

There are many strategies for conflict resolution that can result in better performance of the search algorithms. The principle on which these are most commonly based is that when, in a given situation, several rules could be applied, these are taken in order according to some stated priorities; the following are the priorities most commonly adopted.

(1) A subset of the rules is chosen by applying certain meta-rules.
(2) Priority is given to those rules for which the left part is the most detailed: this is because such rules give the most precise conclusions.
(3) Priority is given to those rules that use information most recently acquired or deduced.
(4) Priority is given to those rules that give the greatest number of conclusions.
(5) The rules are taken in an order depending on the importance of their conclusions for the goals to be achieved.
(6) If the conclusions are weighted, the rules are taken in decreasing order of the weights.

There are several methods for allocating the relative priorities:

(1) By an algorithm built into the inference engine, which computes at every stage the best order according to the criterion adopted.
(2) By meta-rules which select the rules according to their content, using

criteria that can depend on the particular problem being attacked. This method is sometimes used in conjunction with (1)

(3) By a step in the compilation of the rules, performed at run time by the knowledge acquisition module: this is done in Snark [Vialatte, 1985; Vignard, 1985]. Some systems exploit here two basic properties of expert systems called, respectively, structural resemblance and temporal redundancy. The first refers to the fact that in many cases the premises of several rules will have clauses in common, and use of this can reduce the number of tests that have to be made; the second, that there are often only a few changes to the working memory between successive iterations of the inference engine. Improvements of several orders of magnitude have been achieved by use of this latter by the de Rete algorithm in the Ops-5 engine [Forgy, 1981]. Improvements have also been achieved by use of the work of Ghallab [1980] and of Dufresne [1984].

Inference engines of Level 0 (propositional calculus) and Level 1 (first-order logic)

An examination of the two examples of clauses given in Section 1.2.2.2 will show that there is a fundamental difference between them. The first refers explicitly to some single patient for whom the cholesterol level is known, whereas the second assumes that there can be several resistors, among which the inference engine has to find if there is one with the stated property. Only constants enter into the first example, and we say that this concerns the propositional calculus; in the second the engine has to test several different resistors for the particular property, so this involves the concepts of variables and the existential ('there exists . . .') and universal ('for all . . .') quantifiers, the concern of the predicate calculus. We have here again the distinction made in Section 1.2.2.1.

This distinction suggests a classification of inference engines into different 'levels'. When the rules are expressed as predicate calculus clauses a single rule can be triggered as many times as there are combinations of values of the variables that satisfy each clause. This can be a large number; thus if a rule is of the form

if $P(x)$ **and** $Q(y)$ **and** $R(z)$ **then** $S(x,y,z)$

where P, Q, R are predicates and each of x, y, z can take ten values, the rule can be triggered 1000 times. It is thus essential to have a strategy to avoid this combinatorial explosion, and this must involve:

(1) the choice of the rule to be applied, made according to one or other of the methods described in Section 1.2.2.3; and

(2) for each rule chosen, the ordering of the instantiations according to the couples (variables and corresponding instantiations) that satisfy the left part. This of course applies only in the case of predicate calculus rules, because in the propositional calculus there are no variables and a rule can be triggered only once.

The methods adopted vary from one engine to another but are all based on one fundamental principle: the most restrictive clauses have the highest priority [Lourent, 1984 and McDermott and Forgy, 1978]. The reason is obvious: if one has to find whether certain elements are common to two or more sets one first tests to find if they belong to the smaller set and only afterwards tests the larger. Two consequences follow: the first, that any clauses containing no variables (i.e. only constants) are evaluated first; the second, that any clauses involving the equality operator are evaluated before those involving less precise operators such as less than, different from, etc.

We must not forget that when a rule is evaluated, the effect of assigning a constant to a variable is propagated throughout the system immediately; this can affect the ordering of the clauses and therefore this ordering has to be recomputed. Finally, if the main constraint on the process is the time taken to find a solution it is only common sense to take care that an optimal method does not spend more time ordering and reordering clauses than a nonoptimal but simpler method, possibly using the clauses in random order, would take for the complete process.

Approximate reasoning

So far we have assumed that all the data and knowledge that are necessary for the solution of the problem are available and are known exactly. In practice, however, this ideal situation seldom occurs: the factual information is usually not all available and what there is is often imprecise or even wrong, whilst the knowledge (the rules) may be uncertain and incomplete. We have therefore to be able to quantify and to manipulate uncertainties and to carry these through the chains of reasoning, so as to take account of the indeterminate nature of our problems. The classical methods of dealing with uncertainties use the calculus of probabilities, as for example the expert system Prospector uses Bayes's formula to compute the probability of finding a given mineral at a given location in the earth, given various items of geological information. But this requires certain formal conditions to be satisfied, which is seldom the case in practice. Other methods, derived from probability theory, have been developed; Mycin uses 'certainty factors' whose values can range from -1 to $+1$, computed by an empirical formula derived from Bayes's, a commonly used method found in many expert systems. Another generalization of the Bayes's formula is found in the Dempster–Shafer theory [Shafer, 1976] based on measures of 'credibility' and particularly well adapted to the approximate reasoning of many systems. Similarly for the techniques for the propagation of uncertainties based on theories of 'possibilities' and 'necessities' [Zadeh, 1979, Dubois and Prade, 1982 and 1985], which are similar to the theory of fuzzy subsets due to Zadeh. The idea of 'fuzziness' has been used successfully to take account of lack of precision in data given to an expert system, for example in statements such as 'the readings of the instruments X and Y are close' or 'most of the spots are yellow circles'.

It is a fact that all present methods for handling uncertainty involve at some stage a numerical quantification. We may hope that eventually methods will be developed that use purely symbolic processes or more advanced types of logic, such as modal logic.

1.2.2.3 Advantage of knowledge base methods

Methods using a knowledge base depend fundamentally on the *independence* of the rules, so far as their implementation is concerned. Thus if there are two rules A **and** B $\Rightarrow$ C

$$C \Rightarrow D$$

there is clearly a logical link between the two, but in the implementation neither makes any appeal to the other and they will be linked only by the inference engine in the course of the reasoning process. It follows that:

(1) the rules can be put into the knowledge base in any order – thus in the example of p. 26 the rules can be reordered in any way without affecting the reasoning;
(2) there is no need state in advance how any particular rule is to be used;
(3) the knowledge contained in the base can be examined easily, because each rule includes explicitly the conditions under which it applies;
(4) the system can easily show which rules have been used in the reasoning.

This brings many advantages, and in fact this approach is the only one that is feasible when the knowledge to be implemented has to be acquired over a period of months from experts who cannot be expected to deliver this on demand, quickly, completely and without errors.

Thus representation of knowledge in declarative form is an important feature of expert systems. Nevertheless, there are types of knowledge that are best expressed in procedural form, and, as we shall see later, there is a strong case for developing models that enable the two forms of representation to be mixed.

1.2.2.4 Advanced architectures for expert systems

We are now witnessing an increasing sophistication in the formalisms used for representing knowledge. Much that used to be expressed dynamically as inferences is now given in static or structural form, thanks to the development of methods that were only at a rudimentary stage – for example, in the language FRL – in the early days of expert systems.

Inadequacy of adopting a single formalism
Consider the following simple rule:

> **If** sex (patient) = male **then** pregnant = NOT

As a production rule, this representation is unsatisfactory for several reasons:

(1) it conveys 'static' knowledge; pregnancy characterizes only one sex and there is a link between the two attributes but no 'conclusion' – we do not argue 'now, this is a male and therefore . . .';
(2) common-sense relations of this type are very numerous in every field and it would be very burdensome to have to state them all in this way;
(3) pregnancy is a characteristic of the female and this is not stated explicity but is inferred by default;
(4) if this form is used then the characteristics of a given sex cannot all be obtained in one step.

In the early days of expert systems, and still in many cases today, it was usual to mix different kinds of knowledge:

(1) Control statements.
(2) Relations between parameters:
  (a) hierarchies, in the sense of specialization or generalization of concepts;
  (b) logical exclusions;
  (c) indications of parts that comprise a whole.
(3) Dialogue management, as for example in certain systems for which the ending of a rule with a particular parameter is a signal to output a message concerning that parameter. In a more fully structured program it is the object to which the parameter relates that determines the content of the message, and information on when the message is to be sent is specified in the system and detected by the inference engine.

(4) Propagation of a value from a general concept to a more particular one, performed explicitly by a production rule.

The following is an example of the burden, with consequential inefficiency, of giving static information in the form of a rule:

if type (vehicle) = R25 **then** marque = Renault

Many properties of the general class Renault are inherited by the particular member R25 and it is much more important, as well as conceptually more satisfying, to have a relation between the two that allows certain characteristics to be transferred automatically from Renault to R25. Such a method for knowledge representation is described in the next section.

Object-based languages for representation of knowledge

We first introduce some commonly used terms. An object has a number of *aspects* or *attributes* which are the names of properties by which it is characterized, and these are specific to the type of object: thus we speak of the *center* and *radius* of a circle or the *name, sex, address* and *profession* of a *person*.

Each aspect has a number of *facets*, which are sets of associated items. Thus one facet can be *possible values*, the set of values that can be taken by the aspect in question and another is the *default value*, the value to be assigned when nothing more specific is stated. The object *automobile* will have an aspect *top speed* for which the facet *possible value* could be any number between 0 and 250 (km/h) and *default value* (say) 150.

An object can be represented in a hierarchy in which there are objects both more and less general than itself: *bird* is less general than *animal* but more general than *duck*, for example.

A most important feature of object-based (or object-oriented) programming is that is requires only a small number of concepts to be introduced. Everything depends on the four ideas of object, class, inheritance and message. A program is organized around objects, which are entities characterized at the same time by their attributes and by the actions they can perform, which actions can be triggered only by messages sent to the object. An object can be a particular instance of a generic class, in which case it can, through the mechanism of inheritance, possess some or all of the properties of that class including its actions. The ideas of class, inheritance and attribute have arisen from the work on the language Simula, on semantic networks and on schemas respectively.

There are several programming languages in working existence that are based on these principles, in particular Logo [Papert, 1980] and especially Smalltalk due to A. Kay of Xerox PARC [Kay and Goldberg, 1977]. The original aim of this work was to meet the software engineering requirement of easing the writing of large programs by exploiting the possibilities offered by this formalism for rapid production of prototypes: ease of modification, reuse of code already written (made possible by the inheritance mechanism) and the possibilities for leaving many details unspecified until the last stage of the implementation. A significant number of object-oriented languages are now in use, most of them implemented in symbolic languages; for example, Loops, Flavors, Ceyx, Mering, Formes, Kool, KRS and Orient-84 are written in Lisp; ESP and Looks in Prolog; Objective−C and C++ in C and Object-Pascal and C-Pascal in Pascal.

These properties have proved very useful in AI generally for knowledge representation because they make the following possible:

(1) structuring the knowledge base;
(2) separation of the knowledge content from the technical details of its storage in the computer memory – an essential consideration from the point of view of performance but not pertinent for the implementation generally.
(3) simultaneous use of different formalisms for knowledge representation;
(4) mixing knowledge and reasoning.

Much fruitful work in AI is now centered on object-oriented representation, which is tending to become general in knowledge base systems.

A structured object can be regarded as a prototype, that is, an 'ideal' object to be used as a standard for comparison with actual objects that have to be studied. It is possible no actual object matches exactly the prototype so defined.

The prototype object can just as well be an abstract entity – a situation with certain features, for example – as a physical object. The comparison will usually reveal differences from the prototype, even though the two have certain basic properties in common, and these differences may reflect exceptions to the general rules expressed by the prototype – thus an ostrich is a bird that does not fly – or simply the fact that not all possible details were foreseen when the ideal was defined. This idea of comparing a test object with a standard or prototype has been much used in problems of diagnosis, medical and otherwise: for any individual patient influenza will show a general correspondence with the prototype but also some aspects that are peculiar to that patient.

The majority of representations by objects allow default values to be given which can be replaced by actual values if such become known later.

This possibility is most important in human reasoning but is not allowed in formal first-order logic; it is usually called nonmonotone logic.

We have already emphasized that whilst representation in declarative form brings many advantages, a procedural form can be better in certain cases. Representation by objects allows the two to be mixed by allowing 'procedural attachments' to be made to certain attributes. The language KRL [Bobrow and Winograd, 1977] allows two types of procedure here: 'housekeeping', which says what has to be done so as to carry through certain operations, for example to find the value of an attribute; and 'demons', triggered when certain conditions are satisfied. This is not in fact new, for the idea of a 'demon' [Selfridge, 1959] is very old in AI.

Some writers maintain that it is important to be able to look at the same event from different points of view. For example, Bobrow and Winograd, in KRL, describe an event that can be discussed either as a journey to a particular place or as a visit to a particular person; in the first case the interest centers on the destination and the method of transport, in the second on the people concerned.

There is no general method that will decide if a prototype corresponds closely enough to the situation that has to be identified; usually some of the attributes that are considered to be important will have the required values but checks on other properties widen the gap between the case under consideration and the ideal. It may be possible to say what should be done if it becomes clear that the prototype will not be matched; for example, if 'influenza' explains most of a patient's symptoms but not a 'loose cough' then the complication 'bronchitis' should be considered.

Thus object-oriented programming enables us to represent static (i.e. structural or hierarchical) knowledge and certain types of reasoning, particularly what we may call 'common sense', in a way that is both natural and intellectually satisfying. We shall now consider how this can be used to complement the more classical method of production rules so as to give a particularly powerful and flexible for expert systems, what we call a hybrid architecture.

Hybrid architecture

Hybrid architecture is the form towards which many expert systems are tending; it is shown diagrammatically in Figure 1.4. The knowledge base consists of at least two complementary formalisms, usually production rules and hierarchies of structured objects; all this is interpreted by the inference engine. This forms the working expertise and is surrounded by at least four modules, with these functions:

(1) implantation of expertise in the knowledge base; this will include syntactic, semantic and logical checking;

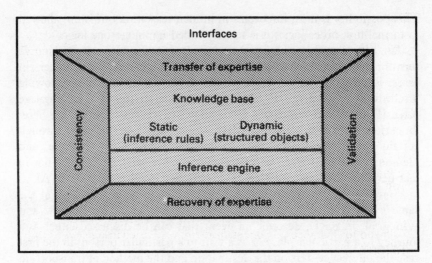

Figure 1.4   Target architecture for an expert system

(2) recovery of expertise from the base, usually by means of a dialogue with the user;

(3) maintenance of the integrity and consistency of the knowledge base;

(4) testing and checking.

The interfaces with the user are usually graphical – for giving explanations, for example – and there are elaborate editors for adding new knowledge items. We describe these tools and consider the criteria for their choice in Section 3.4.4.

Example of hybrid architecture: a building contract

This example has been derived from a study of an expert system for planning construction projects, commissioned by the company Dumez-Bâtiment [Cognitech, 1985c]; the study has led to the specification of the software tool TG-2, using a formalism described later.

Analytically, a construction project can be regarded as the set of tasks that has to be completed in order to create certain intended physical structures. These are of course interrelated with various physical constraints – the roof cannot be put on a building before the foundations have been laid – together with economic requirements. Our purpose in giving this example is not to go into the details of the planning of the various tasks but to develop a model that is both descriptive of the needs and realistically operational and that could be used as a basis for an application of this type.

Figure 1.5 is a block diagram showing the objects that have to be considered and the links between these; the links are relations such as 'IS_PART_OF . . .', 'IS_SUBCLASS_OF . . .' etc. We can in fact say that these relations are themselves objects and this will allow us to set up types of inheritance among objects that are much more varied and flexible than the traditional 'sub/superclass' or 'is a . . .' of the majority of object-oriented languages.

Consider first the object we have called 'STOREY'

```
Object: STOREY          ; name of object
Generalization: OBJECT  ; ancestor in the hierarchy
  AREA                  ; name of attribute
    data type: R+       ; domain of values of attribute (positive reals)
    cardinality: 1      ; number of values of attribute that can take (1)
    linked to: instance ; one such attribute for each instance of STOREY
  HEIGHT
    data type: R+
    cardinality: 1
    linked to: instance
  STOREY
    data type: R
    cardinality: 1
    linked to: instance
IS_PART_OF: BUILDING
IS_BELOW: STOREY
```

There are a number of points of be noted in connection with this essentially simple object:

(1) the relations 'IS_PART_OF' and 'IS_BELOW' have themselves the structure of an object. For 'IS_BELOW' for example:

```
    Object: IS_BELOW
    Generalization: RELATION
      DOMAIN: STOREY
      FIELD: STOREY
      INVERSE: IS_ABOVE
```

No particular inheritance of properties is implied in this relation.

(2) Each attribute of the object has a facet 'data type' that can be used as a first-level check on the value; in the case here of the attribute 'HEIGHT', for example, it is assumed that there is an object R+ that describes the set of positive real numbers. Such use of type checking is also a significant aid to documentation in cases where a large number of objects have to be defined.

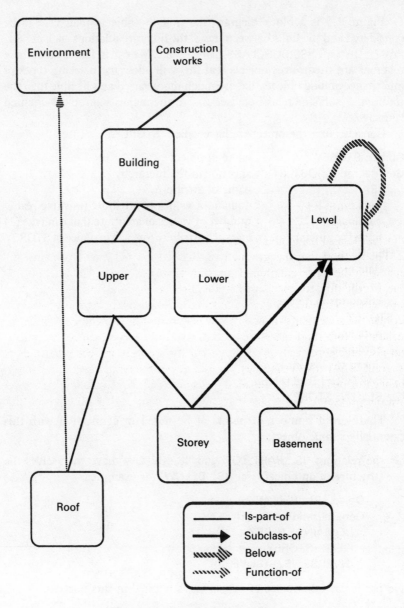

Figure 1.5   Representation of objects

The problem of checking and maintaining consistency within and between objects is extremely complex and merits giving more attention to the problem itself and to possible methods for ensuring this consistency. We now describe some particular cases and indicate how they could be treated.

Constraints on the allowable values of an attribute
Here we can use the attribute 'data type' as a check, as already indicated; and the use of a 'restrictive grammar' will give great flexibility. For example, the object ROOF has an attribute TYPE—OF—ROOF which can take only three (symbolic) values; we can represent this as

TYPE—OF—ROOF
data type: pitched **or** flat—with—parapet **or** flat—without—parapet
default: pitched

Returning to the attribute HEIGHT, suppose we wish to state that the height of a storey must be not less than 2 metres and not more than 3; we write a test for this in either of two ways. For one, we define a new type which we can call ALLOWABLE—STOREY—HEIGHT and write

Object: ALLOWABLE—STOREY—HEIGHT
Generalization: DATA—TYPE
PREDICATE: (and (≤ 'value' 3) (≥ 'value' 2)

For the second we associate a 'demon' with the attribute HEIGHT, which is triggered whenever an attempt is made to assign a value to this attribute.

Intuitively, it is easy to see that defining a new type, as here, is a sensible thing to do only if it plays some role elsewhere in the program.

Constraints involving several attributes of the same object
As soon as a constraint involves more than one attribute the problems of which attribute it is to be applied and when and how it is to be checked arise. Let us extend our model of STOREY slightly by adding two further attributes LENGTH and WIDTH. Suppose we wish to add the 'constraint'

AREA = LENGTH * WIDTH

The simple solution would be to define a demon associated with AREA which would be triggered whenever these values were read – a sort of 'if needed' facet, as found in languages of the type of KRL.

However, experience has shown that the user's ideas about the building are often not very precise: taking this to the extreme, suppose he knows only the area and width of a storey. Our approach would then be to define a very general model for 'constraint' which would be interpreted at run time by creating the necessary links:

Object: CONSTRAINT__ON__STOREY__AREA
Generalization: CONSTRAINT__PRODUCTION
 DOMAIN: STOREY
 CONSTRAINT: (= AREA (*LENGTH WIDTH))
 TYPE: VARIOUS

Constraints involving attributes of different objects
This is undoubtedly the most complex case. We start with an example that shows how a relation can be used to update the value of a particular attribute. Suppose we have an object ENVIRONMENT having an attribute GEOGRAPHICAL__REGION__OF__PROJECT, the value of which is to be chosen from a list of regions of the world, for example Europe, N. Africa. ... It is not difficult to imagine that for each region there are local customs and restrictions that will affect our building project. Thus we can suppose that the default value of the attribute TYPE__OF__ROOF of the object is determined by the region in which the building is to be constructed, and this can be expressed by means of a relation that enables the value of TYPE__OF__ROOF to be modified, by an inheritance mechanism, according to the value of GEOGRAPHICAL__REGION__OF__PRO-JECT. This is summarized in Figure 1.6. This type of inheritance was suggested by the language SRL [Wright & Fox, 1983].
 The objects involved in this relation have the following forms.

Object: ENVIRONMENT
Generalization: OBJECT
 GEOGRAPHICAL__REGION__OF__PROJECT
 data type: **either** Europe **or** N. Africa
 cardinality: 1
 linked to: instance

Object: ROOF
Generalization: Object
 TYPE__OF__ROOF
 data type: **either** 'pitched' **or** 'flat'
 cardinality: 1
 linked to: instance

Object: FUNCTION__OF
Generalization: RELATION
 DOMAIN: ROOF
 FIELD: ENVIRONMENT
 INHERITANCE__BY__TRANSFORMATION: LINK__ROOF__
 ENVIRONMENT

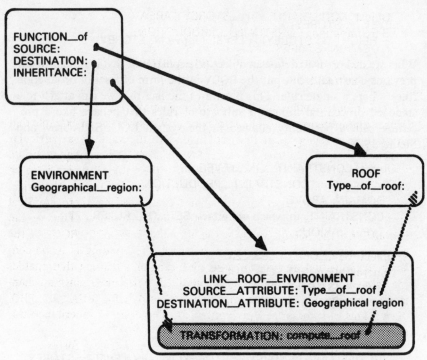

Figure 1.6 Constraints among several attributes of different objects

Object: LINK—ROOF—ENVIRONMENT
Generalization: METHOD—INHERITANCE—BY—TRANSFORMATION
  DOMAIN: ROOF
  FIELD: ENVIRONMENT
  DOMAIN—ATTRIBUTE: TYPE—OF—ROOF
  FIELD—ATTRIBUTE: GEOGRAPHICAL—REGION—OF—PROJECT
  TRANSFORMATION: compute—roof

The function 'compute—roof' produces the correspondence

  'Europe' → 'pitched'
  'N. Africa' → 'flat'

Constraints defined by production rules
Our last example shows how production rules can be used to express a constraint. It concerns the height above ground, which we shall call LEVEL, of a STOREY; there is an obvious relation between this and the LEVEL of the STOREY next above which we can write in a shorthand form as

LEVEL (x: STOREY)
+ HEIGHT (x: STOREY) = LEVEL (above (x: STOREY))

What we do here is to define an object (the constraint) that is similar to our previous constraints but put the BODY in the form of a set of production rules – here a single rule. This illustrates the fact that we can attach to a standard procedural linkage a subbase of rules that behave like a procedure call, a possibility allowed in the system LOOPS [Bobrow and Stefik, 1983].

Object: CONSTRAINT_ON_LEVEL
Generalization: CONSTRAINT_PRODUCTION
  DOMAIN: ABOVE
  CONSTRAINT: to which we attach SET_OF_RULES_23
  TYPE: VARIOUS

Object: SET_OF_RULES_23
Generalization: SET_OF_RULES
  RULES: RULE-3 RULE-4
  STRATEGY: "one rule at a time"

Object: RULE-3
Generalization: RULE
  if   (BELOW x: STOREY y: STOREY) (known (LEVEL x: STOREY)
                                    (known (HEIGHT x: STOREY)
  then   (LEVEL y) = (HEIGHT x) + (LEVEL x)
Object: RULE-4
Generalization: RULE
  if   (BELOW x: STOREY y: STOREY) (known (LEVEL x: STOREY)
                                    (known (LEVEL y: STOREY)
  then   (HEIGHT x) = (LEVEL y) – (LEVEL x)

We have tried, in this very condensed account, to show the advantage to be gained from a 'hybrid' representation in which objects, rules, procedures and demons can be mixed; and further have emphasized the importance of mechanisms that ensure the consistency of the information in relieving the genuinely 'expert' part of the system of the most burdensome tasks. Our study has shown the importance of choosing the most appropriate type of representation for each item of knowledge and of distinguishing between genuine inferential rules and more structural relations between items.

Multi-expert systems

One of the present limitations of expert systems is that they generally use only a single knowledge base, whilst there are complicated problems that require access to a variety of sources of knowledge; this is another way of saying that certain problems require the cooperation of experts in several different fields if a solution is to be achieved [Haton, 1985]. Various architectures have been suggested as a way to achieve this cooperation, giving what are called multi-expert systems and modeling a 'community of experts'. This has been the approach, for example, in the automatic recognition of speech, a problem typifying the need for a very varied stock of knowledge: many aspects such as acoustic, phonetic, lexical, syntactic and semantic have to be taken into account in the attempt to understand the meaning of a sentence. Analogous approaches have been made in the cases of image processing (see Section 1.3.2.13) and medical diagnosis (Section 1.3.2.3).

A particularly important model from this point of view is the 'blackboard'. For the reasons just given this was first applied to speech understanding, in the Hearsay-II system developed at Carnegie-Mellon University, [Lesser *et al.*, 1975], but it is more general and, as we shall see, can be used in many situations in AI. The underlying principle is the treatment of a number of knowledge sources as independent processes that share a complex data structure, the blackboard, and communicate (with each other and with the rest of the system) only by means of messages sent to the blackboard. The blackboard constitutes the facts base for the system and in Hearsay-II is structured in levels corresponding to the successive levels of abstraction of the speech signal, from acoustic to semantic, as shown in Figure 1.7. It also contains the hypotheses gen-

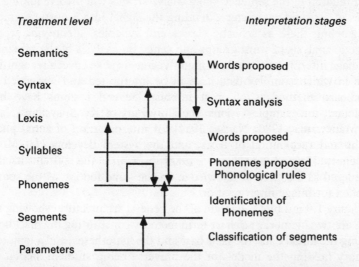

Figure 1.7 Blackboard levels and part of the hypothesis-generation process

erated in the course of the analysis – suggested words – in the attempt to understand the sentence; a knowledge source generates or modifies an hypothesis each time it is activated, that is, each time some particular set of conditions is found to hold. Thus a source appears as a couple Condition–Action, a model for the generalization of a production rule, and in this case the Action part can be as complex as necessary. A knowledge source can be equally a classical production rule or a very complex procedure.

It is worth noting that the blackboard model allows declarative and procedural knowledge statements to be mixed.

To illustrate these principles we will briefly study the working of Hearsay-II, basing our study on the architecture shown in Figure 1.8. Each knowledge source takes part at one or more levels of the blackboard whenever it is activated by the monitor, and if there is a conflict created by several knowledge sources trying to gain attention at the same time, a queue is formed, the order being decided according to some prearranged strategy. This allows very complex strategies to be used, for example to concentrate on one particular aspect of a problem according to some set of criteria – the 'focus of attention' strategy. It is essential to be able to adopt strategies of this type when attacking complex problems, because it is impractical to explore all possible solutions and there must be some means for keeping only the most promising hypotheses.

Each knowledge source brings to its level its own contribution to the further development of a partial solution, that is, a new hypothesis that in this case is sufficiently consistent with the data to constitute a possible interpretation of the sentence being analyzed; this will involve finding the values of acoustic parameters, dividing the signal into acoustic segments and labeling these as acoustic classes and syllables, identifying words, syntactic analysis of word groups and semantic analysis of the sentence.

Image interpretation and computer vision are, like speech recognition, fields in which complex data have to be interpreted and for which the blackboard method is of great interest. Several systems have been developed, for example Visions, the University of Kyoto system [Nagao and Matsuyama, 1980; Nagao, 1984] for interpretation of aerial photographs and recognition of faces, and the system developed at McGill University [Levine and Nazif, 1982] in which the system itself is considered as a source of knowledge on the same footing as the sources supplied for image interpretation.

Figure 1.9 is a block diagram of the general architecture, showing that there are two memories: a short-term memory constituting the blackboard holding the initial data, the facts base and the hypotheses, and a long-term memory holding the models of the universe being studied, shared and

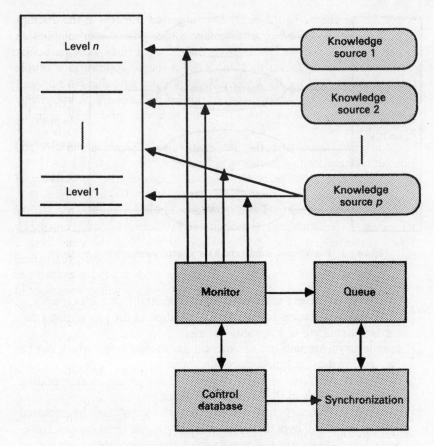

Figure 1.8 Functional architecture of Hearsay-II

accessed by the knowledge sources. Such a system can handle the low-level visual tasks of interpretation of two-dimensional scenes, such as preprocessing and segmentation.

The blackboard model has been used equally successfully for signal processing, for example in HASP/SIAP [Nii *et al.*, 1982]. The purpose of this system is to detect and identify marine structures of various types, including surface vessels and submarines, from data provided by hydrophones and using such knowledge as the 'acoustic signature' of such structures. Several other projects with the same aim use the same approach.

To summarize, the blackboard model has features that are important to the design of advanced architectures for expert systems:

(1) the possibility of cooperation between knowledge sources of very

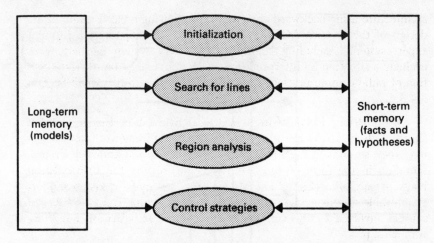

Figure 1.9   Blackboard architecture for a pattern-recognition system

varied types, mixing declarative and procedural forms if necessary;
(2) the Condition–Action couple, a generalization of the production rule, for representation of knowledge items;
(3) parallel asynchronous use of different knowledge bases, which can be implemented as multiprocessor hardware;
(4) solution of problems at different levels of abstraction, corresponding to different levels in the blackboard hierarchy;
(5) possibility of incremental construction of the solution by repeated refinement of the hypotheses provided by the different experts represented in the system; this results from the opportunistic method of working, in which at any stage the currently most informative data can be acted on;
(6) possibility of incorporating very elaborate controls, that can deal equally with forward and backward chaining.

Several tools for aiding the development of blackboard-based expert systems have been designed with these properties in mind.

Hearsay-III [Erman, *et al.*, 1981] This, as the name suggests, was derived from Hearsay-II but is not in any way limited to speech recognition; it uses two types of blackboard, one for the hypotheses and the associated knowledge items, the other for control of the system. We have already seen that the model allows the system itself to be regarded as one special knowledge source.

AGE [Nii and Aiello, 1979] AGE (Attempt to Generalize) provides the developer with a blackboard architecture and also a more classical architecture using backward chaining, thus allowing great freedom in the design of the system. AGE has been used to develop several different expert systems, including Hannibal, a military system for helping to evaluate a situation by interpretation of data obtained from the interception of radio communications. We discuss this system further in Section 3.4.3.4.

MXA [Rice, 1984] Written in Pascal by SDI in England, MXE (Multiple Expert Architecture) provides a general framework of developing expert systems, using a blackboard architecture and knowledge representation in the form of rules. It has been used by the British Royal Navy in particular [Lakin and Miles, 1984], to give a decision-support system able to amalgamate and interpret data coming from a variety of sources involved in the command and control activities of a military command post.

These tools are powerful but are also complex, and can be used only by highly skilled knowledge engineers who have a firm command of AI languages and concepts. However, they may be made more widely available in the future as a result of additional software facilities.

1.2.2.5 Current limitations of expert systems

Present-day expert systems are still very rudimentary, even though they often give spectacular results. Among the main limitations, now the objects of research, are the following.

(1) The over-importance of one individual expert in establishing the knowledge base, giving too strong a personal stamp. This will be reduced by the appeal to other experts for evaluation and criticism of the prototype, but the basic knowledge remains that of the leading expert.

(2) The almost complete absence of any learning capability. An expert system does not improve itself by using its past experience and, except in a very few cases, cannot add to its knowledge base. Much work is now being done on this aspect; some capacity for learning will become essential for the semi-automatic assembling of very large knowledge bases, because of the cost and laboriousness of acquiring this knowledge from human experts.

(3) The restricted coverage of the field being studied, and the fallibility of the system at the boundaries.

(4) The limitations imposed by the methods for knowledge representation now available, despite recent improvements, especially for multimodal representations. As MacCarthy commented over 20 years ago, 'common-sense' knowledge is extremely difficult to represent and to

use, and apart from a few special cases such as the medical system CASNET [Kulikowski and Weiss, 1982], causal relations are usually badly exploited in the reasoning process.

(5) Superficiality of the knowledge in the base. Expert systems do not have the deep knowledge of issues surrounding the problem that would help them to improve their reasoning. Thus the knowledge available to a system for diagnosing machine breakdowns is essentially a set of heuristic rules of the form Symptom(s)–Cause(s); what there should be in addition is a functional model of the machinery in question, together with a store of fundamental knowledge of, say, mechanics, which the system could use to argue from first principles as a human engineer would.

The attempt to find qualitative models of physical phenomena provides a rich field for AI research, and is of great importance for many fields of application. Thus a crucial requirement in the development of advanced industrial control systems is the simultaneous use of heuristic rules and a knowledge of the basic physics and chemistry of the processes to be controlled.

(6) Limited reasoning methods. The use of numerical coefficients to indicate probabilities, plausibilities, likelihoods and so on, found in most expert systems, does not resolve the difficulties of handling uncertainties and conducting approximate reasoning. Symbolic methods, not necessarily numerical, would seem to offer a better approach for the future; these future systems must be able to reason about uncertainties, and not only in an uncertain universe, in a way similar to that of a human expert, so as to deal with complex situations.

(7) Time-dependent reasoning, i.e. the type of reasoning that has to be conducted when dealing with phenomena that evolve in time [Vere, 1983a and b], as in surveillance, industrial process control, response to alarms, plant maintenance, decision support and so on. This is discussed further in Section 1.3.1.2. It usually entails working in real time, and the response time imposes a constraint on the expert system which must take this into account dynamically, modifying its reasoning process according to the time available. The present solutions to this problem are rather limited; for example, the medical diagnostic system VM, mentioned in Section 1.3.2.3 below, uses the change in values of certain parameters between successive instants. Reality is usually more complex than can be accounted for in this way; for example, changes over time are very often a reflection of relations between events, and a model for these events is needed that is adequate for giving an understanding of these relations, including cause-and-effect. Much research work is going on here also, into both

the fundamental aspects, such as the connection with temporal logics, and the development of advanced models.

(8) Limited ability to provide explanations. The ability of an expert system to show the successive steps in its reasoning – for example, the succession of rules applied – is as important to the experts and knowledge engineers concerned as it is to the inexperienced user seeking to improve his or her technique. However, this alone is not enough if the system is to be used as a teaching aid; here, as in (5) above, the system should have deep knowledge of its own field and also of teaching methods and of the pupils. It is likely that in the long term expert systems will have a profound influence on the whole subject of computer-assisted learning (CAL); see Haton and Haton [1985].

(9) Inadequate interaction with the external world. This concerns communication between the system and humans, whether the expert, the knowledge engineer or the user. Natural language and graphical images play a major role here; for example, a version of Tom has been produced in which a videodisk is used to display the symptoms that may be shown by tomato plants. The criticism applies equally to the links between the system and the physical system or process to which it relates; a great amount and variety of information is necessary for good reasoning, and for this the expert system should have connections to networks, databases, measuring instruments and other devices.

1.2.3 Questions to an expert

Q: Two questions are always coming up in connection with expert systems. First, about their performance, now and in the future, compared with human experts; and second, about their advantages over what's usually called classical information science. Taking the first, how do you feel? Can an expert system do as well as a human?

A: The strength of the human mind is undoubtedly its capacity for handling fuzzy concepts, implications and pieces of information that are imprecise or even mutually contradictory; and to see analogies between different cases when the relations aren't immediately obvious. It also has an ability to short-circuit what is not going to be useful and to sort out the relevant from a mass of detail. This makes it particularly well adapted to solving difficult problems by being quick to see the right approach and looking at only a few possibilities out of the many. The computer, on the other hand, is renowned for the speed and precision with which it can calculate and for its effectively infinite memory capacity, which together enable it to recover any item of information that has been given to it, systematically and with practically no risk of error.

The aim is that expert systems will combine these two sets of properties, that is, will formalize the human reasoning processes while keeping the combinatorial powers of the computer. In applications where this can be done the expert system will be more powerful than the human, but where the reasoning has the characteristics of an art the human will continue to have a great advantage. The fields in which this latter applies are still very important.

Q: That's all very general – could you be more precise? For example, can expert systems improve themselves?

A: This is the question of self-teaching. AI researchers have already developed some programs with learning abilities for a few simple problems, such as psychological tests, recognizing geometrical figures and so on. For an expert system, learning initially means knowing how to modify its rules – to improve them – as a result of having been given from outside some assessment of the quality of the results it has produced. The next level is that the system should be able to learn how to discover new rules, for example by inductive generalization from individual cases. Both these require the system to examine its own reasoning process; this will usually be represented by a graph, and what is required is to find those nodes at which a better path could have been taken. The number of possible combinations is enormous, so the number of cases supplied to the system must also be very great; and even if enough can be provided to cover all possibilities – which is a vain hope in any complex system – there is no guarantee that an improvement gained in one region will not be accompanied by a deterioration in another. Further, for many problems there are several solutions, or a list of solutions in descending order of plausibility, and this makes the learning process that much harder. And lastly, it can happen that the true solution is known only a long time after the system had produced its solution.

For all these reasons, there is yet no working expert system with true learning capabilities.

Q: But isn't the ability to learn an essential condition for 'intelligence'?

A: 'Intelligence' as we define it has many components, of which learning ability is one; and from this point of view expert systems do not qualify. But we must be careful not to jump to the conclusion that they are therefore 'unintelligent': after all, the ability to learn is very much the prerogative of the young – should we say that an old man is unintelligent simply because his learning capacity has deteriorated? Then again, components other than intellectual qualities certainly enter into human learning, motivation, for example. The objectives with which an expert system is constructed are bounded by the reasoning that it will perform; simulation by electronic equipment of essentially biological phenomena is part of AI research, but lies outside the field of expert systems.

Q: But isn't that a drastic simplification of the problem? Aren't there, after all, unbridgeable gulfs between humans and machines where creativity and the ability to innovate are concerned? Could an expert system, for example, adapt as well and as quickly to a new situation as can a human?

A: That depends on what you mean by a new situation. If it's simply that the data are new – different input parameter values – the answer is yes, it can; but if it means a new type of problem for which no provision has been made, the answer will usually be no. However, a human expert equally may perform badly on a problem of a type he isn't used to; the extent to which he performs less badly than an expert system will depend on the reasoning powers – of analogy, for example – that he can bring into play in order to visualize a possible solution.

Q: How does an expert system behave when given problems that are outside its field?

A: An expert system seldom differentiates between a problem that it can't solve because it needs knowledge that hasn't been given, and one that it can't solve because the data are incomplete or contradictory. This inability is due to a lack of general knowledge and to the system not having those layers of *meta-reasoning* that would give it the ability to reason about its own reasoning processes. Don't forget that so far expert systems have been built with specific ranges of tasks in mind, and without any intention of raising the general problem of intelligence.

Q: There is another fundamental difference that shouldn't be overlooked: expert systems don't have any organs of perception. Now, psychologists have shown that perception, far from being a matter of passive reception by the relevant organs, is really an intelligent activity, in fact that it *is* intelligence, on the same level as other faculties such as reasoning.

A: But there are expert systems with perceptive devices, for example some military systems and systems for pattern or image recognition; and this will be essential in many applications in the future. So far, the greatest advances have been made in vision, hearing and touch; taste and smell will certainly prove much more difficult, because there are so few experts there.

Q: If expert systems were as intelligent as you seem to be saying, shouldn't they be able to reproduce themselves?

A: A few attempts have been made to write programs that will help to build expert systems, but it would be a great exaggeration to say that these are 'experts'. Further, any real expertise needs at least ten years to develop, and no one, anywhere in the world, has an expert system so old.

Q: Taking all in all, could one honestly say that expert systems really are intelligent?

A: We mustn't forget that our ambitions are limited to making systems that can reason in very narrow fields; in other words, general intelligence in your sense of creativity, motivation and reasoning by analogy is not the aim of our study. But if we define intelligence simply as the capacity for solving problems there is nothing against considering the computer, or the expert system, as intelligent. Where intelligence is the question, the computer is usually judged more severely than the human: if the machine gives a correct answer the reaction is 'Of course, it was programmed to do that'; if not, 'it doesn't understand anything'. Don't forget that the level of correct communications between humans is far from high, nor that the number of mistakes we make every day is hardly consistent with intelligence as presently defined.

Q: I can see what it is that, in your view, differentiates the 'intelligence' of an expert system from the expert himself; but what differentiates an expert system from an ordinary computer program?

A: At present – and these differences are likely to become blurred as time passes – it's mainly in the way in which the reasoning is represented. In an expert system the rules are kept separate from the machinery for interpreting them, whereas in a classical program the two are combined. It follows that the route followed by an expert system is not decided in advance but is constructed dynamically by the inference engine as it applies the rules; in the classical program the sequence of decisions is programmed explicitly. Thus knowledge-based systems offer greater possibilities for modifying the knowledge held in the system and for explaining the line of reasoning they have taken, and for taking account of knowledge items without the user being aware of this.

Q: Greater ease of maintenance is often given as a decisive advantage of expert systems over standard programs; but if an expert system becomes very big, isn't there a risk of its containing contradictory rules?

A: A system with a good knowledge-acquisition module can usually detect repetitions of rules or internal contradictions. If a contradiction cannot be detected statically, that is, without running the system, because it arises from an interaction of certain rules, then matters are more difficult and more elaborate methods have to be used. Purely logical contradictions can be detected by many systems. But don't forget that human experts contradict one another; they don't arrive at a common consensus, because their experiences have been different, and their differences are perfectly justified. Resolving possible contradictions between reasoning rules can be very beneficial for the progress of science and technology, and expert systems can and should contribute to this.

Q: You just said that an expert system constructs its problem-solving path dynamically: is this not very different from what goes on when using a standard decision table or tree?

A: I said then that everything in a decision tree is programmed explicitly. If the program can be written without any errors and if there is little likelihood of the need to change it later, then this is perfect and there is no need of expert systems. But if complex strategies like back-tracking have to be used in the reasoning process, or several sources of information called on that are not necessarily available simultaneously, or fuzzy concepts, then the decision tree method is ill-suited. It can happen, however, that a program based on expert system principles is seen, *after the event*, to be reducible to a decision table, and it is then sensible to rewrite it in that form; but the apparently unnecessary detour will have been worthwhile, because it will have made clear the details of the expertise and of the reasoning processes and possibly have led to some simplification of these.

Q: How do you justify the distinction made between a knowledge base and a database, which at first sight seems quite arbitrary?

A: In two ways, mainly. First of all, databases are much more bulky, because they are primarily reflecting the memory aspect, that is, the ability to store and recover a very large number of items; whilst knowledge bases reflect the reasoning aspects and contain methods for solving problems. With a database it is the user's job to conduct the high-level reasoning and to interpret the data that it provides; it is in fact a tool for the expert who knows how to use it and not for what we may call the ordinary user. An expert system (because of its knowledge base) knows how to use the data and how to manipulate them so as to provide advice or a decision.

However, I grant you that 'intelligence' is effective only when it is coupled with a significant body of factual knowledge: strong reasoning powers and a good memory are complementary and this is why the two approaches are starting to converge. For many applications, such as banking, administration and industry, an expert system must be able to access a body of information that is relevant to the problem under consideration and to use this intelligently. A very large number of items of information can be involved, and these are often structured in the form of a database, the set of such bases constituting the collective, and continually evolving, memory of the enterprise. The links between these and the knowledge base proper are of fundamental importance to the expert system, which must be able to extract from the general body all the information that it needs in order to conduct its reasoning, without putting a series of questions to the user. There are not many systems that can be relied on to do this. A few prototypes have been developed as research projects attempting to integrate relational or more complex database management systems and AI work on reasoning, giving, for example, DBMSs more or less closely coupled to inferential systems; Prolog is used here, mainly. Work is being done also on hardware architectures oriented towards such systems; in Japan the relational database machine DELTA, one of the ICOT ('fifth generation') projects, is an indication of the knowledge base processing machines of the future.

A useful intermediate stage between the completely separate database and knowledge base and complete integration of the two is provided by the 'deductive database'. This contains both data items, given in relational form, and knowledge in the form of general rules for deducing new facts not stated explicitly in the facts base. Such an arrangement offers the user new services similar to those of an expert system, such as handling incomplete information and giving more informative replies to questions, as well as deducing new facts. But the reasoning powers are still very limited, and much work remains to be done here.

Q: One last question, if I may: aren't you afraid the expert systems are, after all, just a fashion?

A: 'Fashion' is a phenomenon that appears and disappears without our having much idea of why. Here we are bringing in a new style of computer programming that is influencing all those information scientists who can see its advantages. If no one is talking about us in a few years' time that won't mean that it was just a fashion but that our ideas have become integrated into the technique.

Q: So it's not just a fashion?

A: No.

1.3 WHERE ARE EXPERT SYSTEMS USEFUL?

1.3.1 Types of Problem for Expert Systems

There are certain types of problem that are suitable for attack by expert system methods (and by implication others that are not). It is extremely important to know these, because a problem that does not fall into one or other of the categories described below will best be dealt with by the more classical algorithmic methods, or even be out of reach of present methods because of the difficulty of formalizing the necessary expertise.

1.3.1.1 'Fixed instant' or 'nonhistoric' diagnosis

The problem here is analogous to that of medical diagnosis, a matter of interpreting a given set of data by choosing from a list, prepared independently in advance, the situation that best explains these data, or the several situations when several give equally good explanations. The diagnosis need not be unique, for various reasons:

(1) the data may be incomplete, and lack those that would discriminate between a number of possibilities;
(2) there are several different causes of the phenomenon observed;
(3) a diagnosis is a kind of ideal object characterized by a certain set of properties and may exist only in the mind of the specialist, whilst the phenomenon to be explained is something from the real world and seldom matches the ideal exactly.

The term 'fixed instant', or 'nonhistoric', means that the decision has to be made for a given instant in time, t say, without concern for the past or future; and if there is such an interest, past or future is treated in an overall sense and not as a series of observations at successive instants.

This is the type of problem that is most easily attacked by existing methods, because it usually requires the analysis of a single 'object' (possibly composed of a number of sub-objects) defined by a set of symbolic values, usually discrete, which can be manipulated by reasoning rules obtainable from human specialists. The set of possible conclusions translates into a set of goals to be reached by the system, which therefore works mainly by backward chaining.

The following problems come into this category:

(1) the many problems of classification;
(2) medical diagnosis, at a fixed instant;

(3) diagnosis of breakdowns of any physical device, such as a computer, a car engine or a domestic appliance; often a maufacturer's leaflet or manual will give elementary 'expertise' on repairing the fault;
(4) diagnosis of fabrication faults in materials;
(5) risk evaluation, for example that undertaken by a bank in lending to an enterprise or to an individual. In the case of the bank the diagnosis takes the form of some measure of the level of the risk; in a geological case there will be observations that show that earth movements occur with certain frequencies at certain locations, and therefore provide a set of parameters that can be used to compute the risk of these occurring at a given site;
(6) advice and guidance in matters governed by rules and regulations, particularly when these are complex and changing. Setting insurance premiums, for example, is essentially an algorithmic process, applying established formulas to given values of certain parameters; but the complexity of the situation can make an expert-system approach preferable. It is not a question here of using an expert system as such, for strictly speaking there is no expertise, but rather of using expert system types of programming methods.

1.3.1.2 Evolving situations

Situations that change with time are more complicated to deal with than those that do not, for now the system must contain not only the diagnostic rules but also rules for state changes, for prediction and for checking predictions. It must be able to show how the situation responds to external influences and to advise on how to make it evolve in such a way as to solve the particular problem.

A basic medical example is understanding the development of an illness or other medical situation so as to be able to act in time – the complementary situation to 'fixed-instant' diagnosis. Crisis management is another example, but with the major additional restriction that decisions have to be taken quickly, in an hour rather than a week or a month, and this implies a certain efficiency in the system. In both cases it is the events that guide the actions to be taken: if no event occurs there is no reason to change the state; thus the system will use inference engines that work mainly towards the future, although at certain times it may be necessary to pursue a given goal and therefore to use backward chaining. Further, there must be some means for checking that the actions suggested by the system have actually been performed – either reporting by the people concerned or some automatic recording of the changes made. A system of this kind is thus very appropriate for any 'chief officer', taking that term in its most general sense and including, for example, the head of a fire brigade or a medical service, or the colonel of an infantry regiment.

Understanding an evolving situation is more complicated than deciding whether or not a set of parameters has the same value at two different times, t and t' say; for now we have to decide also if any difference is significant, and if it is, what this means.

1.3.1.3 Task ordering and resource allocation

Task ordering is the name given to an important class of problems of which the characteristic is to decide the order in which a given set of tasks is best executed, under certain imposed conditions; the most usual constraints concern time, such as the requirement that a particular task must be completed before a given date or within a given length of time, but there may be intertask constraints such as that task B cannot be started until task A has been finished, that tasks T and U can be performed simultaneously, or even that task V should not be performed unless it rains. Whilst algorithmic methods have been used here, the most-used method being PERT, it seems that the use of expert systems will bring advantages.

The algorithmic method is perfectly satisfactory when the conditions can be stated clearly and precisely, and there is then no need to use expert system methods; but the latter can be useful when:

(1) the user needs the help of an expert in the field of the problem, to make precise the constraints that seem fuzzy to him; or
(2) the full set of constraints cannot be satisfied together and there may be priorities among them that are difficult to express algorithmically but susceptible to decision by heuristic rules; or
(3) the constraints themselves change rapidly with time and updating by classical methods is too costly.

Resource allocation can be either a problem in its own right or a part of a task-ordering problem. Since resources are limited their allocation to a set of tasks that has to be performed within narrow limits imposes constraints that are difficult to satisfy. If there are no considerations concerning the times taken to perform the tasks or the availability of the resources then we have a pure resource allocation problem; otherwise, an allocation problem coupled to a task-ordering problem.

The difficulty here is to find the right expert – there are no 'resource allocation experts'. Those who claim any such expertise usually operate very approximately with fuzzy constraints which they do not apply rigorously and bring in other constraints that may be subjective and are never written down.

1.3.1.4. Selecting the relevant information

The classical methods of information science have not successfully handled problems where there is too much information. Such information can block a system that has to work in real time unless there is provision for what can be called 'intelligent filtering'. An expert system can act as such a filter, eliminating noise, compressing signals, transforming numerical data into symbolic items, deriving higher level semantic information and so on.

The problem can arise in, for example, a military information system, a fully automated message transmission system or a system in which information arriving from a large number of sources has to be integrated. A very particular type of inference engine is required, which must be able, for example, to halt its own progress and remain halted until it receives a particular message; it is very likely that such an engine will work mainly by forward chaining, because it is the new information that will set it going again.

1.3.1.5 Specification and design

A typical example here is the production of plans for a house to be built, or the configuration of an information processing system to meet a given specification. The way in which the various components are assembled to give the final object is not fixed; the optimal or desirable way may depend on the level of success achieved in satisfying the constraints, which may be imprecise – 'the drawing room must be at least 40 m^2, for example – and satisfiable in several different ways. Some constraints may be more important than others, and there may be a case for abandoning a constraint if that brings worthwhile benefits – 'going 1% over the budget will give 10% greater value'. The good designer is one who knows when to relax constraints because they cannot be satisfied or because satisfying them would cost too much.

A fundamental consideration here is that the design of each component interacts with that of every other and therefore cannot be conceived independently of the rest; neglect of this may necessitate back-tracking when a constraint tested later is found not to be satisfied. The method of attack is to determine the main components in outline, leaving the internal details, which will not interact between components, to be settled later. The process is one of breaking the given problem into a number of subproblems, but the difficulty is that the details of this breakdown are specific to the particular type of problem and it does not seem easy to give a method that is both general and efficient.

Problems such as this involve handling large numbers of objects and usually require variables for their formulation; they can lead to a very strong combinatorial explosion unless there are good heuristics to guide the process of solution. Computer-aided design (CAD) is making more and more use of expert systems to design objects whose complexity grows without cease, such as VLSI circuits.

1.3.1.6 Concept formation

The development of an expert system in a particular field has often had the effect of improving the expertise in that field, as a result of the work put into classifying and formalizing the knowledge provided by the experts. The methodology can also be used in this way, to help fix ideas in fields where expertise is scarce and what little there is not well understood. It is not so much a matter here of constructing working systems as of assembling knowledge bases that can be used later to improve existing systems.

One example of this second case is computer vision, in particular the interpretation of images having a very complex technical content such as those that have to be interpreted in electrophoretic analysis of colloids, a new technique for which there are few high-level experts. Another is automatic recognition of speech, where a very difficult problem is the interpretation of the acoustic (vocal) signal in terms of phonetic units such as phonemes. Everyone is 'expert' in this process for his native language, but the expertise, acquired in earliest childhood by innate learning processes, is unconscious and completely inexplicable – differing, for example, from the professional expertise in diagnosing railway engine failures that an engineer acquired by experience in adulthood. However, there is a way to build up knowledge concerning this decoding, using a *sonogram*.

A sonogram is a graphical representation of sound showing the variation of frequency and amplitude with time, much used in phonetic studies; Figure 1.10 shows the sonogram for the French word '*idéale*'. A phoneticist, as a result of studying many sonograms in the light of his knowledge of phonetics, will develop an ability to segment the record into successive phonemes, and to identify these, with a success rate higher than that of any existing automatic equipment. This expertise is very difficult to acquire because it depends very much on visual perception, but its formalization enables great progress to be made in understanding the

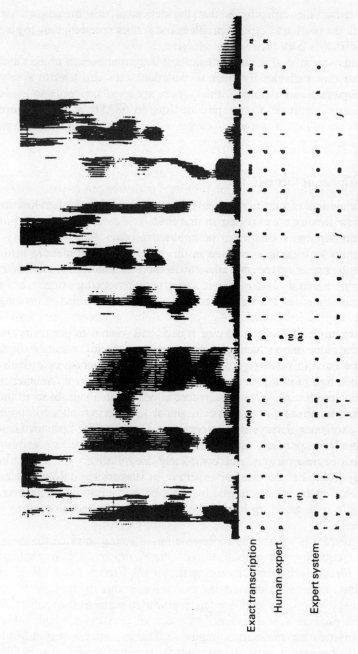

Figure 1.10 Sonogram of the French word *idéale*, showing interpretations by a human expert and the expert system APHODEX [Carbonell *et al*, 1986]

phenomenon of live speech. Several projects using this approach are being pursued. At CRIN (Centre Récherche en Informatique), Nancy, the system APHODEX has been developed for spoken French, with over 350 rules and complex reasoning strategies deduced from a study of the way in which an expert phoneticist works [Fohr, *et al.*, 1985]. Figure 1.10 gives the interpretations provided by the human expert and by APHODEX, the inference engine of which was specially designed for this type of problem.

1.3.1.7 Computer-aided instruction (CAI)

CAI programs are not usually expert in the field in which they aim to teach. They neither conceive the problems that they put to their students nor do they solve them; they are just programs, and therefore they cannot show how they conduct their reasoning. Only facts can be learned from them, not strategies for solving problems.

The idea of using expert systems for teaching arose because they explain their method of reasoning, and display the stock of knowledge on which this is based. This does not mean, however, that an expert system can be used just as it is for this purpose, that is, with only its problem-solving capabilities: it must be given the ability to generate problems of stated levels of difficulty. The system itself will solve these problems, but it must also have the teaching skills necessary to decide which are tricky problems, to set a series of problems of increasing difficulty and to decide what the pupil has to learn in order to be able to solve them and when he or she has reached the required standard. It is probably vain to hope that a universal teaching program can be developed, but it is reasonable to look forward to systems that will provide teaching for a range of problems – in diagnosis, for example – coupled to problem solvers. The first will have rules that operate on a facts base and comprise both what the student has learned already and what rules are still to be learned; the second acts as a facts base for the first.

Figure 1.11 shows the architecture for an expert system designed for teaching.

1.3.2 Fields of activity covered

1.3.2.1 Finance and insurance

The banking, financial and insurance sectors are concerned with several types of problem, principal among which are:

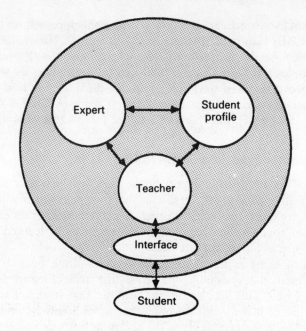

Figure 1.11 Architecture for intelligently assisted teaching by computer

(1) fund management, especially of investment portfolios;
(2) advice on loans, for the private individual;
(3) risk analysis for bank loans (steadily replacing traditional 'credit rating');
(4) management of a company's finances;
(5) drafting insurance contracts;
(6) assessment of industrial risks, for setting insurance premiums.

We consider these in turn.

Portfolio management The client states how much he wishes to invest and whether his concern is for security or for riskier high capital gain, also if he has any preferences where his money is invested, and so on. The system then suggests a set of investments, which it can modify if the client then states further requirements. Some French banks are already contemplating introducing such a system as a service for their customers, along the same lines as they made access to accounts available over the Minitel network. A system of this kind would need a diagnostic module (to identify the type of client making the enquiry) and an operational research module (to find solutions to a set of linear relations); and because it would be intended for direct use by the general public it would have to be adept at working with natural language.

The Cognitive Systems company has produced a prototype system for the General Bank of Belgium; and a folio management program Folio [Cohen, 1983] has been developed at Stanford.

Loan advice This requires access to a large body of data concerning what is being offered by the market, giving all the rates and surrounding conditions; in France there are at least 250 possibilities to be considered, of which about 60 are concerned with public funds. This information is widely dispersed and not easily collated. It is clearly impossible for any of a bank's agents to hold all this in his memory, and experience has shown that an agent will suggest to a client only those possibilities with which he is very familiar. Thus for any particular problem concerning raising finance the client will find that an expert system provides a better set of possibilities, which usually represent a much more complex arrangement than the single contract he would have entered into because of lack of information and time. The expert system provides an important alternative to the traditional but expensive method of giving special training to the staff; it is a more economic proposition to put in an expert system for helping to sell financial packages than to mount a comprehensive and continuous training program when it is realized that any one of the agents so trained will only rarely make use of his training.

Loan risks This concerns loans to companies and is a matter of examining their economic state to find if this is healthy, and hence to assess the risk that a bank undertakes in lending them money.

Company funds management This has to take account of forecast income and expenditure and to allow the managers to make decisions concerning lending or investing funds when there is a credit balance, or borrowing when in debit. The problem is more complex than those previously dealt with because it requires a complex situation to be followed in time.

Insurance contracts This is a very important problem for insurers, although it is logically very simple. Many contracts differ in only a few clauses, depending on a few special particulars in the case in question. Thus whilst there is much repetition, it is rare for two contracts to be identical, and expertise is necessary to identify the few points of difference.

Insurance premiums Setting these for an industrial enterprise usually involves bringing in an expert on each separate type of risk to which the enterprise is exposed. Although the process for assessment is algorithmic in nature it has to use many rules that embody complex legislation arising from many particular cases and change continuously.

Little has been published concerning this fiercely competitive financial field; little is known about the most advanced applications, because their developers seek to retain the competitive advantages that they believe these systems give them. However, the liveliness of the field is shown by the number of 'expert system factories' that specialize in such applications – their clients remaining unknown. The firms Syntelligence, Cognitive Systems, Palladian, Helix and Applied Expert Systems all claim to do much work of this kind. Applied Expert Systems has recently announced a combined hardware and software package, Plan-Power, consisting of a dedicated work station and an expert system shell specially adapted to the development of banking applications; and both SRI International and the Gartner Group have important projects.

1.3.2.2 Law and public administration

The most important problems here concern interpretation and application of legal instruments and drafting formal documents such as contracts, deeds, acts, etc.

The first includes helping individuals and companies to find from complex documents what financial or other benefits they can claim, and how they should go about doing so. Because of the many changes made by most people in the course of their lives – marriage, retirement, change of dwelling, forming a company, etc. – few can know all the many steps that have to be taken; and since everything is usually expressed in jargon, or the conditions governing applications are difficult to interpret, the formal procedures are seldom easy for the nonspecialist to understand. Expert systems for helping here could be made available not only to the general public but also to the public officials who have to operate the services. This would undoubtedly save time and improve communication between the two sides, and in addition would bring advantages resulting from the clarification of some of the older texts in the process of formalizing the expertise they represent [Kowalski and Sergot, 1985]. With such ideas in mind the Ecole Nationale d'Exportation, working with Cognitech, has developed ten expert systems for helping the customs authorities to find their way through the jungle of documents, concerning customs, excise, transport, insurance, currencies, etc., that govern exporting.

Drafting contracts has already been mentioned in connection with insurance, and what was said there applies equally to any class of document for which the general form is fixed but the detailed wording depends on a large number of parameters whose values vary from one person or one transaction to another. The expertise consists in choosing, for each particular situation, the appropriate words, paragraphs and legal clauses to 'fill in the blanks' in the standard form.

As a general principle we can say that any administrative problem that involves handling large masses of symbolic information, such as formal rules and regulations, is a good candidate for solution by means of expert systems. Whilst the reasoning processes used in these problems are essentially algorithmic, a program so based would be extremely costly to maintain because of the frequency with which the code would have to be modified in order to keep up to date with the continually changing regulations; the ease with which such updating can be done for expert systems gives them a decisive advantage. The theoretical feasibility of using expert systems in this way has been shown in a thesis study on payroll and personnel administration [Levesque, 1983] but much still remains to be done to overcome various technical obstacles arising from poor performance in practice, in particular inadequate speed of processing and of access to large databases.

1.3.2.3 Medicine

The medical field has the paradoxical distinction of having been the first for which expert systems were developed and the last to make effective use of them. This reluctance is explained in part by the 'sanctity' attributed to the object of the study, here the human body – even though the final decisions would be made by a responsible doctor who would use the advice provided by an expert system in the same way as he would that provided by the medical literature. The authors, however, take the view that the main reason lies in the high opinion that many doctors have of their own art, leading them to believe that no computer system could possibly equal them; or conversely, in the case of some others, in an irrational fear of being outclassed by a machine endowed with a better memory than their own. The two arguments may seem mutually contradictory, but in fact both are held by different groups of doctors.

Whatever, the case, whilst doctors may be hostile to the idea of spreading their expertise widely through the medium of the machine, diagnosis being the most dignified part of their activity, they are entirely happy to have the machine help them in the more routine parts such as maintaining patients' records, sending out reminder notes for visits and preparing and recording drug issues. They also recognize the potential of expert system methods for teaching.

Many laboratory prototypes have been developed for what we have called 'fixed instant' or 'nonhistoric' diagnosis in special areas, for example kidney infections or diseases of the liver; given the symptoms observed and the results of laboratory tests on the patient, they provide the most probable diagnosis or diagnoses and usually also suggest an appropriate treatment. A good example is Mycin [Shortliffe, 1976]. More recently, several researchers have attacked the problem of following a patient's medical history and the development of an illness as time passes; an example here is the system VM for giving respiratory aid to a patient in intensive care [Fagan, 1980].

The special nature of medical reasoning has led a number of researchers to design models that differ to a greater or lesser extent from the normal, either

(1) by extending the usual types of production rules, for example in SAM [Gascuel, 1981] Sphinx [Fieschi, 1981] and others; or
(2) by combining several different methods for representing knowledge items and reasoning processes; for example, hierarchical representation, Internist [Pople, 1982]; frames and Bayesian reasoning, PIP [Pauker *et al.*, 1976]; semantic nets and rules, Casnet [Kulikowski and Weiss, 1982]; hierarchical 'community of experts', taking into account the different contributions of general practitioners and specialists; and representations in terms of concepts, MDX [Mittal and Chandrasekaran, 1980]; and others.

The teaching aspect is evident in some systems; and the possibility is emerging of systems that will be used by the patients themselves to help them understand their illnesses and deal with them. Diabetes is in this class, especially for patients dependent on insulin; for such patients must not only give themselves daily injections – if they are capable – but also regulate their diet: cf. Mariot *et al.*, [1986]. A recent study [Bétaille *et al.*, 1984] concerns hemodialysis in the patient's home, which could be of help in certain kidney disorders.

1.3.2.4 Agriculture

The most important problem in agriculture is the improvement of crop productivity, and this means battling successfully with different predators. We started this chapter with an extract from the very large-scale French project concerned with vegetable pathology, Tom [Blancard *et al.*, 1985]. This can take into account over 200 symptoms connected by a network of relations, and has 180 inference rules; it 'knows' some 60 diseases of the tomato, some due to parasites (16 fungal, 4 bacterial, 6 viral such as the mycoplasmose virus), some not (deficiency diseases, toxicities, genetic anomalies) and several pests (leaf miners, bats, aphids, flea beetles), and for each can advise on a treatment which it puts out as a few lins of text. It can also use the information in its database, for example on resistant strains, to suggest a change of variety for the next crop.

Tom is now being extended to cover the 30 main European crops; and within the ESPRIT program a consortium comprising Cognitech, General Electric and the Laboratoire de Recherches en Informatique d'Orsay is developing a self-teaching system to be incorporated into Tom.

A group at the University of Illinois has developed a prototype system called AQ 11 [Michalski and Larson, 1978] for testing methods for teaching. Given descriptions of several hundred affected soya plants, together with the relevant diagnoses, they have constructed inference rules which, used with other data, have given better results than a program developed by the classical method involving consultations with experts.

The project ARPEGE is being pursued at the Centre Mondial Informatique et Ressources Humaines with the aim of helping with farm management.

An important possibility for the future is the use of robots to identify affected individual fruits or vegetables during sorting and packaging. However, computer vision is not yet sufficiently well developed for this, nor is there any program that can recognize such symptoms as 'gray mold on gray-beige spots scattered over the upper surfaces of the leaves'.

1.3.2.5 Geology

One of the most important geological practices is that of getting the best possible knowledge of the subsoil, either to increase the probability of success in prospecting for mineral or other valuable products, or to reduce the probability of accidents resulting from lack of knowledge of its structure. The following are some of the expert systems developed in this field.

Prospector [Duda *et al.*, 1979] This is in effect a consultant in mineral geology which, given data relating to the subsoil and the upper layers, advises on the probability of there being deposits of certain minerals in that area. It uses partitioned semantic networks and efficiently compiled production rules; around it have been developed various useful tools such as KAS (Knowledge Acquisition System) [Reboh, 1981] for helping the designer construct new models or change those already existing.

Litho [Bonnet *et al.*, 1982] This interprets measurements of physical properties of the rocks, such as density, electrical conductivity and radioactivity; it calls on general information relating to the geological context of the site, for example its geographical location, from which follows information about the general geological features of the region, its paleontology, its petrography, its mineralogy and so on. Litho uses an inference engine Elitho – related to Litho as Emycin is to Mycin – developed on a Vax machine in the language Franzlisp. The interpretation is a technical description of the successive layers traversed by a borehole, with a precision of 0.15 m; this can then be used by programs dealing with fluid flow to determine the regions in which petroleum is most likely to have accumulated.

Cessol [Ayel *et al.*, 1984] This is a system designed to help the planning of geotechnical surveys and the evaluation of their findings, undertaken in connection with building construction. This integrates knowledge relating to various fields, including mechanics, hydrology, geology and building science.

1.3.2.6 Warning and management of crises and catastrophes

Human experts can usually explain why an economic crisis has occurred after the event, using a variety of theories that are not necessarily consistent among themselves; but they can very rarely predict such an occurrence. No one today can say just how far the dollar will fall nor when it will start to rise again. If an expert in forecasting is asked if a certain event can be predicted the reply will usually be 'Yes – afterwards': in other words, by hindsight.

On the other hand, there are certain types of natural disaster, such as earthquakes, landslides, floods and volcanic eruptions, for which the favorable conditions are fairly well known and for which there are enough observations for general rules – physical laws, in effect – to be inferred, which can be explained by geologists and other relevant experts. It is thus possible to identify those regions of the Earth where the risk of some natural catastrophe is highest. The earthquake zones are well known; regions where landslides are especially likely could be identified equally accurately and the necessary precautions taken. Some regions, such as the Charente in France, are flooded every year at the same time; an expert system could detect the warning signs and set in motion precisely planned operations, its strength residing in its rigorous approach and its memory of similar events of past years.

Forecasting could be improved by operating with expert system techniques on very large databases built up from observations on past disasters.

Not only is forecasting feasible, but it is also realistic to envisage the use of expert systems to organize rescue operations. This is not the simplest of problems, because it has to involve several of the techniques we have described earlier, such as allocation of limited resources (when all the constraints may not be satisfiable simultaneously) and the following in time of a changing situation, filtering the relevant items from a very large body of information when it is known that not all items are of equal importance nor of equal reliability. The experience of some recent natural disasters has shown that the ensuing panic and lack of coordination among the various rescue services could be at least partly avoided if there were an expert system that kept a clear head and remained tireless and available for 24 hours every day.

1.3.2.7 Information science

Strangely enough, information science has not so far given rise to a great number of expert systems, apart from those concerned with configuring computer systems. The following applications are projected or are in the process of development.

(1) *Choice and use of large software systems*, for example packages for calculation of strengths of materials, statistical systems, optimization – e.g. EXADS [Rogers and Barthelemy, 1985] – or mathematics generally. One very well-known system is Macsyma [Moses, 1967], for formal manipulations in algebra (including solution of sets of algebraic equations) and in differential and integral calculus; this performs very well and in the USA is used over a network by more than 4000 workers.

(2) *Program writing.* The Pecos system at Stanford [Barstow, 1979] is an aid to programming in Lisp and Fortran; it is in fact part of a more ambitious project, PSI [Green, 1976], aimed at automatic programming. KBPA (Knowledge-Based Programming Assistant) was developed by IBM Palo Alto and the University of Illinois to help the programmer through the different stages of program construction – design, coding, implementation and testing.

(3) *Program generation* from a library of previously developed modules.

(4) *Analysis of software failures.* The Prime company has developed a system that examines, automatically, the traces of a program's execution, stored and preserved in case of incident.

(5) *System configuration.* The aim here is to enable a computer manufacturer to offer a configuration of component items that will meet a customer's requirements. Most such systems are concerned only with hardware but some consider also the software needed for the applications that the customer has in mind, for example Siemens's Siconflex

[Lehmann *et al.*, 1984]. Almost all the major computer manufacturers have systems of this kind: DEC (R1/Xcon with over 3000 rules, which has successfully configured Vax systems with 98% success), [McDermott, 1980 and 1984], ICL, BULL (Spec), Sperry, NCR, Nixdorf (Conaid). Such systems could be made available to the public to advise on the choice of hardware and software suitable for a stated problem.

(6) *Running large computer systems.* IBM in particular has a teaching system to help here.

(7) *Program translation.* The Lexeme Corporation [Electronics, 1985] has a system that will translate programs written in Fortran or Cobol into Ada or C, which halves the cost of hand translation.

1.3.2.8 Industry

Expert systems have already made an important impact on industry and will do so increasingly in the future; the applications are in a variety of fields, as follows.

Computer-aided design (CAD)

Structures The SACON system [Bennett and Engelmore, 1979] provides advice on the choice of programs for structural engineering computations; the ADROIT system of the British consultancy Scicon is an aid to the design of aircraft structures.

Electronics A great deal is done in connection with the design of VLSI (very large-scale integration) circuits: the PALLADIO system at Xerox [Brown *et al.*, 1983], Fairchild (checking that the circuit meets the specification), Fujitsu (production of masks from a specification in a high-level language) [Maruyama *et al.*, 1984], IBM (design of printed circuit boards and of integrated circuits), NTT.

Building A long term project TECTON has been developed to act as an expert collaborating with an architect, by leaving the design and final choices to the architect but working out the consequences of the choices made, indicating any internal contradictions that may arise and putting questions to elicit missing information. The KEOPS company has a prototype system for producing working drawings, with all the accepted industrial conventions, from sketches of a building design. Four French organizations, GAMSAU, IIRIAM, MATRA and BETEREM, have collaborated in producing a system for evaluating costs in the early stages of a building project. The Centre Scientifique et Technique du Bâtiment (CSTB) and INRIA are looking into the possibilities for using new languages and software tools for attacking the special problems of building, using INRIA's general engineering design system SMECI. Finally, the Ecole Polytechnique Fédérale de Lausanne and the Dumez construction company have collaborated in producing a system for helping the design of the outer shell of a building [IN.PRO.BAT, 1986]

Diagnosis of breakdowns, incidents and manufacturing faults
Here again are many developments. Expert systems are important both because they provide a nonalgorithmic solution to the problems of detecting failures and also because they make it easy to update the database in step with changes made to the physical system, such as repairs, improvements and new electronic circuits. They are used in a wide variety of applications. IBM has DART, 'An expert system for computer fault diagnosis' [Bennett and Hollander, 1981], Dassault Electronics has DEDALE for faults in hybrid electronic circuits; systems have been developed for radar, for railway traction such as General Electric's CATS-1 [Bonissone and Johnson, 1983] and the Rufus system described in Section 1.2, for telephone networks such as Bell Labs ACE [Vesonder *et al.*, 1983] in the USA, and for power stations, both fossil fuel and nuclear. For industrial incidents, the petroleum company Elf-Aquitaine has SECOFOR for diagnosing possible causes of drill jamming during the sinking of a well [Hollander *et al.*, 1983].

For manufacturing faults, an interesting British development is a system for detecting defects during glass manufacture [Mitra and Parker, 1984]; and in the same field Cognitech has produced a program to deal with metal casting, for one of the world's major metallurgical companies: this is activated by a signal from the casting-shop foreman and can identify the cause of the fault and say what steps should be taken to get rid of it. Systems of this kind are of very great importance in the improvement of industrial productivity, especially in the developing countries.

Production engineering
In the manufacturing and production industries the increasing complexity of the equipment that human operators have to control, and the move towards ever increasing automation, are ensuring that AI will become steadily more important in these industries. Present developments concern a variety of components of an integrated production system.

Process command and control This is a difficult problem generally, the solution demanding real-time working, complex time-dependent reasoning and the processing of a very large mass of data coming from many measuring and detection devices – several thousands, possibly. Examples of systems that have been developed for this are PICON on the Lisp

Machine at LMI [Moore, 1984] and PILOTEX from the French company ITMI. Some prototypes for helping operators are working, for example for a Danish cement works [Martin Larsen, 1981] and for continuous processes such as nuclear power generation in the USA [Nelson, 1982], in France [Ancelin, 1985] and in Japan [Yamada and Notoda, 1983]. In all cases of this type the operator – and the expert system that is available to help him, and possibly later to replace him – has only a limited amount of time in which to take a decision in a complicated situation. Since it is not possible to examine every possibility, the need is to collect the values of those parameters that are relevant to the particular situation and to select from the knowledge base the items that are most likely to lead to a solution [Sauers and Walsh, 1983].

Task planning and ordering Expert systems offer much greater flexibility than the usual mathematical methods of operational research, as is shown by the IMS system for integrated manufacture, a broad program of development by Carnegie-Mellon University and the Westinghouse company in the USA [Fox, 1981], and in France by the Compagnie Générale d'Electricité's SOJA [Le Pape and Sauve, 1985]. Studies have been made also of a variety of manufacturing operations, in France in particular at the University of Grenoble with the GARI system [Descotte and Latombe, 1981]; and of aids to project management and control, for example Dumez's PENELOPE for laying out the schedules for large-scale construction projects [Cognitech, 1985c].

Robotics This has now become integrated into manufacturing. The new generations of robots contain increasing amounts of AI, for example for computer vision, geometrical reasoning, trajectory construction, generation of action plans and rescheduling of tasks after some incident.

A matter of major importance in industry is the integration of expert systems into the general hardware and software environment of each undertaking, and for this an essential requirement is the linking of the system with the local information network. Some standardization is occurring in this field, as shown by the standard MAP adopted by Boeing and General Motors, with which PICON, mentioned above, is comparable.

1.3.2.9 Management and office work

Expert systems will certainly be used here in the future, even though at present there are few products available. The hoped-for outcome is increased productivity resulting from better handling, dissemination and exploitation of information; the following are the potential applications.

(1) *Modeling information flow* in an enterprise or administration.

(2) *Automatic analysis and distribution of documents*, possibly combined with computer scanning and recording.
(3) *User-friendly interfaces* that will make different information systems easily accessible to nonspecialist staff.
(4) *Automatic provision of office services* such as mail, arrangements and agenda for meetings, etc.
(5) *Access to information* in databases, either within the enterprise or outside. The general problem of interfacing an expert system to a database is still not completely solved, even though, as shown in Section 1.2.2.3, it is of great importance, especially in management.

A few relevant products have appeared recently, among which we may quote XSel ('Excellent Selling Assistant') [Polit, 1985], an expert system developed by DEC to complement their configuration system Xcon (see Section 1.3.2.7 above) and intended to help their sales staff draw up orders for Vax machines. This has a knowledge base of over 4000 rules and provides a complete and consistent set of information, including prices and delivery times.

1.3.2.10 Chemistry

The first expert system ever produced, Dendral, by Edward Feigenbaum at Stanford in 1969, was in this field. As we have already said, Dendral can determine the structure of a compound given its molecular formula and the results of mass spectrometer analysis; it can perform better than any human expert and is in daily use by many researchers over a telecommunications network. Many other systems have been developed for other tasks, in particular the following.

Identification of elements. The system EXSYLA [Lamboulle *et al.*, 1985], developed at CRIN, Nancy, in collaboration with the University of Metz, uses mass spectrographs to identify the elements in organic or inorganic compounds.

Computer-aided (organic) synthesis. Synthesis of organic compounds is of great economic importance in the creation of new products in such fields as pharmaceutics, plastics and fuels. Several algorithmic systems have been developed, but these are cumbersome and inflexible and do not allow the use of heuristic methods that would exploit large structures provided by expert organic chemists. This heuristic approach would include the search for new methods for synthesizing new compounds, evaluation of the costs and the risks, study of methods already used by other workers and so on; the expert system methodology provides the right framework for developing 'intelligent' systems for synthesis. Several projects may be mentioned here. SECS (Simulation and Evaluation of Chemical Synthesis) [Wipke *et al.*, 1978] is an interactive system for helping the chemist find and evaluate possible routes for a synthesis; it uses a knowledge base that includes details of chemical reactions, information about reactivities of compounds and basic principles of chemical synthesis. SYNCHEM 2 [Gelernter *et al.*, 1984], the culmination of more than 15 years' work, uses heuristic methods to find routes for organic syntheses; it has a very broad knowledge base and can bring into play information about a very large number of reactions.

1.3.2.11 Military applications

Expert systems have recently become important in military applications and the potentials are numerous and promising; the characteristics of military activities – scarcity of expertise, very high level of performance required, highly stressful surrounding conditions, etc. – make this method of solution very attractive.

Some applications made to serve military ends can be valuable also for civil purposes. This is especially true of systems for diagnosing breakdowns, aimed at increasing the availability of technical equipment; several such have been financed by the military, for example in France DRET (Direction de la Recherche et des Etudes Techniques) has financed one for aircraft failures, at Avions Marcel Dassault. To be more specific, military applications are concerned with the following three major fields, found in large-scale projects such as the Strategic Computing and Survivability Program (SCSP) financed by DARPA.

Indentification and pursuit of targets

Target identification has been the object of many studies over the past 20 years and more, using pattern-recognition techniques, in particular statistical techniques. Recognition can be improved, and errors corrected, by calling on an expert system that makes use of the context in which the target is found. Systems of this type have been developed in the USA by Martin Marietta and Hughes Aircraft, leading to the idea of autonomous target-seeking vehicles for operation on the ground, in the air or under water (e.g. tanks, helicopters, aircraft and robot submarines). Many design studies for such vehicles have been made, and prototypes have been built by Hughes, Honeywell, Westinghouse and several American universities. In all cases the vehicle has a group of expert systems that cooperate to carry out the following tasks:

(1) *Vision:* interpretation of data provided by visual sensors such as cameras or telemetered lasers.

(2) *Planning:* generation of routing plans according to the objectives of the mission and the obstacles encountered.
(3) *Integration of information* from different sources, to provide a description of the state of the vehicle and its environment.
(4) *Reasoning:* using this information in connection with specialized knowledge bases.

Aids to control of military vehicles

The control of modern vehicles, especially aircraft, is becoming ever more complex and is making ever-increasing demands on skill and attention. Expert systems can help here in at least four types of task:

(1) *diagnosis* of the state of the vehicle and its environment;
(2) *navigation*, identifying reference points, setting and following routes;
(3) *tactics*, recognizing targets, cf. AIRID [Aldridge, 1984]; analysis of risks when attacked, forming action plans;
(4) *recognition of enemy vehicles*, evaluation of threat.

Such systems will undoubtedly be common in future generations of military aircraft.

Command and control

Expert systems can give invaluable aid to the man in charge of an operation, in tasks such as:

(1) preprocessing information coming from different sources and combining this to make more effective use of it possible;
(2) interaction with databases to extract the information needed in order to reach a decision.

A great deal of research is being done in all the fields described although little has been published. Among the systems already developed are TECA, by the Rand Corporation, for naval threats; TATR, also by Rand [Callero *et al.*, 1984] for deciding the best tactics for attacking an airforce base; Multisensor Esm (SRI International) for interpreting the data from multisensors on bombers (cf. p. 43); and a system for interpreting the signals received in ocean surveillance. This last uses the 'blackboard' model (*loc cit*); a similar model is used in the SUS system, developed for the British Royal Navy for interpreting multisensor data received on ships [Stammers, 1983].

1.3.2.12 Aeronautics

The main problems encountered in aeronautics are:

(1) diagnosis of faults on the ground;
(2) diagnosis of, and recovery from, faults in flight;
(3) giving help to the pilot;
(4) training, of flight crews and others;
(5) modeling of the aircraft's subsystems and management of the flight;
(6) formatting and presentation of data in the cockpit;
(7) planning of individual flights and of air traffic.

Diagnosis of aircraft and helicopter faults on the ground is most important. Very often items of equipment are replaced when they are perfectly serviceable, simply because there is neither the time not the competence at the airport for a proper diagnosis to be made. In France work is being done on this problem at the CGE's (Compagnie Générale d'Électricité) Marcoussis laboratory and at Dassault, the latter having developed CECILIA [Champigneux, 1984], an expert system for diagnosing faults in electrical and in hydraulic circuits; there are developments also at Bell Helicopters in the USA and at Westland Helicopters in Britain.

The 'intelligent co-pilot' is the next stage of flight automation after the now-classical autopilot, which is limited to certain parts of the flight: American studies have shown that most flight incidents are the result of human failures. Important work is being done at NASA on incorporating the human pilot into the control loop for aerospatial systems, providing him with as much help as possible by means of expert systems for diagnosing and recognizing situations as they arise. Elsewhere considerable effort is being put into modeling the behavior of the human pilot, in the form of rule-based or message-exchange systems: for example, the system MESSAGE developed at CERT for Airbus Industries [Boy, 1983].

The Dassault company has developed ALICIA, an expert system for flight management and MARIA [Champigneux, 1985] for simulation of aerial combats; and the University of Illinois has a qualitative model for the Turbojet engine [Rajagopalan, 1984].

The problem of air traffic control has been tackled by many workers; we may mention AIRPLAN [Masui *et al.*, 1983], for traffic management at an airport and AUTOPILOT [Thorndyke, 1981].

Expert systems have been developed for planning individual flights:

(1) ICEX (Icing Expert) uses meteorological reports to predict zones where there is risk of icing;
(2) NASA Langley has used a simulator for the aircraft's behavior to study the flight-planning problem.

1.3.2.13 Image processing

Numerical processing of images is increasing in economic importance in a wide variety of fields, including robotics and production engineering, medicine, space, biotechnology and office work. Up to the present the methods used have been purely algorithmic, involving a number of processes applied to the image in a fixed and predetermined order. This approach is not feasible when one is faced with the complexities of interpreting and understanding images: thus no one is capable of writing an algorithm that will enable a robot vehicle to navigate a part of the real world, or to interpret a tomographic image. In such circumstances we have, at one end of the scale, to bring in a wide range of knowledge, and, at the other, to study the elementary constituents of the image ('pixels' or 'pels' for a screen image) in order to perform such intelligent tasks. Further, successful interpretation of images often requires expertise that is acquired only with long experience, and the importance of expert systems here is that they enable this expertise to be captured.

Several experiments have been made along these lines, for example, to help analyze industrial images [Nazif and Levine, 1984] or biomedical images [Chassery and Garbay, 1984]; Cognitech, the Louis Pasteur University at Strasbourg and CRIN at Nancy have collaborated to produce an expert system for interpreting radiological images. In our previous discussion of multi-expert systems and blackboard models (cf. p. 43, also Matsuyama and Hwang [1985]) we pointed out that a complete system for image interpretation must involve complex interactions between expert systems of different types and between these and various knowledge bases. Also such a system must allow heuristic and procedural methods to be mixed, in particular for handling the physical data provided by the sensors. Such developments, in which the best use is made of both AI and algorithmic techniques, are a good illustration of the complementary nature of the two approaches.

1.3.2.14 Biotechnology

The concern of biotechnology is to use the methods of biochemistry, microbiology and engineering science in combination to control the activities of cellular organisms and large molecules such as enzymes and proteins; it is certain to become of very great importance in the future.

Several applications of expert systems have already been made in this field: MOLGEN [Martin *et al.*, 1977] for help in the design of experiments on cloning and molecular genetics; SEQ ([Clayton *et al.*, 1981], exploited commercially by the Intellicorp company) for interpreting nucleic acid sequences; and we have already mentioned the use of Dendral for determining chemical structures [Buchanan and Feigenbaum, 1978]. In view of the complexity of the processes that are to be controlled we can say that AI and expert systems will play an important role in the future, particularly for:

(1) improvement of instrumentation, by making it possible to extend the scope of instruments in fields such as the protein-related industries;
(2) used together with image-processing techniques, helping to interpret patterns in electrochromatography;
(3) automation of methods for crystallization and purification of proteins;
(4) interpretation of electron density maps, to determine the three-dimensional structures of proteins – the Crysalis system [Englemore, 1979] represents some preliminary work on this problem.

1.3.3 A prime field for AI: space

We conclude this survey of AI applications with a more detailed review of the developments now being made in space research; for the space industry provides a picture of how industry in general will probably be using AI in the not very distant future. This may be because it is an initiator of, and experimenter with, the most advanced technologies, or that it employs the most complex decision systems, or again that its activities are subject to the most severe constraints; whatever the reason, it has made the most spectacular applications of AI and in so doing has stimulated equally spectacular advances in the subject. Whilst this is the field for which the most sophisticated applications have been developed, it is also the one in which these are closest to full operational status [cf. Cognitech and ESD, 1985].

The applications of expert systems here have a number of special features. We shall mainly describe applications made on the ground rather than to space vehicles in flight; in-flight applications are no less promising, as is shown by the numerous systems developed in the USA for managing the subsystems of the future space station [Georgeff and Firsheim, 1985]. The variety of expert systems under development or projected is a measure of the range of activities encountered in this work and of the technological challenges it presents. We shall discuss some applications that differ greatly among themselves; in terms of the fields of activity of the European Space Agency (ESA) these can be put into two broad classes:

(1) systems concerned with design;

(2) systems concerned with operations – diagnosis of faults and failures, control, planning and revision of plans.

These applications concern both the 'ground' and the 'space' segments, and vehicles and other devices of all types, satellites, launchers, probes, shuttles and space stations. We first look at what is alraeady being done in Europe and in the USA, dealing with the major projects; and then consider what seem to us to be particularly promising applications that illustrate the advantages to be expected from these systems and the problems that they present, such as real-time working, use of databases and linking of diagnostic and planning systems. Finally we consider in greater detail the application to the management of the batteries in a low-orbit satellite.

1.3.3.1 Activities in the USA

A large number of expert systems for space applications have appeared in the USA since 1984; one of the exponents of this work is NASA, which has undertaken many developments and theoretical studies, especially in its research centers at Ames, Langley Jet Propulsion Laboratory, and to a lesser extent Lewis, and at its operational centers Johnson and Marshall. Among the industrial organizations who have recognized at an early stage the possibilities of expert systems for attacking certain space-related problems the following deserve special mention: Ford Aerospace, Boeing, Martin Marietta, Lockheed and, to a lesser extent, Hughes Aircraft, TRW and General Electric.

Applications to design

NASA Langley. This center, in addition to its considerable work on robotics, has developed EXADS – EXpert system for Automated Design Synthesis [Rogers and Barthelemy, 1985] – to help users of the design system ADS, an optimization package developed by and for NASA. ADS is a complex program providing about 100 options (strategies, optimization methods, etc.) which, in view of the possibilities it offers, is badly underused. EXADS, written in Franz Lisp for Vax, has about 250 rules and uses the inference engine AESOP, also developed at Langley.

NASA Johnson. This center has developed FDS – Flight Design System – for determining the essential parameters of a mission such as the time and direction of launch and the orbit required by the aims of the mission. There is an intention to couple an expert system with a CAD system (IMI) to help the engineers plan the maneuvers of the shuttle when approaching the future space station.

Application to operations

Classical automation and control theory are very powerful tools in this field; certainly men would never have landed on the Moon had it not been for the Kalman filter. They are very effective both for optimization (of a trajectory, for example) and for real-time control, for which they are much faster than a man. However, they are intolerant of failures, whether hardware or human, and ill-adapted to taking high-level decisions; whilst expert systems are much less good at optimization and real-time control but much better at handling incomplete or erroneous data. Above all, expert systems are designed to conduct reasoning as a human expert or group of experts would, and their stock of knowledge can be easily modified at any time. Appreciation of these complementary strengths and weaknesses has led several American aerospace teams, both at NASA and in industry, to envisage systems in which AI and control theory would be mixed. Such systems would be developed mainly for controlling physical subsystems, with detection of anomalous behavior, diagnosis of failures, generation of action plans and revision of plans 'on the fly'. The following are some of the projects being undertaken.

Jet Propulsion Laboratory. Planning, diagnosis of failure, revision of plans. Steve Vere at JPL was one of the first to become interested in the use of AI in space research. In 1975 he implemented a plan generator, Deviser, that correctly took into acccount the notion of time, not limited to the simple idea of 'before' or 'after' but associating a 'time window' with each elementary action [Vere, 1983]. This has been used to produce plans at various levels of detail for the Voyager space probe; one of these plans provided for 200 goals and 700 events, all with time constraints. However, Deviser has been used only by the people who designed and built it, because the interface with the human user, now being improved, is too demanding.

JPL has developed another plan generator, Switch, an extension of Deviser with capabilities for revision of plans and better management of consumable resources; and in parallel with the work on plan generation, an expert system, Faith [Friedman, 1984], for diagnosis of failures. One of JPL's aims is to couple Switch and Faith so as to produce a system that will revise the plan after a failure has been detected and diagnosed; for example, that some resource is no longer available. This is the project PEER (Planning and Execution with Error Recovery), the architecture of which is shown in Figure 1.12.

NASA Ames. This is probably the most active center for development of expert systems for aerospace applications. Among other activities it is

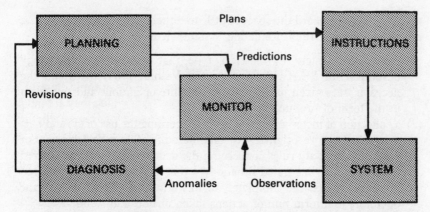

Figure 1.12   JPL PEER (Planning and Execution with Error Recovery) system

undertaking theoretical researches in collaboration with Stanford (knowledge representation and acquisition), with MIT (use of fuzzy logic for failure diagnosis) and with SRI International (procedural methods for reasoning in expert systems). Ames has made many applications of expert systems. Two of these will now be described: KAOS (Kuiper Astronomical Observatory Schedule) and HORSES (Human Orbital Refueling System Expert System).

KAOS [Nachtsheim and Gevarter, 1985], developed with the help of the software tool MRS [Genesereth, 1984], aims to produce a flight plan for a C-141 plane carrying a telescope, so as to maximize the time available for certain celestial observations. It has to take account of a number of very different linked constraints:

(1) those of observability, concerning both the telescope and the bodies to be followed;
(2) embargoes on overflying certain areas, such as military zones;
(3) fuel consumption, and flight time.

KAOS is linked to two purely numerical systems whose tasks are respectively:

(1) determining, for any given date and aircraft position, the time during which the bodies are visible in a given observational window;
(2) generating a flight plan, given a launch date and a series of points in space at which observations are to be made.

KAOS is already able to generate, within an acceptable time, plans for making a limited number of observations.

The aim of the operational version of HORSES [Boy, 1985] is to help the astronauts on board the space shuttle to refuel satellites in space, using the system ORS (Orbital Refueling System). It is in two parts:

(1) An expert system of classical type that uses the methodology developed for SEAGOS [Kessaci and Vesoul, 1984] to extend the decision trees given in manuals for satellite operation, and put them in the form of production rules.

(2) a collection of meta-knowledge, part concerning the use of (1) and part – which is more original – to take account of human factors. For example, there are rules concerning the degree of automation desired by the operator in a stated situation, so that the system can be required either to take charge completely or to work in collaboration with the operator, to inform him of actions taken or not, and so on.

NASA Johnson. This, in Houston, Texas, is the second center for NASA's expert system work, responsible to the central direction of NASA for manned flights. It has had an AI laboratory since 1984 where many expert systems are being developed, five of which are prototypes for operational systems. In particular, several are for the control and fault diagnosis of the physical subsystems of the future space station, for example for cabin pressure, for cabin air purification (FIXER) and for energy management (EXEPS). Other expert systems for the space station are being developed at other NASA divisions.

The Johnson team has produced NAVEX – Navigation Expert system – for flight monitoring during the re-entry phase into the Earth's atmosphere. This, developed with the help of the tool ART described in Section 3.4.3.6, is a good example of the coupling of an expert system with control theory. The Mission Planning and Advisory Division (MPAD) of NASA provides real-time support for shuttle flights during launch and landing, including control of a processor, HSTD (High Speed Trajectory Determinator), that uses the data coming from three radar stations, together with Kalman filters, to determine the position and velocity of the vehicle. The operations are normally carried out by three people at a control desk, and the aim of NAVEX is to reduce this team to one person helped in certain tasks by the expert system; the two will share the work as follows:

(1) the operator initializes the HSTD before the flight, communicates verbally with other operators at the control center and provides NAVEX with data that it cannot get by direct telemetry, such as separation of the fuel tanks;

(2) NAVEX keeps the operator informed of any problems that arise, advising him if necessary of any requests to be made to the people determining the flight trajectory.

Boeing system control. Boeing has undertaken important research work in AI and has created a center of excellence in Seattle, whose activities include expert systems and interfaces with natural languages. Among many expert system applications in aeronautics it has produced a subsystem control for the future space station, ECESIS (Environmental Control Expert System In Space) [Dickey and Toussaint, 1984]; this is for the Environment Control/Life Support System (EC/LSS) that purifies the cabin air, in particular removing the excess carbon dioxide produced by the astronauts in breathing, and extracting oxygen from this. Automatic control is essential in view of the complexity of the station and the high cost of any onboard work. ECESIS was developed with the help of the YAPS tool [Allen, 1982] on a Symbolics 3600 machine; it has an attractive graphical interface and is linked to a subsystem simulator.

The way in which the designers of ECESIS went about their task is significant for the application of AI methods to the problems of space technology. Atmospheric regeneration is a new and complex technology requiring electrochemical, chemical, mechanical and electrical devices; control has still to be flexible because no one yet knows how the regeneration process interacts with other systems connected to the same resource, for example the thermal regulation system. Rather than try to find if a control theory approach would be best, the designers preferred to demonstrate the feasibility of an expert system.

ECESIS, however, does go against the accepted rule that to build an expert system you must have an expert. The problem of environmental control in a space station, like many others in this field, is characterized by the development of novel physical systems that make use of advanced technologies for which there is no operational experience and therefore no expertise. ECESIS has been conceived as a development tool that offers various methods for representing knowledge and various control strategies; the expertise is at present limited to 'plausible' knowledge, to be replaced by true expert knowledge when this becomes available.

1.3.3.2 Activities in Europe

Whilst several companies and national and European organizations have started to become interested in these new methods of attack on aerospace problems, especially operational ones, the number of applications here is small compared with those in the USA. Apart from the study made by Cognitech and ESD for the European Space Agency (ESA) [Haton *et al.*, 1986], we may quote two studies now in progress:

(1) the 'Study of Expert Systems for Spacecraft Management', by a consortum of European companies (Laben, CRI and MBB/ERNO),

for an onboard management system for an autonomous space vehicle;
(2) a study led by CNES (Centre National d'Etudes Spatiales), with several subcontractors, of the control of satellites and diagnosis of faults.

One of the European applications is XX.CDMS, by MBB/ERNO, an experimental expert system developed in 1984 for fault diagnosis and planning of repairs for the command and data processing systems of Spacelab. This is unusual in that its software architecture is based on three languages, Prolog, Common Lisp and Modula: the type of knowledge representation is declarative for diagnosis and procedural for repair. The expert system Giotto AOCMS [Garrido *et al.*, 1985] is also experimental and exists in three versions, in Lisp, Prolog and Pascal; its purpose is fault diagnosis for the AOCMS subsystem in the Giotto probe that controls attitude and orbit. The greater part of the expertise used here comes from the operations manual for the probe; the system arrives at its diagnosis on the basis of telemetered data and develops a plan of action which is sent to the probe as a sequence of commands; it has several hundred rules.

1.3.3.3 Some potential applications

We give here some potential applications in space work that represent the state of the art; the list, which is related to the different fields of expertise available within the ESA, is not meant to be exhaustive.

Heat transfer
The models developed here must take account of heat transfer between the satellite elements both by radiation and by conduction. Radiation is now well understood and there are mathematical models depending on methods such as albedo calculation or Monte Carlo that give good results. Conduction calculations, on the other hand, are much more empirical and depend on the practical knowledge of heat transfer engineers. The published literature provides values for 'thermal contact resistance' between pairs of materials, such as aluminum on aluminum for example, but these have been determined under ideal conditions and do not take account of such things as clamping forces, the states of the two surfaces, their form and any bonding and are sometimes affected by convection – which of course is absent in a satellite in space. An expert system can help the engineer to choose values for these thermal coefficients, taking into account:

(1) the published values;

(2) the practical experience gained with certain types of structure (e.g. multilayered) and certain materials (e.g. aluminum);

(3) the factors, such as those above, that may affect the transfer.

A system such as this would have the advantage of having a knowledge base that could be easily modified by the engineers concerned, and could act as a common reference work.

Configuration of physical subsystems

The aim here would be to help with the preliminary designs for subsystems in the early phases of a study, before inviting tenders; the applications would concern feasibility studies in the light of the client's requirements, preliminary designs and estimates of costs. Initially at least, a single expert system would deal with a single physical system such as the electrical or optical system, antennae, solar panels or control of attitude and orbit.

We must not forget that space technology is advancing very rapidly indeed and even the basic ideas of satellite design may be questioned: for example, new materials that gave significant savings in weight could affect the choice of other components such as batteries. Any expert system of the type considered here must therefore be very flexible, especially in its architecture.

Operational control of satellite

The operational control of a satellite requires a team of several people to be permanently on duty to interpret the data telemetered by the satellite and to send back commands, especially in the case of faults or failures. Such a team will consist of an engineer in control of the mission and five or six operators directed by a technician. An operations manual (Flight Operations Plan) will have been provided by the builder of the satellite to deal with faults or other anomalies. Unfortunately, and inevitably, the manual cannot foresee all possible situations and the need often arises for an expert in the subject of the particular failure, mechanical or electrical engineering for example, or heat transfer; and further, it will be of fixed structure and not necessarily easy to use.

The idea would be to employ an expert system that combined the procedural knowledge of the instruction manual – these being generally written in the form of decision trees – with the more intuitive knowledge that the experts have not been able to express in the manual and which consists of heuristic rules for using the procedural knowledge. Several studies have been made along these lines and several models built; in France there is SEAGOS, already mentioned, and in America Ford

Aerospace, using the tool KEE [Kehler and Clemenson, 1984] have built a prototype system for control and fault diagnosis of the electrical subsystem of a satellite [Golden and Siemens, 1985]. This latter works as follows: an alarm activates a 'guardian' program that localizes the problem, using a set of rules in backward chaining; it then hands over to a 'monitor' – effectively the expert in the field in question – that attempts to diagnose the fault, asking the operator to carry out various procedures. An expert system of this type could embody blackboard-type architectures (cf. Section 1.2.2.4) to integrate items of information of different types; the idea of scenarios [Schank and Abelson, 1977] could also be very useful, especially in carrying out procedures and detecting errors in these.

Diagnosis of launch faults during countdown

During the 30 hours preceding the launch of a vehicle – the countdown period – synchronized sequences of test and check operations are performed on a very large number of parameters, involving passive sensors in the launch gear and payload; the purpose is to find out if any parameter value is outside its required range.

Interrupting the countdown can be a very costly business and can risk abandoning the launch; it often results from failure or too high a sensitivity of a pressure or temperature sensor or, as in the recent case of the Ariane launcher, a calibration error. The sensors in question are usually the same from one launch to another, so expertise can be built up concerning their mode of failure. Thus an expert system for diagnosing sensor faults could be an effective aid in crisis conditions, where several experts are acting together and a decision has to be made very quickly – within the order of tens of minutes – so as not to miss the launch window. Such a system need at first concern itself only with certain specified sensors recording from functional systems or the pressure in the fuel charging system on the launch pad: this latter is the case for the LOES (Liquid Oxygen Expert System) developed at NASA Marshall for the space shuttle [Scart *et al.*, 1984].

Such an expert system would need to have knowledge of two types:

(1) functional descriptions of the sensors, in the form of structured objects (cf. Section 1.2.2.4);
(2) a rule base for the modes of failure and the corrective measures.

Determining the orbit

Determination of the position and velocity of a satellite just before the firing of its motors at apogee is most important; this firing, in fact, is a most delicate operation on which the rest of the satellite's life depends. For this determination the control center has data from several different ground stations; but these signals can have errors or be corrupted by noise. Thus the problem is knowing something about the presence and nature of errors in the signals and about the noise levels, to find a method for computing the speed and velocity that will minimize the error in the final result. An expert system could help here in two ways:

(1) using relations between the data from different ground stations to decide which signals were corrupted or wrong;
(2) guiding the choice of method of calculation.

This application should be compared with what was said in general terms about the use of expert systems for helping the choice of numerical methods – finite elements or statistical, for example – in connection with the NAVEX system.

1.3.3.4 An example: the management of a satellite's batteries

The problem
We are concerned here with the application of an expert system to managing the electrical storage batteries on board a space satellite. These batteries are of vital importance to the satellite, especially in the low orbit case, and skillful management can have the beneficial effect either of prolonging the operational life of the satellite or of allowing lower capacity, and therefore lower weight, batteries to be carried, and thus increasing the useful payload.

Batteries are not well understood, and at present there are no good numerical models; so an expert system approach to the problem, which can make use of the knowledge and experience of the designers, should be a good alternative. Management involves a sequence of charge/discharge cycles carried out in a laboratory, and the expert system is intended to help the test operators both with the short-term management and with the study of the batteries' behavior over long periods, this latter with the aim of optimizing their use and increasing their useful life. Work is going on along these lines at Martin Marietta [Dietrich and Imamura, 1983], where an expert system is used for interpreting data derived over time from a battery in operation; the system is thus concerned with time, and at both short-term and long-term levels [cf. Section 1.2.2.5]. This system is in several respects more representative of space-technology applications than those we have mentioned previously, and its approach seems to be one that should be adopted in other space applications and also in other fields of advanced industrial technology. Further, the energy management problem that is being dealt with here is one that will appear, with much greater complexity, in future space stations [cf. Imamura *et al.*, 1983].

Other features of this application are as follows.

(1) It has to handle a very large body of information and thus opens the way to other space-related expert systems that also have to handle large masses of information. In this context we may note that the task of sifting through the data transmitted to Earth by space probes and observational satellites is enormous, and some intelligent processing on board would be very valuable.

(2) It is a ground-level application that will help its users – designers of electrically powered space systems for ESA – to envisage applications of expert systems in control centers and on board satellites. So again the approach seems to be one to be recommended, by which the engineers tackling space problems can acquire expertise in AI, concentrating first on ground-based applications and later, when the technology has matured, on onboard possibilities.

(3) It is a good example of an expert system that combines AI with control theory. The data it has to handle are measures of voltage, current, charge and power, made on a battery that is being cycled under test conditions. The charge/discharge phases are controlled by a real-time system linked to the sensors and regulators, a typical cycle being discharge, then charge at a specified constant current until a specified voltage is reached, then charge at constant voltage until the time for the next discharge. The role of the system is to interpret certain data obtained at the end of the cycle, in a broader and deeper way than control theory could alone; this interpretation will take account of the battery's history and of the predicted demands to be made on it by the satellite, and suggest changes to be made to the relevant parameters for the subsequent cycles.

The expertise and the knowledge representation

Provision of the knowledge necessary to this system requires the participation of an expert in battery design for satellites, who has extensive experience of a battery's life cycle, its ways of failing and deteriorating and of ways in which the effects of this failing or deteriorating can be overcome.

The need to take time into account and to process large volumes of data demands a novel architecture. About ten measures (voltage, current, etc.) are made at each cycle; with a cycle time of 90 minutes and a total time of 2–3 years this gives about 175 000 measurements to be analyzed. It would not be sensible to deal with all these data in one block (at the end of the period), nor would it correspond to the way a human expert would go about the task: he would make (provisional) interpretations as the data came in, and would be able to ignore progressively the large amount that seemed irrelevant while concentrating on what seemed significant to the problem being studied – deterioration of the battery, for example.

The architecture chosen for this system is based on the principle that it too should be able to 'forget', to recover past events if necessary and to combine items of information so as to discover tendencies. The system as realized has short-term (single cycle), medium-term (several cycles, corresponding to 2–3 days) and long-term (historical record, in particular for deterioration) memories. It is shown diagramatically in Figure 1.13.

1.4 THE EXPERT SYSTEMS MARKET

1.4.1 The general situation

Figure 1.14 gives a simplified picture of the position of AI in the Information Technology (IT) market.

The main characteristics of the AI market are the following.

(1) It is set in the context of a world market for IT that is estimated to be worth 1000 billions (10^{12}) of dollars (US) by 1990. This enormous sum represents only the automation of a single activity, that of numerical calculation, which forms only a minute proportion of the total human intellectual activities; whilst AI opens the way to automation of a large number of such activities, such as logical reasoning, understanding natural language and perception. These simple considerations lead to the view that is being more and more widely accepted that in the long term the AI market will be several times greater than that of IT as we now know it.

(2) Among the different segments of the IT market, AI is the one that will grow fastest over the coming decade. Although its total dollar value now is only 150 millions, it will, according to a study made by the American company International Resource Development Inc. (IRD), reach 8.5 billions by the end of the decade; and the Arthur D. Little company estimates the American market alone as 60 billions by the end of the century. An annual growth rate of around 60% over ten years puts AI in the forefront of the high technologies for development; this growth will be stimulated in particular by the big international research and development projects, such as the European Esprit and Eureka, the British Alvey, the Japanese 'Fifth Generation' and the American MCC (initiated by the information science industry) and military projects SCSP and SDI (Strategic Defense

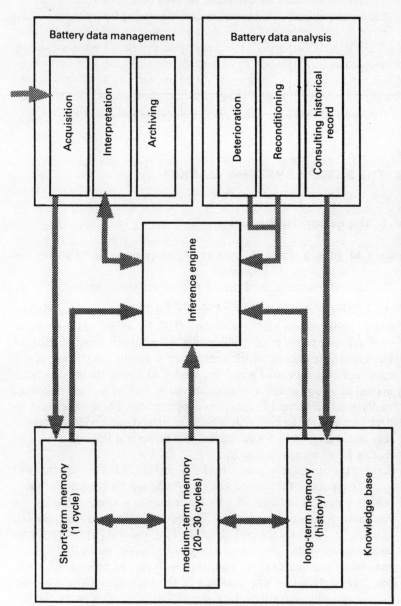

Figure 1.13　Block diagram of expert system for satellite battery management

Total IT market $1000 billion

Artificial Intelligence $8.5 million	Hardware	Software	Services
	29%	62%	9%

Figure 1.14   The AI market: predictions for 1993 (*Source: IRD*)

Initiative – 'Star Wars'). All of these make AI a top-priority channel for investment.

(3) The world market can be divided, classically, into three sectors: hardware, software and services. The prediction is that the hardware sector will remain stable at about 30% over 1983–1990 whilst the software sector will increase to about double, from 29% to 62%, at the expense of services which will decline from 38% to about 9%.

1.4.2 Segmentation of the AI market

This can be studied from two points of view: that of the technologies exploited and that of the activities developed.

1.4.2.1 AI technologies

AI makes its main impact on the market through four technologies:

(1) expert systems;
(2) understanding natural language;
(3) man–machine comunication;
(4) image interpretation, and more generally computer vision.

The four have certain basic concepts and technical methods in common which link them and justify their grouping together under the name of AI, and also explain their use in combination by some specialist companies such as the French Industrie et Technologie de la Machine Intelligente (IMTI) which has combined the techniques of expert systems, computer vision and robot control.

Each of these technologies opens a considerable field of potential applications, all more or less long term. That of expert systems is the most developed operationally and is the one for which industrial demand exists already and is growing; the market here is concerned with scarce knowledge, its acquisition, preservation, up-dating, reproduction and dissemination. Thanks to the techniques developed here, expertise has acquired a new status: previously merely a *service*, available only by personal attendance of the expert himself, it has become a *product* and thus merchandisable, able to be produced and distributed in large quantities at low cost, and thus widely available at all times and in all places. The preceding sections of this chapter have described some of the existing or foreseeable applications; as we have seen, the techniques are important to all sectors of activity without exception.

A longer view must be taken for the other three, but their potential market in the long term is at least as great and possibly greater. Thus mastery of machine understanding of natural language, and in particular of speech, will open the way to unconstrained communication between humans and machines, available to everyone. This will remove the main obstacle to this communication, the need to use artificial languages, and is essential to the automation of office work. It is essential also to the spread of expert systems, for many of these are justifiable economically only if they can have very many nonspecialist users. The IRD study already quoted estimates the market as 35 millions (US$) in 1985, doubling annually to reach 1000 million in 1990.

Image understanding and pattern recognition are necessary for giving many automatic systems the ability to organize and control their own behavior: for example, robots for industrial, space or military activities. They are necessary also to improve the productivity of humans working on tasks that require the use and interpretation of large numbers of images, such as teledetection, medical images and biotechnology.

1.4.2.2 AI activities

These can concern either the industrial market or the general public.
Industrial activities can concern:

(1) manufacture and sale of hardware, specialized or otherwise;
(2) development and sale of industrially oriented software packages: this is estimated to be worth 19 millions in 1983 and 5.3 billions in 1983;
(3) services, in two broad classes: training, advice and consultancy in one, design and implementation of systems to a client's requirements in the other; such activities characterize SSII (Société de Service en Ingéniérie Informatique)–type enterprises, typical of which in Europe, for classical IT, is CAP-Gemini-Sogeti. According to IRD this market will grow from 25 millions to 770 millions in the decade.

For the general public, professional or domestic, the activities will be the design of software packages intended for very widespread use, and the large-scale production and marketing of these. Non-AI examples of such products are Lotus 1-2-3, Multiplan and D-Base III, of which the numbers of copies sold run to between hundreds and thousands.

1.4.2.3 The market segments

The interactions between the 'technology' and 'activity' criteria lead us to define eight market segments; these are summarized diagrammatically in Figure 1.15.

Segment A: manufacture and marketing of AI hardware

The argument continues between the advocates of standard hardware and those of specially designed machines dedicated to AI work, such as the Lisp machines mentioned in Section 3.5. The mere existence of this debate – which, because of the stakes being played for, is more like a battle – is evidence, if any were needed, of the importance that virtually all the big computer manufacturers attach to this future market. At present the dedicated-machine market, although being vigorously developed, seems to be restricted mainly to research laboratories, whether in the public or the private sector, and government organizations such as defense departments. This is due partly to the high cost of such machines together with the level of skill needed for their use and their inadequacy for use within the constraints of industry, and also to the difficulty of transporting applications developed on them to more normal IT environments – a problem that is not made any easier by the absence of standards. However, we can expect that most of these difficulties will be relieved within the next five years; but the important question is whether the manufacturers of standard equipment can take advantage of this delay and bring their machines up to the level of performance needed for AI work. At the moment standard equipment has solid advantages of price and usability, the latter especially in interfacing AI applications to the enterprise's general data processing and IT activities; but its performance in AI is poor compared with that of special machines. Whilst this relatively low level of performance may be acceptable today, taking into account the current state of application development which is mainly of demonstrator programs and prototypes, it will not be so when realistic operational applications come to be developed. The manufacturers who are most sharply aware of the future need are developing solutions of their own, such as adding specialist coprocessors to their standard equipment – an attitude favored by Texas Instruments, for example, who have developed

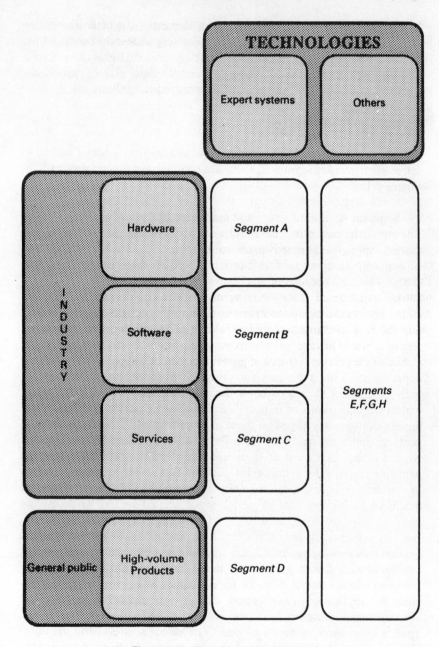

Figure 1.15   Breakdown of AI market

a Lisp microprocessor – or integrating AI languages and tools into their basic software. IBM, for example, have followed this second course with their Lisp-VM and Prolog-VM.

Altogether, the standard v. special machine argument will be settled by some compromise on cost/performance/ease of use, while waiting for the ultimate solution, the arrival of genuinely inferential machines with integrated parallel architectures.

Segment B: commercial production of industry-oriented software packages

Industry-oriented software packages are of two types, those for general application in production control and management and those specific applications.

Tools of the first type enable the industrial user to design, develop, maintain and exploit expert systems, integrating these into his production facilities and perhaps even into his products; see, for example, Section 3.4. Entering this segment of the market will require a major change in the financial structure of software companies: even if a few companies in Europe have been able to mobilize the resources needed to develop such tools, the R & D effort required is beyond the capabilities of the usual software house. However, it is a major opportunity for these companies and a need that cannot be side-stepped, for these reasons.

(1) The opportunity is that the demand for *genuine* industrial tools – a term explained in Chapter 3 – will explode in the near future, whilst at present there is very little on offer.

(2) The *necessity* is that these tools will form the means for production on which the turnkey operations of these companies will in future depend. Thus the viability, the independent existence even, of these companies will come to depend on the quality and availability of such tools. The recent quarrels between some European and American software companies show how greatly exposed to risk are high-technology enterprises whose production depends on agreements for technology transfer made with foregin companies.

More generally, Europe must not depend on foreign suppliers for its production of expert systems: the restrictions imposed regularly by the American authorities on the export of the more powerful tools show clearly the need for autonomy in this field.

Tools of the second type are aimed at solving the major particular problems of modern enterprises, for example availability of plant, automation of production, flexible manufacturing, security, training and so on.

The main factor limiting entry to this segment of the market is the degree to which the software companies have access to the finance needed to support the R & D effort. Here Europe is far behind, for example, the 14 million dollars invested by Ford in Inference Corporation or the 600 million that the US Department of Defense has put into the SCSP program – with the spin-off for the R & D subcontractors that can be imagined.

Segment C: consultancy and turnkey services in expert systems

This is the most active segment today, and accounts for the greater part of the turnover of the specialist companies. The present immaturity of the technology is shown by this situation, for which there are several explanations.

(1) It is an invariable characteristic of emerging technologies that more money can be made in the early stages by *saying* rather than by *doing* – and *a fortiori* than by *getting done* – which is the real sign of industrialization.
(2) In direct relation to the industrial immaturity of the technology, few of the tools developed by these companies are worthy of the name of *product*: most are 'semi-products', often needing a great deal of training and professional support for their effective use.
(3) Finally, there is the influence of the academic background of the founders and initial staff of these companies.

The companies selling these services who will be the first to escape from this situation will be those that, faced at an early stage with a large number and variety of industrial problems, are able to develop a methodology by using their experience.

Segment D: provision of expert systems for the general public

There are many applications that could find a market in the public at large, several examples of which have been given in the introduction to this book. Three main factors distinguish the large-scale production and distribution of these products:

(1) Their penetration into the general world depends very much on that of microcomputers into professional and domestic environments (or of links to networks such as Teletel) and on the level of general familiarity with decision-aiding software.
(2) The skills required for success in this market segment are not those that characterize the software companies that specialize in AI. Producing and distributing software for the general public requires an

industrial and commercial maturity that few such companies possess.
(3) Finally, the levels of investment required are beyond the financial resources of these companies.

The last two points lead one to suspect that the market will be monopolized quickly be those few of the world's companies that can simultaneously mobilize the production skills, the marketing experience and the financial resources needed for the task: for example, Lotus development of Microsoft. It is very clear that it is in this segment that the greatest profits are to be made: IRD predicts that office and domestic applications will account for almost 75% of the total AI market in 1993.

Segments E, F, G, H: products for the general public derived from other AI technologies
We mention these segments only for the record. They are for the very long-term territories awaiting development, Eldorados now inaccessible of whose conquest the high-tech adventurers dream; but today rather morasses in which the ill-advised venturers would sink without trace.

1.4.3 Features of the demand

As we have seen, the scale of the investment required for implementing operational expert systems is such that only a limited number of enterprises will be active in this field. Even subcontracting the undertaking can represent an investment of several million dollars, to which must be added the costs of use and maintenance; acquiring industrial mastery requires several times this amount. This means that today few organizations are able to afford the entry costs, and over the next five years they will be essentially the following:

(1) Enterprises with more than 5000 employees, in industry, food and agriculture, distribution, services. This means some 210 French or 470 European companies; these French companies account for over 80% of the total national investment and half of them employ more than 10 000 people.
(2) The major banks;
(3) The major insurance companies;
(4) Publicly owned or controlled organizations: airlines, telecommunications, railways, defense laboratories, etc.
(5) Organizations whose scope is European (ESA, CEE, etc.) or international (NATO, OECD, WHO, etc.)

Growth in this market will result from:

(1) reductions in the cost of developing expert systems;
(2) accumulation of successful industrial applications;
(3) the influence exerted on small- and medium-sized enterprises by their main customers.

1.4.4 Features of the offers

A simple way to describe the current state of availability of AI products is to take the diagram of Figure I.2, showing the different functions involved in an AI project, and superimpose on it indications of which of these are, and which are not, undertaken by the various types of organization considered. This is done in Figure 1.16; the following comments relate to these organizations.

(1) The general body of organizations that do no AI work as such, but simply make what use they can of expertise in their field of activity.
(2) Organizations that are beginning to take an interest in AI, making perhaps rather random approaches to strategic project management.
(3) Customers for AI such as the big governmental or international agencies, who undertake these activities in order both to understand their own needs and to be better placed to assess the offers made to them. Their concern is not to build expert systems themselves but to have them built, and in this they can, and in the case of some bodies such as ESA do, play a determining role in the evolution of industrial production of such systems. They insist in imposing their own quality standards on this novel software, and under their influence the contractors have developed standards for specification, documentation, validation and quality assurance that in the long term can only benefit the entire expert systems industry.
(4) The exceptional bodies that are self-sufficient in AI and able to integrate this into their production and R & D facilities and into their long-term development plans.
(5) Consultancies, specialized or not, who introduce AI into their clients' activities in the process of instructing them in project management and strategic decision taking. These are of two types.
   (a) Software houses of the usual type, for example, CAP-Sogeti and SEMA in France; CAP in the UK; and the American SRI International. It is a natural and necessary course for such bodies to introduce AI into their products. They hold two strong cards, their professionalism in IT and their customer base; but against

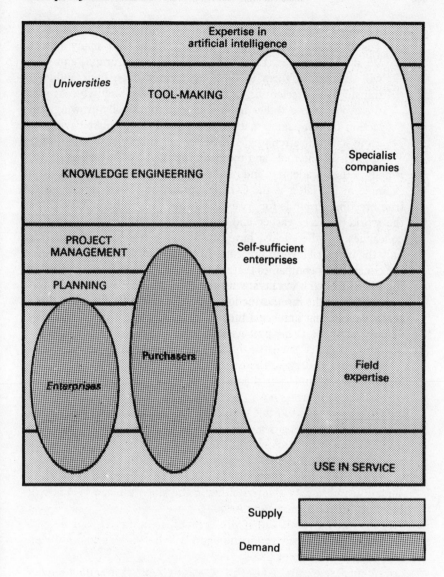

Figure 1.16 Sources of supply and demand

this their inbuilt culture – consultancy pure and simple – and their traditional attitude towards investment and the idea of a 'product' give most of these bodies little inclination to provide the resources needed to gain a real mastery of AI. Their keyword is 'opportunism', and their clients the only investors.

(b) AI specialists: in France, Cognitech and ITMI, in the USA Teknowledge, Intellicorp, Carnegie Group and many others. What characterizes these is their science-based origin, and what will distinguish them in the long term will be their ability to transform this scientific capital into industrial activity. Around these bodies is a rather indefinite, but continually growing, collection of companies that work in this field without having the same scientific strengths, satisfied to act simply as distributors or appliers of the tools and methods supplied by the leaders.

(6) Finally, the academic and industrial research laboratories – an example of the latter is the CGE laboratory at Marcoussis; these are true breeding grounds for AI expertise and it is to be welcomed that the workers there, earlier and with more determination than their colleagues in other fields, have attacked the real-life problems that only the industrial world presents. An important fact is that several of the consultancy companies that specialize in AI have been founded by high-level research workers, with the result that today AI shares with biotechnology the rare distinction of being a scientific discipline that is really penetrating industrial life.

2
Choosing the first application: the impact study phase

2.1 WHY STUDY THE IMPACT?

2.1.1 Reasons for a rational method

The choice of a subject for an expert system should be the outcome of a process that guarantees the following:

(1) the field has been surveyed thoroughly, so that there is no danger of a better application having been overlooked;
(2) the strategic aims of the enterprise have been taken into account, and the proposed system will make a real contribution to achieving these;
(3) the management, the relevant experts and the potential users have all been actively involved in the choice, so that there is no risk of the proposal being turned down or shelved;
(4) the general applicability of the results to be provided by the experiment, so that general lessons can be learned from them;
(5) the success of the project, in the sense of its acceptance within the enterprise: failure of the first expert system can result in the enterprise cutting off funds for further investments in AI, and so in the end losing competitiveness.

2.2 AIMS OF THE IMPACT STUDY

The aims of the impact study are:

(1) to increase the enterprise's awareness of the importance of AI and of the fields of its application, regarding both its scope and its limitations;

(2) to identify the most promising, and at the same time the most realistic, application (within the enterprise), taking into account the needs of future users, the current state of the art and the skills and other resources available;
(3) to define a properly thought out project for the enterprise.

The study requires a collaborative effort by the best-informed people in the enterprise, both in the analysis of the activities and in the choice of the first applications, and thus constitutes very much an alerting of the enterprise to these new techniques. All those who will participate in the implementation of this first system – top management, project leader, subject experts, users, as discussed on p. 3 – must be involved in its choice so as to give the project the best chance of success. The outcome of the study will be:

(1) an evaluation of the potentialities for use of expert systems in the enterprise;
(2) a documented proposal for a pilot application that can be developed straightaway, as a fore-runner to a first full scale trial.
(3) a general strategic plan for AI activities.

2.3 METHODOLOGY OF THE IMPACT STUDY

We suggest that there should be four phases as shown on Figure 2.1 [Cognitech and ESD, 1985]:

(1) making the case;
(2) study of potential applications;
(3) choice of a pilot study;
(4) detailed specification and justification of the pilot study.

2.3.1 Making the case

This is the phase of alerting the enterprise to the potential for improved productivity offered by AI and in particular by expert systems. It comprises four tasks, as follows.

2.3.1.1 Task 1: setting up and training a steering group

The job of this group is to guide the study and ensure that it progresses. The group should consist of five or six members of the enterprise, chosen

ES—H

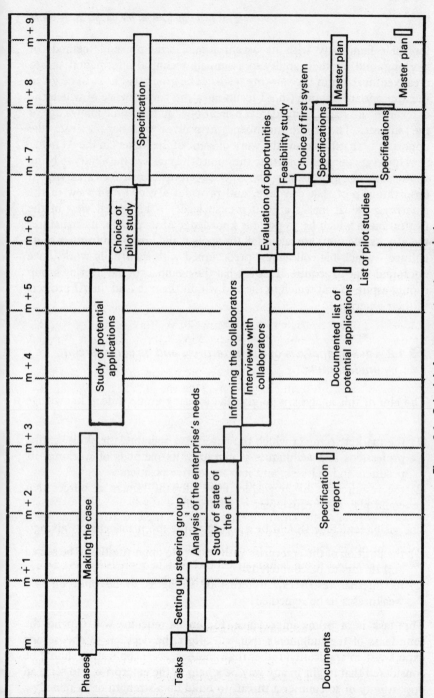

Figure 2.1   Schedule for an expert system project

for their familiarity with its organizational structure and methods of working, and for their ability to assimilate technical information and to create enthusiasm in the working teams. The group will need to be given the appropriate training (in AI techniques), in consequence of which the enterprise will reap the incidental benefit of acquiring some knowledge of the subject. The group members themselves will benefit from the opportunity to get to know the work of some of the leaders in the AI field.

However, the real benefits to the enterprise concern the ability to bring about and manage change. The steering group is in effect a privileged observation post that can take, and provide, a very broad view of the enterprise. What marks a good project leader is his global view of the institution in which he works, his knowledge of its people, its structure, the way its decisions are taken, all the spoken and unspoken features of its culture – which his colleagues, preoccupied with their daily work, have not found time to acquire. This is what the members of the steering group should aspire to and which in the end will fit them to lead the AI projects in their enterprise.

2.3.1.2 Task 2: analysis of the enterprise and its commercial environment

The aim of this analysis is to give the steering group a deep knowledge of:

(1) the market sector in which the enterprise operates, the skills, crafts, professions and techniques it employs, its methods of working, its products and markets, and its competitive position;
(2) the resources it has available, especially the human resources that could play an effective part in AI activities.

The visible outcome should be a report to the top management, giving:

(1) the position of the enterprise with respect to opportunities to be seized and threats to be countered;
(2) its internal resources, in terms of strengths to be built on and weaknesses to be remedied.

This task is of prime importance, for on its outcome will depend the soundness of the judgments that will affect the decision to choose one expert system application rather than another: *every* application should be considered that might in any way be a help to the enterprise – to seize an opportunity or to counter a threat, to build on a strength or to remedy a weakness.

2.3.1.3 Task 3: Study of the state of the art in fields important to the enterprise

Following Task 2, the purpose of this is to identify the main achievements in these fields and to fill the gap in mastery of the relevant techniques between the enterprise and its competitors. To this end links must be forged with a number of information networks, both in the enterprise's own country and abroad, as follows:

(1) research centers, both in the universities and privately operated;
(2) the country's scientific attachés in its embassies and consulates;
(3) industrial sources, in particular the AI consultancies;
(4) the technical media specializing in AI; the bibliography gives a list of these.

It is also worthwhile taking part in the main AI events such as conferences and exhibitions; we hardly need to comment that in this context foreign travel can be profitable as well as pleasurable.

By using these different sources of information the group will be able to identify those workers (wherever they are) who seem likely to have most to contribute to the study in progress. These should be contacted and interviewed and whenever possible asked to demonstrate any expert systems they have built or been concerned with.

Finally, the literature should be surveyed and a critical report written, giving the state of the art in the fields being studied.

2.3.1.4 Task 4: Informing the collaborators

By collaborators here we mean members of the enterprise, not belonging to the steering group, who because of their general ability, their experience and their position in the organizational structure have the best knowledge of the different trades, crafts and professions that it employs and of how these are in fact employed; there should be at least one collaborator for each of these skills, as identified by Task 2, and when the same skill is employed at each of several different sites it is worth having a collaborator for each site. Thus there may be several tens of collaborators associated with the impact study.

The collaborators represent the points of view of the actual users of any system that may be developed and it is their responsibility to identify the potential applications. Thus a potential application is one that is seen to be useful by the collaborators.

The task of informing – educating, perhaps – the collaborators consists first in giving a number of general lectures or seminars along the lines of Chapter 1, so as to familiarize them with the basic concepts of AI and with the main ways in which these can be applied; followed by summaries of what has been found about the enterprise in Task 2 and about the relevant state of the art in Task 3. The criteria to be applied in deciding on potential applications, which will be described in section 2.4.2 below, are then explained in detail. The result of all this should be that the collaborators return to their regular work with the ability to look at this work critically with the possibility of expert system applications in mind.

The alerting of the enterprise to the possibilities of expert systems is achieved by spreading the reports generated by these tasks and also the contents of the lectures and seminars given to the collaborators; and with these documents the collaborators are equipped to identify the areas of their own field of work that seem to be the best candidates for the second phase of the study, the analysis of potential applications.

2.3.2 Study of potential applications

The first thing that the collaborators have to do on returning from their lectures and seminars is analyze the activities in their sectors of the enterprise with the aim of identifying potential applications of AI methods. The steering group will then conduct in-depth interviews with them, so as to gather all the suggestions for applications; in these interviews each collaborator will be required to give detailed information for each application proposed, as follows:

(1) the type of work it relates to, and the staff involved;
(2) the problem being tackled;
(3) the scale of the problem – frequency of occurrence, number of people affected, financial aspects, etc.;
(4) the person(s) in the enterprise with the ability to solve the problem;
(5) the reasons why the problem cannot be solved by classical methods;
(6) the areas of the problem in which expert system methods are expected to be advantageous;
(7) the criteria applied in choosing the application that have led to the favoring of the expert system attack;
(8) the value to the enterprise of a satisfactory solution to the problem, in particular the impact on the strengths/weaknesses and the opportunities/threats questions;
(9) the general benefits to be expected from the introduction of an expert system and the fields in which these will be experienced, such as economic, human and social relations, technology, etc.;

(10) the input data needed for the system, and their sources; the output expected and the form(s) in which it will be given; the interfaces, if any, with other information systems;

(11) the conditions under which the system can be used, and the operational environment required;

(12) the minimum performance required of the system for it to be of real use.

All this will be summarized in a descriptive document for each potential application, and a standard form of document should be adopted in the interests of later implementation. This phase is completed with the dissemination of the combined set of such documents, thus listing, with full details, all the proposed applications.

2.3.3 Choice of a pilot study

In this third phase the potential applications identified and documented in Phase 2 are put in order of preference, using criteria of opportuneness, on the one hand, and feasibility on the other.

2.3.3.1 Projects that are opportune

The choice here should be made by a specially convened committee of senior members of the enterprise, who will be able to take into account economic, organizational, personnel and other criteria that will have been outside the scope of the collaborators and even of the steering committee. That is, this group will look at the proposals from a strategic point of view, and will be able to make a judgment based on opportuneness.

This evaluation committee will be briefed with whatever information it needs on expert systems and the main applications already made of these, and criteria for judging opportuneness that will be described later in this chapter (section 2.4.3). The outcome will be a list of applications in order of preference according to these criteria, and these, starting with those at the head, will then be studied by the appropriate experts for their technical and economic feasibility.

2.3.3.2 Projects that are feasible

This next stage of selection should be undertaken by one or more AI experts from outside the enterprise; they should meet those members of the enterprise who are experts in the fields to which the proposed applications relate, and at the outset these field experts should be given a general briefing on expert systems and how they are built, and if possible have a system demonstrated to them.

The AI experts will ask the field specialists to explain how they go about solving the problems that they meet in the course of their work; and in listening to these explanations will assess the quality of the expertise under discussion, its availability, the extent to which it is formalized, the motivation that the specialist has in communicating it to others, the kind of knowledge brought into play and the methods of reasoning used. The criteria applied here are described in section 2.4.4 below. As a result of this assessment some of the potential applications passed on by the evaluation committee will be discarded, either because they are not a matter for AI or because the problems cannot be solved by existing practical AI methods within the constraints of time or economics that must be respected, or again because the necessary expertise in the field seems to be lacking. The AI experts should be told in particular that they must reject any proposed application that would require nonindustrial tools to be used or would involve too-advanced concepts or methods.

The result of this final sifting is the list of possible pilot applications: that is, applications within the enterprise that are at once useful according to the collaborators, opportune according to the evaluation committee and feasible both technically and economically according to the AI experts and the field specialists.

A final request to the AI experts, to complete the documentation, is for a costing of the development of each of the proposed pilots, in both manpower and money. Such an economic evaluation requires the experts to have good experience of the industrial development of expert systems, in addition to their scientific knowledge. Actually, the total cost of bringing an expert system into operation is often several times the development cost, and this discrepancy is not always clear to experts whose experience has been solely in the academic world.

The list of possible pilot applications, with all the relevant information generated in this study, is then submitted to the evaluation committee and it is for them to choose one to be implemented. This final choice is of critical importance, for on the outcome will depend the fate of the new technology in the enterprise: if this first application is successful, expert systems will quickly become incorporated into its fabric; but if it fails it will be 'back to the start' and recovery will take a very long time.

2.3.3.3 Choice of the first application

Several criteria must be applied in making this choice:

(1) It must have a good chance of succeeding. There are already enough

unavoidable difficulties in the way of implementing even a very simple system without adding to these by tackling complex problems or trying to use very advanced AI techniques; and all concerned should be wise and modest enough to recognize this. For example, it is courting unnecessary risks to choose as a pilot a problem that involves nonmonotonic reasoning or time as a variable; and wholly unreasonable to expect to succeed with one's first system integrated into some real-time process. AI experts carry a heavy responsibility here if they take their research dreams for operational realities.

(2) Though simple, it should not be trivial. The system must solve a real problem, one that the enterprise has not been able to solve by classical methods.

(3) Its impact must be widespread; and as well as interesting those in its particular field the system must show that it can be extended so as to interest specialists in other fields. This implies that the problem chosen for the pilot system must be one that concerns a broad spread of people within the organization – or at least can be understood by a broad spread – rather a narrow specialist group or a confidential matter.

The body that makes the final choice must consider very carefully, and so far as possible anticipate, the personal and psychological problems that the exercise might give rise to: rivalries between different power groups, quarrels between experts from different fields, worries of staff who are unsure of their jobs or their status, and so on.

2.3.4 Detailed specification and justification

This last phase is one of synthesis of what has gone before; it is a matter of documenting the pilot study in full detail and specifying the expert system in a standard form that is described below. This documentation is then submitted to top management, together with a report showing where and how AI methods could be incorporated into the enterprise's activities. The actual implementing of the pilot system can either be undertaken by the enterprise itself, if it has the necessary resources, or be subcontracted to an outside specialist organization; in the second case the specification drawn up in this phase will be a key document in the invitation to tender.

2.3.4.1 Form of specification of an expert system

When the problem is one of constructing a computer program of the classical type, software engineering can offer tools and methods of proven value; and an approach along these lines is especially necessary in the case of large-scale projects involving many people, both to ensure that the final product meets the client's needs and also to estimate, even if only approximately, the resources that will have to be committed. But unfortunately these methods cannot be applied directly to expert system construction, because of the following features:

(1) the type of data involved and the predominance of symbolic processing;
(2) the central role of the expert, throughout the project;
(3) the incremental style of the building of the knowledge base, which enables spectacular reductions to be made in the delay between the identification of the need for a representation of a particular knowledge item and the production of the software for this. This possibility of quick production of a prototype can be a major asset for the expert system methodology from the point of view of the quality of the product, which it would be a pity to give up in exchange for a more rigid procedure. One should, rather, accept the possibility that the initial specification may change in detail – under the control of the client – in the course of the development, and even regard this as an advantage.

Thus specially tailored methods for specification must be developed, that take account on the one hand of the need for a basic description of the needs to be met and the objectives to be pursued, and on the other of the peculiarities of expert systems in general. This is an exacting task, and one must look for guidance to what has proved successful in software engineering. A good starting point would be the work done for the European Space Agency [Cognitech and ESD, 1985], in which the software engineering standards of BSSC (84) 1, recommended by ESA for space applications, are used as a basis for expert system specification; the framework given below follows the general lines of this work. As a general principle, the greater the care with which the study has been documented, the easier it will be to draw up the specification.

High-level definition of the product

This will not pay any attention to practical details or difficulties of implementation or use. Most of the information required can be got from the documentation of the impact study.

(1) Users' needs; with a detailed identification of the potential users.
(2) Objectives of and limits to the project.
(3) Overall system within which the expert system is to be integrated.
(4) Main functions and services to be provided by the expert system.

(5) Main operational constraints on the expert system: environment within which it will be used, how it is to be made available to the users, degree of portability expected, and machines and operating systems on which it is to be run.
(6) Economic aspects, in particular cost/performance goals.
(7) Justification for AI approach: discussion of the different possibilities offered by AI and comparisons with more classical methods if any are applicable.

Detailed specification

Functional specifications
(1) Functions to be incorporated.
(2) How these functions are to be realized.
(3) Interactions between functions and hierarchies.
(4) The product as a whole and its components, e.g. inference engine, knowledge base, facts base, knowledge-acquisition modules, interfaces, etc. This must make clear the various technical aspects of the problem, in particular:
    (a) the AI techniques to be used in knowledge representation: identification and representation of the basic concepts (parameters) to be manipulated in the field of application; basic knowledge items (rules, objects) and the relations among them; information the system must be able to get from external databases;
    (b) the mechanisms for reasoning and checking needed to achieve the stated aims with the knowledge available;
    (c) the techniques to meet possible needs for communication in natural language: lexical features of the application and its use in practice.

Some comments on these points are given in section 3.4.

Expected performance
(1) Main timings: data acquisition and updating cycle, response time to queries, average session length, etc.
(2) Storage capacity for active information.

Integration into the global information system
(1) Origins of the various sets of data used by the expert system: field expert, user, physical sensors, other applications, archives, etc.
(2) Hardware interfaces across which the expert system must communicate: host machine, host operating system, file managers.
(3) Software interfaces: database management systems, various utilities.

Operational environment
(1) Interaction with the global system: degree of autonomy of the expert system, etc.
(2) Interaction with the user: 'help' services, tolerance of mistakes, etc.
(3) Interaction with the expert: e.g. means for examining the knowledge base.
(4) Interaction with the knowledge engineer: editors, test routines, consistency checks, etc.
(5) Security provisions: extent and frequency of dumps, provisions for restoration of a previous state, protection of knowledge base, protection against user errors, etc.
(6) Provisions for maintaining the knowledge base.

Resources to be employed (Section 3.5)
(1) Languages.
(2) Host computer:
    (a) processor: basic speed needed, real and virtual memory, high-speed numerical unit (if necessary), mill time and elapsed time needed for start-up and for routine use;
    (b) operating system: multitask/multi-user provisions, interrupt system, virtual memory management, security provisions, file management;
    (c) availability of other machines.
(3) Storage media – magnetic disks, optical disks, magnetic tape; capacity required at start-up and for routine use.
(4) Terminals: alpha-numerical, graphical, color video, bit-map.
(5) Communications: interfaces (V4, RS232C, etc.); links with local area network(s).

Test and validation (Section 3.6)
(1) Test standards, tools, codes to be used.
(2) Tools for testing and validating the knowledge base.
(3) Test procedures for the inference engine.
(4) Definition of battery of tests, criteria to be applied.

Documentation (Section 3.7)
(1) Detailed specifications: these will be outlined after the first demonstration of a working system and the details filled in after the later stages of prototype and advanced demonstrator have been completed.
(2) System architecture.
(3) Reference manual for maintenance of the code and the knowledge base.
(4) Users' manual.

(5) Test manual, giving details of all the tests and the results expected; this can be used to ensure correct performance of the system after any modifications to the knowledge base or the software tools used.
(6) Detailed description of the knowledge base and how it will change over time:
  (a) rules;
  (b) parameters and the values these may take;
  (c) objects;
  (d) cross-references between rules, parameters;
  (e) etc.
(7) Tools for self-documenting by the expert system.

Methodology and development
Description of the development cycle, design – coding – test – maintenance, is discussed in detail in Section 3.3. This should give, for each of the four phases:

(1) the objectives;
(2) the input;
(3) the output
(4) the activities performed;
(5) the resources used.

Man–machine interface
(1) Maximum effort required of the user in using the system.
(2) Maximum time required for learning to use the system.
(3) Types of output devices used by the system: graphics, multiwindow, colour, videodisk, voice, etc.
(4) Types of input device used by the user: keyboard, touch-sensitive screen, menu, mouse, voice, natural language, etc.

Feasibility
Most of the information required here can be got from the documentation of the impact study, particularly from Phase 3, choice of a pilot study.

(1) Main difficulties foreseen, with possible solutions: risks involved in the development, possible technical obstacles, competition arising, risk of obsolescence.
(2) Main technical advantages possessed by the enterprise for overcoming difficulties foreseen: R & D resources, experience in related fields, etc.
(3) Main benefits expected.
(4) Main weaknesses of the enterprise that could reduce or cancel these benefits.

Management of the project (Section 3.8)
(1) Paperwork: reports, documentation, coding sheets.
(2) Schedule: phases, checkpoints, etc.
(3) Budget: resources required in man-days, machine hours, etc.
(4) Development team: selection of members, especially of experts.

2.4 CRITERIA FOR THE CHOICE OF AN APPLICATION

We have seen that the choice of an application should be the outcome of a collaborative study involving the potential users, the field experts and the top management of the enterprise; the aim of the impact study just described is to produce this consensus, which provides the only guarantee of success for a project as essentially risky as putting one's first expert system into operation.

In the course of this study each individual involved in the selection will look at the applications in the light of criteria that are relevant to his or her own field of interests and activities. Thus there will be one set of criteria for the group we have called the collaborators, another for the final selection committee and yet another for the experts; all these groups of people, however, should have some economic criteria in mind when approaching the question, and it is for this reason that we start this review of the selection criteria with a consideration of the economic aspects.

2.4.1 Difficulties of purely economic arguments

Some attempt should of course be made to evaluate the economic benefits resulting from the introduction of an expert system, to find the return on investment; but necessary as this may be, it risks being little more than a trivial exercise.

A fundamental advantage often claimed for an expert system over a more classical type of computer program is the ease of updating and maintenance. This cannot be denied, and it would seem to be easy to quantify the advantage when one knows the cost of maintaining and correcting errors in software: this repair work accounts for almost 60% of the total cost of software. But after this certainty how many uncertainties remain? What extra IT resources are needed for running an expert system? What does any conversion of basic software cost? Staff training?

An expert system may be used to solve a new problem, and in this case the evaluation is even more difficult because there is no basis for comparison. The difficulty would seem less when one is concerned with problems that have already been tackled by other methods but with less than satisfactory results; however, can one be sure of knowing how to measure accurately the economic effect on the enterprise of the faster response to enquiries, or the greater availability of plant resulting from failure diagnosis, or the reduction in delays in a chain of manufacturing processes when an expert system is used to help control the machine loadings?

INRA's expert systems for diagnosing plant diseases have certainly improved the growers' yields, but with what effect on their financial balance? Hard to say: will the extra produce find buyers in a market that is already slack? Will the end result be to bring the prices down?

So we can see that whilst a consideration of the economic aspects of expert systems is necessary, it is not at all a simple matter. But if estimating the benefits is often risky, estimating the costs is much less so; and the decision to invest in an expert system is thus always something of a gamble and should take into account secondary benefits that may not be quantifiable in financial terms but are nonetheless real. Consider, for example, the exposition of a certain body of knowledge by an expert in that field with the help of a knowledge engineer; it is generally agreed that this has the beneficial effects of setting out in black and white what was previously obscure, for all to see, and also of exposing this knowledge to critical assessment by other experts, with the possibility of adding to it and improving its quality. Further, most experts recognize that their methods of reasoning are improved as a result of this involvement of the knowledge engineer. Thus an improvement in the quality of the enterprise's stock of knowledge can be counted among the returns from the investment in an expert system.

Finally, it is not at all clear that the criterion of financial return on the investment should predominate in the case of the first experiment with expert systems. What often seems preferable is some sensible compromise between financial return and chances of success: good value would be delivered by a project promising modest financial returns but little risk of failure.

It is for the top management of the enterprise to strike this delicate balance between certain costs and risks on the one hand and uncertain economic returns and unquantifiable benefits on the other. What is re-markable is that large expert system projects have been undertaken in so uncertain a climate; the only explanation must be that not all decisions are taken in the light of cold reason.

2.4.2 Criteria applied by those making the case

The choice of an application must involve some criteria relating to time and others to complexity. A 'good' problem in this context is one that could be solved by the relevant expert in a few hours rather than a few minutes or a few days: the numbers are intended as orders of magnitude rather than as precise estimates. A hardware failure that could be diagnosed by an expert in half an hour represents a problem worth considering.

From the point of view of complexity a 'good' problem lies somewhere between one that can be solved with the help of a check list and one that needs considerable insight. The plain check list can be viewed as the lowest form of expertise; but if it requires tests to be made in an order that is not fixed but can lead to a complex decision tree, it may qualify as a potential expert system application.

We now give a dozen criteria that can help to identify potential applications. They should be applied after the impact study has been completed so as to provide a basis for the selection procedure.

There are recognized experts, available and willing to participate
If many people claim to be able to solve the problem satisfactorily one would be hard put to justify an expert system; so one must look for problems for which there is a distinct difference in performance between the average individual and the expert.

There are of course problems for which there are no experts, particularly in fields that are new or are developing rapidly. An example is failure diagnosis for novel equipment, for which the only knowledge is that possessed by the design and construction teams, and the equipment has not been in use long enough for expertise in its behavior to have been built up. Such problems, however, cannot be simply brushed aside; and an expert system can act here as a collector of expertise as experience is gained.

A good indicator of the feasibility of an expert system project is the time taken to find the relevant expert and get to the point of a consultation, and the length of time the expert will allow for this meeting. If it takes a month and the expert will give only a couple of hours, it would be better to abandon the project straight away: this rare expert will not be able to give the time needed for the study, and still less for developing the system.

No algorithmic solution is known or even possible, or desirable
The commonest case is where no algorithm is known – for medical

diagnosis, for example – and the expert uses heuristic methods, which he has developed as a result of experience but whose success cannot be guaranteed. Another is characterized by there being an algorithm that gives the correct solution unambiguously but which would take too long to run on any existing computer. A good example is chess, where an exhaustive examination of all the situations on the board that could follow from any given move could guarantee avoidance of defeat but would occupy all the computers in the world for centuries.

There are also cases in which an algorithm could be devised but would be unsatisfactory because of the modifications to the program that would be needed in order to deal with changing circumstances; further, an algorithmic solution lacks the well-known property of an expert system of being able to explain its results. A good example is the problem of setting insurance tariffs. These are determined exactly as functions of a number of parameters – though some of the definitions involved could be questioned; but the complexity of the procedures, which require reference to many statements concerning conditions, such as exceptions, and scattered widely through the proposal, and the frequency with which these are changed, make the expert system approach greatly preferable.

It should be noted, however, that in some cases the expert may give the impression of using a deterministic method of solution; this is because the only technique he is familiar with is that of decision trees, and he has subconsciously downgraded the description of his method of reasoning so as to get a working program.

The relevant knowledge is said to be of an intuitive nature

There is a long-standing argument as to whether 'intuition' is really intuition or simply accumulated experience – just as musical improvisation demands a firm technique and a great deal of experience. To avoid getting into this argument we will take 'intuitive' to describe knowledge or methods of reasoning that are difficult to justify, whether or not rational justifications exist in theory. Some maintenance engineers have a 'feeling' for the cause of a failure without being able to justify this, whilst the designers, who know everything about the structure of the equipment and its theoretical behavior, could not diagnose the fault nearly so quickly. It is just this 'short-circuiting' of reasoning by experts that an expert system is intended to reproduce.

The useful knowledge is neither in the books nor taught

There is thus a need to conserve and to disseminate this intellectual capital; even so, an expert system is often justifiable despite the existence of books or lecture courses.

For the most part, books give only theoretical knowledge and say nothing about how this is to be used 'intelligently'. This is certainly the case for the 'intuitive' knowledge of the previous paragraph, and also for the meta-knowledge needed in order to use the formal knowledge. Expertise is often a matter of using different possible methods in decreasing order of probability of success.

The reasons that lead an expert to short-circuit his general method of arguing in certain clearly defined cases are often subconscious and therefore not published in the literature; it is the task of the knowledge engineer to bring them to light.

The existence of instruction manuals in the enterprise can in fact argue in favor of the expert system, because it shows that there are experts and that they are interested in spreading their knowledge.

The information to be processed is more qualitative than quantitative

The aspect presented by the first research projects in AI was of processing symbolic information that was mainly qualitative: this did not of course exclude the need to use numerical results, but such computations did not predominate, nor do they in expert systems. Interpreting visual images or speech necessarily involves a great deal of numerical processing and this presents some difficult technical problems; but the 'intelligent' part of the program, which begins with the expert system, is the final interpretation on a semantic level. This can, for example, require the ability to distinguish between a river and road in an aerial photograph by conducting some complex reasoning involving environmental information.

The body of relevant knowledge is changing rapidly

It is difficult to freeze any body of knowledge, and a major advantage of the expert system approach in this connection is the ease with which the program can be modified. As we have seen, this architecture is in effect a recognition of the fact that it takes time to extract the experience and reasoning processes from a human expert, and to represent these in a computer program, especially if that experience has taken a long time to build up.

The expertise is scarce and is vulnerable

There is the well-known Peter Principle, of rising to the level of one's incompetence. The experts in an enterprise who have built up great competence in the design and construction of some hardware or software product may well have been moved on when the product is put into service; their expertise is only incompletely represented by the manuals provided for the users, and therefore should be 'cloned' before they move on. This can be economically vital for the survival of the enterprise. Another example is the small number of very high-grade geologists in a petroleum company, who often have to spend long periods away from their home base because they are needed at distant sites.

Any proposal should be examined carefully to see if it involves too great a dependence on a very small number of specialists, and is therefore at risk if any of these should fail to come up to the expected standard, go sick or leave.

The expertise is shared among several people

There are problems whose solution requires several people to cooperate and pool their knowledge, because they complement each other. No single human ever has complete expertise: there will always be situations in which one expert will be able to solve a given problem – perhaps because he has met it before – but will be unable to solve another. Forming a consortium of experts, kept together as a permanent body and available for consultation, can give a concentration of expertise that has no human equivalent.

One must, however, take care to ensure that tackling the problems in the field of interest does not call on too many different disciplines, nor on too wide a variety: an expert system is the more powerful the more restricted its field.

The expertise is all held at one place, whilst the users are scattered

The difficulties here are aggravated if the users are a long way from the experts and communications are poor. This is the case of a high-technology industrial process in a developing country, in which the company that supplied the technology has either to maintain an expensive technical team on the site or be prepared to send out one or more experts to deal with the slightest incident; and the same situation could arise in Spacelab, where the astronauts would have to conduct complex scientific experiments in fields well outside their own expertise. A variant is that the experts are available only at certain times of the day and the users at others: managers of continuous production processes know very well that the proportion of scrap is much higher on the night shift or Sunday than in the daytime when engineers and experienced foremen are on duty.

Spreading the expertise by means of training courses would be too costly

In many subjects expertise is badly taught – not enough training personnel or none at all, no manuals or relevant records, and so on; and the time taken in training new staff can make serious inroads into their productive time. So there can be considerable value to the enterprise in having a tireless and always available source of expertise that is frequently brought up to date and can act also as a teacher by helping to explain the knowledge and strategies built into it.

The decisions often have to be taken under stress
In some contexts the experts have to take decisions in conditions unfavorable to calm reflection, such as when there is a volcanic eruption, a flood or an industrial accident, or when an incident requires a space satellite to be controlled. Mistakes can be made because certain parameters have not been taken into consideration, for lack of time – or simply overlooked.

The necessary information is incomplete or imprecise
It can be necessary to take a decision quickly, even though not all of the information required is available: for example, the engineer on duty in a control room when there is an incident. The heuristic reasoning used by the expert system will give a response which, whilst not optimal, will be reasonable and better than nothing. Imprecise information can be either matched against other items or given a weight that indicates the confidence that can be attached to it.

2.4.3 Criteria applied by the evaluation committee

In addition to considering opportuneness and the strategic aspects (cf. Section 2.3.3.1) this committee should apply the following criteria.

The problem that it is intended to solve with the help of an expert system should be sufficiently long term
It should certainly be on a much longer time scale than the probable development time for the system; proposals for expert system attack on problems for which solution by other means – technological developments and organizational changes, for example – can be foreseen in the near future, thus making the expert system obsolete, should be rejected out of hand.

Similarly, fields that lack stability or are developing rapidly should be treated with reserve: it is true, as we have said, that the expert system approach allows rapidly changing knowledge to be handled easily, but it is also true that new knowledge may require new methods of representation that are incompatible with those already in place and consequently destroy all hope of return on the original investment.

There should not be, in the enterprise, a competing project tackling the same problem by different methods
It is good sense to aim to compare an expert system solution with one achieved by more classical methods, but not in the case of a pilot application: the competitive climate can only act as a distraction in circumstances in which the overriding need is for cool and calm thought, and there are already enough opportunities for losing one's head. One goal at a time should be the watchword.

The project should not be on the critical path of any other project
Here again it should never be forgotten that the pilot system is not being developed with the aim of integration into a product or a production process. It must be allowed considerable independence of other projects being undertaken by the enterprise, particularly in view of the fact that the risks that always accompany the first application of a new technique require the project to be planned with reasonably tolerant time constraints.

The managerial sector to which the expert belongs is well informed on the project and enthusiastic for its success
In particular, the management should be quite clear about the effort that will be required. Allowing the expert to give up a significant amount of his time to the project cannot fail to affect the organization of the regular work, and from this point of view it would be prudent to ensure that his colleagues were well informed on the situation, because it is on them that the consequential extra work will fall.

The project must not risk generating irrational reactions in the future users of the system
We have already mentioned the fear of being replaced by a machine in what has always been considered to be an essentially human activity, that of logical reasoning. More generally, it is important to ensure that the project gives rise neither to unreasonable expectations not to too deep a skepticism. The future users, and particularly the information services manager, must take an attitude of welcoming interest towards the system, and must feel convinced of its ultimate genuine usefulness; as we shall see in Chapter 3, the greater part of its evaluation in practice will depend on them, and indeed the decision of whether it is actually used or not.

With the same considerations, projects should be discarded at this first stage if they seem likely to cause disturbances to the services or even to have connections with services that are already disturbed by other causes. In such a case an expert system could be made a scapegoat for other failings and a target for pent-up feelings that were only waiting for a chance to make themselves known. The same applies to any project that plays an important role in the internal politicking of the enterprise or one of its departments, for there the development team would be open to attacks that they were not intended to meet. The risk is particularly great if the project is going to lead to a significant redistribution of power or to demand considerable resources, whether of people or equipment. In such circumstance the likely reactions of the director responsible for the information services should be considered and if possible anticipated; best of all, he should be involved in the choice. It is even more important to avoid choosing a project for covert objectives, like getting a number of experts to agree among themselves or making peace between rival departments. There is no reason to expect artificial intelligence to succeed where natural intelligence has failed.

The project would benefit from the active support of a senior director

Experience has shown that whatever the precautions taken at the start, an expert system project is always subject to threats. The stakes, though not always made explicit, are high, and hidden feelings, often subconscious, are expressed when it is launched. The development team, under contradictory pressures from different directions, can get discouraged or become entangled in clandestine maneuvers. They should be protected from this by the influence of someone high up in the organizational structure who understands the hidden culture of the enterprise.

2.4.4 Criteria applied by the AI experts

As we have seen, the final stage in the selection procedure is the evaluation of the available expertise and of the feasibility of the project by the AI experts, or at least by the knowledge engineers. They should take account of the following factors.

There is an expert in the field of the problem, who is available for participation

This will have been considered already by the collaborators (cf. Section 2.4.2), but, an AI expert from outside the enterprise will be better able to make a judgment on this count.

A true expert is one who can have the last word in a discussion between specialists; this air of authority is essential if one aims to give the system proper credibility, especially when there are no objective criteria for the validity of the results it gives. It is equally important, for both the credibility and the effectiveness of the future system, to distinguish clearly between true expertise in a field, which results from long experience, and merely a knowledge of that field, however excellent: the true expert alone knows the secret ways through the subject – as the poacher knows the tracks of the game. Another essential is the availability of the expert, which is often in conflict with his status as an expert: if he is an expert then he is indispensible, and if he is indispensible then he is unlikely to be available.

The AI expert, taking advantage of his status as an external consultant to the project, should check the amount of time the field expert can give to the work during a year. This must be done formally and as precisely as possible, noting in particular any commitments to travel, either in the home country or abroad.

The field expert will be expected to be able to communicate his expertise to the uninitiated, in short to be a good teacher; he should also be able to go back over an argument, to take it apart and judge it afresh. No one who is engaged for the particular purpose of transferring his expertise should hold back information; rather, they should be attracted by the idea of seeing their knowledge spread around widely, even discussed and criticized by their peers.

One expert, alone, is able to cover the major part of the expertise needed

The development of an expert system should not suffer disturbance by squabbles between different experts; and the role of the knowledge engineer is not that of judge or arbitrator. A single expert, the most distinguished available if there are several, should take part in the development, although others may be associated with the project at a later stage, particularly in the validation. If several experts are needed to cover the complete field of the problem, care should be taken to see that they complement one another rather than compete; and one should be nominated leader, and arbitrate when necessary.

The problem really justifies an expert system, and is reasonably tackled by this method

We have already seen that the problem must be difficult enough to require a nontrivial expert system for its solution, but not so difficult as to be beyond the reach of existing techniques, in particular where large databases and complex reasoning processes are concerned. If it requires only a modest amount of information to be handled it risks giving rise to the view that a more classical approach would suffice, such as a decision tree. Ideally, a first system should require at least 200 and at most 400 rules; a problem needing more can usually be broken into smaller subproblems which can then be tackled separately.

The possibility of breaking down the given problem into subproblems ifself augurs well for the feasibility of attack by the expert system approach. It is both methodologically sound and psychologically encouraging to be able to show partial but significant achievements during the course of the development; in contrast, nothing is more frustrating than working on a project that demands all one's effort and shows nothing in return over a long period. This breaking into subproblems has also the benefit of allowing the development team to cut their teeth on problems easier than the main one.

Finally, the knowledge engineer must make certain that the problem to be solved requires a body of knowledge that is reasonably homogeneous and of reasonable extent. Whilst in theory an expert system can handle a mass of knowledge from a wide variety of sources, in practice limits are imposed by the physical storage capacities available and the times needed for the processing on the computers available. Similarly, problems that need too much 'common-sense' knowledge should be rejected, for this, though easy to state, can require far too many rules for its expression.

There are unambiguous criteria for success

It is most important to be able to decide, without any doubt, whether or not the final system has met the objectives. We have already seen how important is the status of the field expert who provides the knowledge used by the system; the knowledge engineer must ensure that he is equally capable of providing criteria that will not change with time and will be generally acceptable. However, in most cases the soundness of the system can be established by objective performance measurements, and therefore the existence of measures, if any, should be established at the outset, and in particular a set of known cases assembled that can be used as tests.

The problem does not need too many or too complex interfaces with other software

There is always the possibility of wanting to use the system in connection with an existing information system; this raises the problem of linking, for example, to a database management system or in the case of a real-time system to certain physical sensors. Whilst recognizing that this is a common need and that the necessary interfaces can be built, we would not recommend choosing a problem having such a need for a first system: there is too great a risk of the development team becoming enmeshed in these peripheral activities and losing sight of the main goal, which at this stage is the acquisition, representation and reproduction of the expert knowledge needed for solving the problem. It is the 'one thing at a time' principle again.

3

Going into action: implementing the first expert system

3.1 THE FIRST SESSION

Q: Every time I meet a forecasting expert I want to tell him the story of the clairvoyant who heard a knock on the door and called out 'Who's there?'

A: A good story.

Q: Well ... tell me, why do you think expert-system methods could be important in forecasting?

A: If I've understood what you and your colleagues are saying, an expert system can gather specialist knowledge from a small group of experts and make it available to a large number of users of the system. Now, most errors in forecasts are due to the forecasters knowing only a few of the possible methods – and, in particular, seldom knowing their limitations.

Q: So your aim would be to make your own knowledge available to many others; but why is the choosing of a forecasting method so complicated a matter?

A: Well, there are very, very many criteria for choosing a method and the ways of reaching a decision aren't really algorithmic. And again, there are often other aims underlying the term 'forecast' – we often want to describe, to understand, to explain, to check something.

Q: What sort of number of these methods are there?

A: About 100, in about 20 different classes.

Q: Could you tell me a few?

A: First of all there are general classes like exponential smoothing, ARIMA, regression and so on; then in exponential smoothing, for example, there are the methods of Holt and Winter, of Brown, of Lewandowski ....

125

Q: Would it be possible to define a class of users for a pilot expert system for forecasting?

A: Yes, I'd suggest those people in medium-scale organizations who have to do forecasting occasionally – it's not their full-time job. They're experts in their own fields, like cars or babies' nappies, but not in forecasting. In France there are scarcely a dozen forecasting experts worth the name. ... For a first shot we might think of the short- and medium-term forecasters, of whom there are a lot and who represent quite a big economic stake.

Q: You could give me, briefly, an actual example of a problem that could be treated this way, and how you would go about it?

A: Certainly: how about tolls on the western Autoroute? Figures are available for the numbers of vehicles passing through the toll stations each day, and what the management would like to have, at no great cost, is a general forecast of the traffic for say the next six months. After a study of the graph of the time series one might suggest exponential smoothing with adjustment for seasonal changes – Holt and Winters' method, for example – and linear or quadratic trend.

Q: As I understand it, then, there is a basic expertise of recognizing the general graphical form of the series. For a start, could the system just ask a few specific questions about the graphs, and leave the interpretation of these to follow later? Interpreting a curve needs a synoptic view to be taken of it, which is usually difficult to program and anyhow isn't the main object of the exercise.

A: No problem! The program could put questions about seasonal changes, the general form and the trend, and about movable holidays and so on. In a final form of the program these could be extracted directly from the series by a time-series analysis program, for the user to take into account or not, as he chose.

Q: What would be the use of a good forecast in this case? What benefits could one expect from it?

A: The first application would be to forecast the amounts taken in tolls, for financial planning; and for this a simple method using monthly figures would be good enough. After that, it could be used to predict the number of gates that needed to be open at any time, and for this daily or even hourly figures would be needed.

Q: Aren't there other methods than those you've suggested? And what about the consequences of forecasts that prove to be wrong?

A: One could try regression with respect to time, with seasonal variations included; that wouldn't be an 'error' properly speaking, but programming it and getting it to work would be a much more complex job for a result that was barely as good. At the other extreme one could rely on 'finger in the air' extrapolation, but to take into account seasonal variations that would need, well, unusual manual dexterity, shall we say.

Q: It seems to me, then, that the aim of the expert system here is not to suggest the 'best' system in the absolute sense but the best within the limits of the time and money that the user is prepared to invest?

A: In effect, yes: it should suggest the method that gives the best price/performance ratio in some sense. For example, Holt and Winters is fast and doesn't cost much; but a deeper study of the series could be made either by a forecasting method such as ARIMA or a more descriptive method that broke it down into trend, seasonal variations and irregular points, either of which would need a bigger investment.

Q: You know about production rules, don't you? Could you suggest a few simple rules that could be used to make this choice? Just to give me an idea.

A: Plenty! For example, if you want to forecast over a short time ahead and you have a series of records over time past and you want an inexpensive method, then you should consider exponential smoothing. This is a rule that points towards one of the main classes of methods that I mentioned. Another: if you have decided on exponential smoothing and if there are data for different seasons and if the trend is linear and if the number of points is more than twice the number of seasons covered, then you should choose linear Holt and Winters. There!

Q: We've agreed that economic constraints must be taken into account in making this choice; how does one define the cost of a method?

A: That too can be got by a set of rules. Would you like me to tell you how?

Q: Not just now, later. I've a few more general questions to help me understand. For example, are there any experts who know all about the forecasting methods?

A: For short-term predictions, yes; but if you add long-term you have to involve several experts, perhaps only specialists in the type of problem you are concerned with, so as to get a working system. But I doubt if this would be worth the effort – there wouldn't be many users of such a system.

Q: ... which would have a bad effect on the economics of the program. And how can the model be validated?

A: Very simply: you compare its predictions with what human experts gave on past occasions for which the actual outcome is known.

Q: I suppose that's easy enough, compared with other fields of information science – there are plenty of records, aren't there?

That is a true story; the present authors know all about the occasion and its outcome – that a week after this conversation had taken place a small model of the system was running. It must be admitted that all the right ingredients were there: a good subject, a good expert, an experienced knowledge engineer and a good understanding between the two.

The aim of this chapter is to detail the various ingredients that go to make an expert system.

Section 3.2 sketches the portraits – rather idealized, admittedly – of the main workers in the task of construction: the expert, his knowledge engineer and that often underrated person, the project leader.

Section 3.3 gives the main lines of a method of construction. This method certainly does not claim universality or infallibility but it has the merit of having been validated in the building of a large number of expert systems, in a variety of fields, that have actually been used on real problems. So it represents a nonnegligible contribution to productivity.

Sections 3.4 and those that follow describe the different aspects of the method of Section 3.3: choice of tools, validation, documentation, use and maintenance.

The final paragraphs of the chapter deal with some specific features of the construction project, in particular the scheduling and the estimating of the effort needed.

3.2 THE LEADING PLAYERS

3.2.1 The field expert and his knowledge engineer

Success in constructing an expert system depends, in the end, on two people mentioned at the start of this book: the expert in the field of the problem and the knowledge engineer. The relations between these two must be characterized by a sound mutual understanding, confidence in each other and complete absence of any tendency to withhold information: this, and quality of the two, is vital.

We have already outlined in Chapter 2 the qualities that the expert must have: unquestioned authority based on long experience, ability and willingness to communicate his knowledge, capacity for introspection, habit of looking for novel solutions and yet questioning everything, experience of working in a team, availability, patience, tenacity – powers of endurance, even – and the ability not to be misled by incorrect information.

The knowledge engineer must combine a capacity for faultless logical reasoning, a solid basis of scientific and technical knowledge such as one would get from one of the great engineering schools or a postgraduate course at a university, mastery of advanced information science techniques, deep knowledge of AI kept fresh and up to date by constant contact with academic and industrial research, an ability to listen to others or, better, an eagerness to learn, and a good technique for interviewing based on the methods used by practising psychologists.

The expert and the knowledge engineer must get along well together; this means that they must listen to each other yet tread a delicate path between acceptance and criticism: each must take something from the other without losing his own identity. As can be imagined, there is no shortage of obstacles to the building of such a relation; without going into the technical difficulties, let us look at some of the difficulties in the way.

(1) The expert is the experienced man, often the older of the two, whilst the knowledge engineer, working in a new discipline, is usually young. Both good and bad can come from this: the good, something like the traditional eastern master–disciple relation; the bad, all the problems summed up in the term 'generation gap'.

(2) The expert is an important person, the knowledge engineer less so.

(3) The expert is a busy man; the sole job of the knowledge engineer is to importune the expert.

(4) The expert has a stock of capital – his knowledge; the knowledge engineer is paid to extract this from him.

(5) The expert is at the heart of the institution, whose values he knows and helps to maintain; the knowledge engineer is on the edge, even outside – he is a foreign body.

(6) The expert makes himself visible in the process of making his knowledge visible; the knowledge engineer studies and perhaps criticizes this. The expert is the object of the knowledge engineer's activities.

3.2.2 The project leader

Important as the relations between the expert and the knowledge engineer may be for the success of the project, this success depends equally on the care and firmness with which the project is managed, and the responsibility for this falls on a third person, the project leader. As we have seen, on him depends also the likelihood of the system being incorporated into the operational environment.

The criteria here are the same as apply in the case of any other project.

We need only emphasize the importance of experience and of having been with the enterprise long enough to understand its hidden power structure and how to use this in the interests of the project when the need arises – as is more likely than not to happen. The project leader must also be high enough in the hierarchy to be able to arbitrate if anyone should raise difficulties, either in the project team or one of the supporting groups.

3.3 IMPLEMENTING AN EXPERT SYSTEM: THE COGNITECH METHOD

The COGNITECH method can be broken into four parts, shown in the four panels of Figure 3.1 These are:

(1) quick development of a demonstrator, to establish the feasibility of the project and also the conditions for the final product;
(2) a test prototype;
(3) (possibly) an advanced demonstrator;
(4) construction and putting into service the final product.

We consider these in turn.

3.3.1 Demonstrator project

In the sense used here, a demonstrator is a genuine expert system deliberately restricted to some representative subset of the problem that one wishes finally to solve with the help of an expert system, and with such operational requirements ignored as speed of execution and demands on memory capacity. This name is used in preference to 'model' because of the connotations that have become attached to the latter: one can read of 'models of expert systems' that are no more expert than a model of an Airbus is capable of flying. In our study of the choice of a first application we have already emphasized the need for this to be complex enough to be credible.

The objective of the demonstrator is to provide the final decision takers, at the lowest possible cost and with the least possible delay, say three to four months, with a basis for assessing the feasibility of the final project, the performance to be expected and the conditions necessary for its development, such as the resources to be committed and the time allowed. At this stage, construction of the demonstrator, it is advisable not to make any specific investment commitments, either for hardware or for

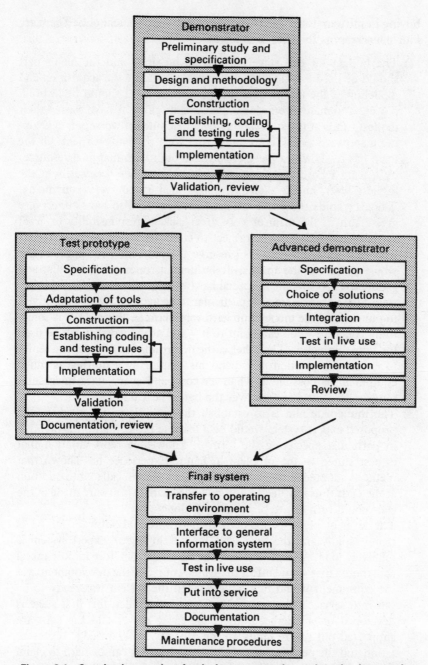

Figure 3.1   Cognitech procedure for design, construction and putting into service of an expert system

buying in software tools – even more, for developing such tools. There are four main reasons for this, as follows.

(1) The budget for this stage is likely to be small and the major part should be used for the main objectives, which are the acquisition and modeling of the knowledge: the main investment should be in brain power. Too many promising expert system projects have wasted their modest funds at the start on buying a machine or, worse, on developing a software tool. The result is that with the budget spent, all the team has to show is a piece of software built with marginal resources by a team whose experience of such work is not necessarily at the highest level, and a skeleton system that is not very convincing. Whoever holds the purse strings will then need to have either very great faith in the team or very great lack of responsibility to grant further funds to allow the project to continue.

(2) The enterprise must always preserve the possibility of canceling the whole project if the results of the demonstrator point to this; and significant investments in special hardware or software will discourage this. There are two traps in particular to be avoided. One is the advice to put most of the money into hardware because 'this at least is something concrete – you can point to it – and at the worst it can be used for something else'. The other is the determination of someone senior to ensure his position or expand his empire by acquiring as much equipment as possible at whatever cost, and every extra microcomputer represents a victory over the baron next door.

(3) The immediate aim is to establish the conditions under which the proposed expert system would be a feasible project, and this involves in particular specifying the form of knowledge representation that is best suited to the problem in hand. Experience has shown that methods adopted at the start of this stage are often called into question at the end; thus any decision to buy hardware or software made at the start could turn out to be a waste of money.

(4) The level of performance of both hardware and software for AI is rising rapidly and the time scale for developing an expert system is relatively long. An early choice of either could therefore impose initial constraints that would affect the whole course of the development, yet the equipment would be obsolete when the system was ready to be put into service. This is very much the case when this first stage is developed on a microcomputer: the basic power and the software supported put severe limits on the capacity for knowledge representation and the performance of the system, and it can be hard to claim that the final system will not be similarly limited.

A clear distinction should be made between the environment in which the demonstrator can be developed and that required for running the final product. The demonstrator can be developed:

(1) on one of the general-purpose machines in the enterprise – if there are none then a service bureau can be used;
(2) with the help of proprietary software specially designed for modeling expert systems. This should be hired if posssible; most suppliers of such software offer hire terms, and even if they do not they are usually open to negotiation.

Thus no significant investment should be made at this stage and, to repeat, no commitments should be made that could reduce the enterprise's freedom to decide whether or not to proceed with the full project, on the basis of the results given by the demonstrator.

There are three stages in the demonstrator project:

(1) preliminary study and drawing up the specification;
(2) construction;
(3) validation and review.

3.3.1.1 Preliminary study and specification of the demonstrator

The first need is to identify a representative subfield of the full problem that, far from avoiding all difficulties, deliberately includes an adequate number and variety of these. Thus if the purpose of the final system is to help a user select from about 50 diagnostic procedures the one(s) best suited to his needs, the demonstrator's choice should be limited to about a dozen, some of which should illustrate different methods of reasoning and others particular difficulties.

The next need is to decide, approximately, the objectives and boundaries of the demonstrator, in particular the input data and where these are to be found, the parameters the system will process and the outputs expected. At this stage the knowledge engineer should define the extent of the problems that can be put to the expert and the resources that will be available for solving these.

Except for a very few classes of problem it is usually very difficult to get an expert to draw up an exhaustive list of solutions to the problems he is asked to solve – giving all possible ways in which a piece of equipment can fail, for example. In some cases the expert's diagnosis is arrived at by numerical evaluation of some expression, such as the likelihood of risks resulting from undertaking some action. In such cases the idea of a 'list of solutions' makes no sense.

Getting all the parameters can take some time, for the expert is likely to use specialist terms in giving his explanations, and the knowledge engineer must make himself familiar with this vocabulary; in some cases it may be necessary to make a glossary of these terms and incorporate this into the system. It can happen that there is no generally agreed vocabulary, in which case a meeting of a group of experts must be arranged, and a set of acceptable terms agreed. In extracting the relevant knowledge from the expert the knowledge engineer must not just ask questions but must also have the expert solve, in front of him, a genuine problem that is simple enough to be handled in this way but shows the type of reasoning that will be used. This is very important, for the human expert will often fail to mention various things that are essential to the solution, simply because they are so evident to him.

Finally, the way in which the demonstrator will be evaluated, and the criteria that will be applied, must be settled; also the characteristics of a set of test cases to be assembled by the project leader.

All the information collected and the decisions made in this study must be recorded in a Functional Specification document for the demonstrator, and this should be approved by all the parties concerned, particularly the expert. This will avoid much argument when the demonstrator is delivered, especially the usual complaint 'But this isn't what I'd been led to expect ...'.

Everyone's agreement having been secured, the project leader can go ahead with planning the construction. The working sessions with the expert must, so far as possible, be fixed straight away, so that he can arrange his diary to take account of these commitments. Experience has shown that lack of proper coordination with the expert is the main cause of slippage in expert system projects.

3.3.1.2 Building the demonstrator

There are two stages:

(1) analysis and design;
(2) construction and implementation.

Analysis and design
This involves the following, in this order.

Analysis. Analysis entails breaking down the goal into subgoals that, so far as possible, are independent.

The inputs and outputs having been settled, the knowledge engineer must clarify the main stages of the reasoning. These may be followed either in a fixed and unchangeable order, with no backtracking, or in an order that is not fixed in advance but is determined either by the information available or by the response to certain questions on which depends the order in which the subproblems are solved. It can happen that these stages are linked cyclically, so that results can be refined iteratively. The choice of inference engine is influenced by these possibilities. The knowledge engineer will need to improve his knowledge of the field of the problem by extensive reading, starting with elementary works and progressing to more advanced, so as to become thoroughly familiar with the specialized vocabulary and the current methods of reasoning.

Design. The expert describes the data he uses for solving the problem, such as readings of measuring instruments or records of the symptoms of an illness or of the socio-economic situation of a person, and the way in which these can normally be obtained, such as reading the instrument, questioning the patient in natural language, extracting from a file written by another program. He says how he expresses the conclusions he comes to: for example a report in natural language giving the cause of the problem, what must be done to solve it, where or to whom to go for further investigations, etc. The knowledge engineer will try to define how the expert relates his data and his conclusions, that is, his reasoning processes and the conditions in which they can be applied. He will take a few standard cases and ask the expert how he would solve these: this will often help the expert to bring to light intermediate steps that he might otherwise have passed over. He should also ask the expert to state the main concepts in the field in question, under which the subsidiary concepts can be grouped; this may seem a hard task at first, but its outcome simplifies the later development of the system and further, it improves the communication between the two people. At the end of this stage the knowledge engineer will have a written statement of a number of rules that will solve certain typical cases; he will also have filled many gaps in his previously skeletal knowledge of the specialized vocabulary.

Finding a formalism. A formalism (or a combination of formalisms) must be found that suits the problem; and the IT tool(s) to be used in the development must be chosen.

Here the knowledge engineer must work on his own, looking critically through what is available to find the tool that can most easily be adapted to the present needs – that is, that will need the least amount of code to be written in order to describe the knowledge. The criteria used here are described in Section 3.4 below.

The knowledge engineer summarizes all this, with his observations on the technical choices involved, in an Operational Specification document.

Construction

Getting the first few rules generally takes longest because the expert has only a rough idea of what is expected of him. He is often set on the wrong track by classical programming ideas, that make him believe that all program structures consist of branches conditioned by the results true/false of tests or the answers yes/no to questions. He can be surprised to learn that much reasoning can be expressed in the form of couples **if** ⟨situation⟩ **then** ⟨action⟩, without any need to foresee where these should be placed in the program. The job of the knowledge engineer is to provide him with a means of expression that will help him display his reasoning.

During this initial stage the knowledge engineer will have to display his teaching skills and gradually show the expert what he needs to know in order to become fluent in expressing his knowledge. He must be careful to avoid being too quick to pour the expert's knowledge into the mold of formalism before having made a thorough study of the expert's natural way of thinking. The best course is to give the expert a great deal of freedom at first and to suggest appropriate methods of representation as and when the need arises. Some experts, for example, need to explain all that they know on a subject, in one go and in the form they are used to, before submitting themselves to the methodical questioning of the knowledge engineer – as though purging their souls before accepting salvation. In extreme cases the knowledge engineer may be reduced to producing a first version of the demonstrator with the knowledge expressed in this natural style, simply to show how inadequate this is. This steering of the expert into formal ways is very tricky to manage: some demand early and rapid treatment whilst others complain that they are being put into an intellectual straitjacket.

This first group of rules, generally the result of a considerable effort, should be put into the system as quickly as possible with the help of whatever modeling tool has been chosen, and the first tests with these shown to the expert. This will enable any gross errors to be corrected quickly, and any lack of realism in the requests made by the program. Once these early faults have been cleared the expert will begin to understand what is expected of him and after a couple of meetings with the knowledge engineer may even be able to write the rules himself: the more he sees results coming from his first efforts, the more his motivation will grow. After this the purpose of the meetings will be to work on the logic and the details of the rules, to polish them up. The program should then be able to solve simple problems satisfactorily.

This work follows a very iterative course, alternating between:

(1) extracting and coding the knowledge, involving for each subtask
    (a) stating the rules for the reasoning
    (b) coding these rules in the chosen formalism
    (c) testing the rules coded

and

(2) testing the system as built at this stage, using the test cases chosen in the preliminary study; returning to (1) if the results of these tests show that to be necessary.

3.3.1.3 Validation and review

After the demonstrator has been made to work, this stage of the project is completed by:

(1) *An evaluation* which, for the project to continue, must show that the demonstrator meets at least a substantial part, possibly all, of the requirements laid down in the Functional Specification. The methods to be used here are described in Section 3.6 below.
(2) *A review paper* in which the expert and the knowledge engineer describe
    (a) what has been achieved: input required and output produced by the demonstrator, performance and limitations, in particular what has been shown by the evaluation, and any problems encountered
    (b) what is needed to develop the demonstrator into a truly operational system
    (c) provisional budget and schedule for further work
(3) *A presentation* of the demonstrator to all who have been involved in the project up to this stage, including the preliminary study and, most important, the top management and the managers in charge of user services.

This will provide all the information needed in order for a top-level decision to be made on whether or not to continue to the next stage, that of building a test prototype.

3.3.2 Prototype project

The aim of this stage is to produce an expert system that can deal with problems requiring any part of the complete field of expertise that is to be represented, and that performs to the satisfaction of a chosen group of experts in this field. So far as precision and reliability of results are concerned, this will give the system as finally required; all that has to be done then is to incorporate it into the operational environment.

There are five stages in this project:

(1) specification of the prototype and of the set of test problems;
(2) (if necessary) adaptation of the development tools;
(3) building and implementation;
(4) validation, by experts and by less expert users;
(5) review and documentation.

3.3.2.1 Specification of the prototype and test problems

This requires the coverage of the relevant field of expertise to be defined precisely, a set of typical problems to be assembled which the system will have to solve correctly and the criteria for the evaluation of the prototype to be agreed. All this will be included in a Functional Specification document, essentially similar to but much more detailed than that written for the demonstrator, and a test schedule.

3.3.2.2 Adaptation of development tools

We have seen that to avoid dissipating resources that should be concentrated on modeling the knowledge, the demonstrator should be built with the help of whatever suitable software tools can be found. These tools, however, will have their limitations. Even if the major part of the expert's reasoning is well represented there will be many details, possibly rather prosaic, that he pays attention to and that will not be treated satisfactorily unless further facilities are added to the inference engine. Further, neither the expert nor the knowledge engineer knows at the start in just how much detail the knowledge has to be expressed, and this becomes clear only in the course of developing the demonstrator; also the boundaries of the expertise and the details of the user environment will be better known at the end of the demonstrator stage. Given the new final objective, the original development tools will probably be found to be inadequate in some respects.

An example of this is provided by the expert system developed by the Dumez Bâtiment company for predicting the times to complete various construction works and used as an illustration in Chapter 1 (p. 71). Initially only a single building was considered; and the system was seen to deal with this satisfactorily, so an extension was planned, to deal with the general case of several buildings together with their entire environment including roads and surrounding land. Whilst it had been possible to produce the first system with the help of an inference engine of level 0 it was clear that it would be much better to introduce contexts as in Emycin [van Melle, 1980], that is, to use typed variables and therefore an inference engine of level between 0 and 1.

Another example concerns the expert system developed by Cognitech [Cognitech, 1985b] for diagnosing motive power failures for the Paris urban railway system RATP (see Chapter 1, Sec. 1.1.2). In the course of this development the knowledge engineer realized that the test made to diagnose one failure could give rise to a new failure, and that the inference engine must therefore be flexible enough to consider several causes – among which would be the true cause – even though the basic assumption made was that any failure had only one cause.

The problem of multiple diagnoses arises also in the agricultural system Tom (Section 1.2.1.1) and has a nonnegligible effect on the way the rules are written. The style of reasoning built into Tom is such that the system does not 'know' that if, because of lack of discriminating information, it is led to suggest several diagnoses, this can indicate the presence of two or more infections. A *post hoc* examination of its own reasoning would of course enable it to discover the true situation. Such limitations in the reasoning process result from the purely formal method of combining likelihood coefficients; this would make it equally impossible to distinguish between a fact that was unknown and one about which no conclusion could be drawn because of two self-contradictory items of information.

Another problem that often arises is that of deciding the weightings in a diagnostic system when many very similar symptoms have to be considered: in vegetable pathology, for example, spots on leaves can indicate any of a dozen different diseases. In such circumstances much more attention has to be given to the meaning of the likelihood coefficients. There has been much argument about the manipulation of these coefficients between the Mcyin [Shortliffe, 1976] and Prospector [Duda *et al.*, 1979] groups, but the two sides do not seem to have realized that they are defined in quite different ways in the two systems: they play a supplementary role in Mycin and an intrinsic role in Prospector.

To sum up, we must note:

(1) there is no universally applicable tool for this work, and a special adaptation will have to be made for each specific field;
(2) the objectives of an expert system project become more precise as the development proceeds; the inevitable redefinitions can require significant modifications of the software tools chosen at the start.

3.3.2.3 Construction and implementation

This follows the same iterative process described for the demonstrator (p. 136) and as in that case requires close cooperation between the knowledge engineer and the expert.

3.3.2.4 Validation

This is done by having a group consisting of experts and less expert users apply the system to the solution or a selected set of real-life problems; this is discussed in some detail in Section 3.6 below. The exercise provides a set of observations on:

(1) the performance of the prototype, revealing any imperfections and any gaps that need to be filled;
(2) the general facilities that it provides for the users.

These can be used to advantage:

(1) to refine the rules as necessary; this will require further cycles of the iteration;
(2) to improve the user interface, for example by changing some of the phraseology used or by using a simpler or less ambiguous vocabulary.

The whole stage is gone through repeatedly until the entire validation group is satisfied with the performance and usability of the system; the effort put in here will have a determining effect on the quality of the final system.

3.3.2.5 Documentation

A *user's manual* must be produced that precisely defines the field of expertise covered by the system, indicating the types of user intended and giving examples of use.

Also needed is *a project review*, reporting the performance achieved, indicating the uses envisaged and the possible future developments, and giving detailed estimates of the costs of putting the system into service, these to include the hardware and software needed, maintenance and costs of user support.

3.3.3 Advanced demonstrator

In some cases it may be desirable, in parallel with the development of the prototype, to make some experiments from a workstation of the kind that would be used with the final operational system: this would reveal any problems that might arise in the transfer to the operational environment and in connection with user acceptance, and thus help the process of deciding if and when to put the system into service. The extreme would be to abandon the project because of what these experiments revealed, even though the system was technically satisfactory.

An *advanced demonstrator* would have to be developed for these experiments, based on the original demonstrator and having the same knowledge base but stressing the user interfaces. It would need to be adapted to the characteristics of the chosen workstation and interfaced to whatever data sources were to be used by the final system, which could be some measuring equipment if the system were being developed to diagnose equipment failures. A robust and ergonomically designed physical interface for the users must be developed. It would be made available to a selected group of users and arrangements made for their use to be observed and their comments recorded.

In the course of these experiments with the advanced demonstrator successive versions of the system could be tried, with the successive changes made in the light of any observations; also various options could be tested and compared. When the study has been completed it must be fully reported, with all the essential observations and the lessons learned, together with details of any actions suggested by the results and of their estimated costs.

3.3.4 Putting the final system into service

When, after studying the evidence from all the activities just described, the enterprise decides to put the prototype system into service, the following have to be done:

(1) adapt the system to the hardware and software of the operational environment;
(2) provide the necessary interfaces with the information sources that will be drawn on – physical sensors, databases, other programs;
(3) carry out user tests and modify the user interface in the light of the results;
(4) provide all necessary documentation, including a users' manual;
(5) set up maintenance procedures, both for fault repair and for development.

All these tasks will be greatly eased, and incidental delays minimized, if the 'advanced demonstrator' route has been followed. The greater the care with which they are carried out, the greater will be the chances of success with the operational system; in fact, success with an expert system, especially in an industrial application, depends on the integration into the existing human, hardware and software environments – in a manufacturing process, for example. Thus the expert system must play the role of a subsystem cooperating closely with the general information system, even if, for convenience, it was developed separately.

Thus the general architecture of an expert system is in three main parts, as shown in Figure 3.2:

(1) The system itself, with its knowledge base, inference engine and subsystems for acquiring knowledge and for providing explanations of its reasoning.
(2) The interfaces with the expert and the knowledge engineer, on the one hand, and on the other with the users; these can include natural language, graphics and videodisks. If the purpose of the system is to control some process in real time there will be connections to data-capture equipment and process controllers.
(3) Links to a local area network (possibly) on which are databases and software packages (and perhaps the experts themselves) that can be of help to the system.

The reader will have observed that questions of AI do not enter at this stage. The reason is that here is a matter for classical IT, with all its established methods, standards of quality and experience of managing large information systems. The transfer from the knowledge engineer to the information scientist will go all the more smoothly the earlier the latter has been involved in the project, the latest stage being the start of the prototype development.

It has to be said that too many AI projects are started outside the information service organization of an enterprise: the situation for expert systems is analogous to that for microcomputers, which have often crept surreptitiously into an organization without any regard for the existing information channels or services, and in both cases great damage will be done if the situation is allowed to continue. The only course is for industrial expert systems to rejoin the mainstream of IT, and a heavy responsibility rests on the information scientists to ensure that this happens.

3.3.5 Summary: distinctive features of the four stages

Figure 3.3 summarizes the main distinctions between the four stages of the development that we have described, using the following five criteria.

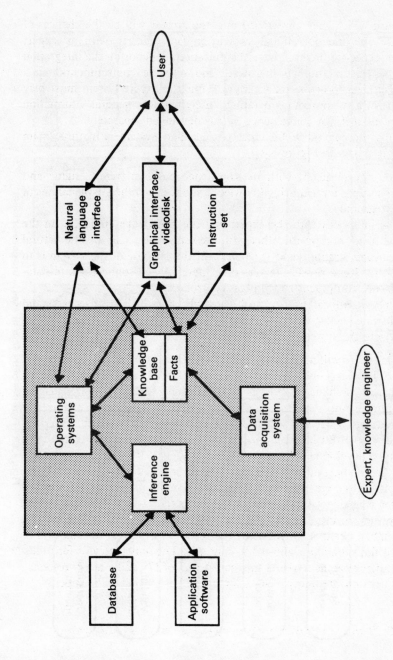

Figure 3.2 Incorportion of an expert system into the working environment

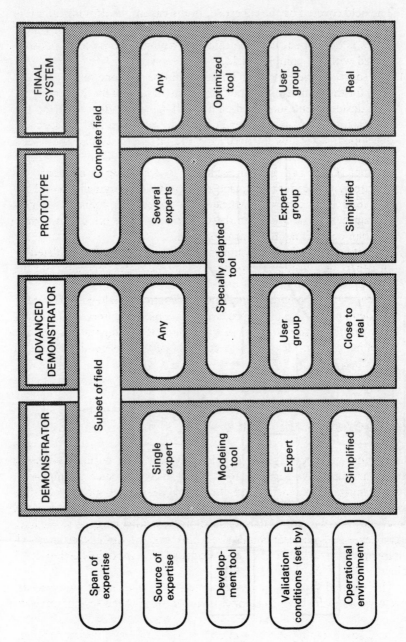

Figure 3.3   Features of the four phases in the development

(1) The field covered by the expertise. In the case of the demonstrator this is limited to some chosen subregion, and the advanced demonstrator, if this is developed, uses the same subregion. The prototype is concerned with the complete field.

(2) The source of the expertise. There should be only one source (one expert) for the demonstrator, but there may be several for the prototype.

(3) The development tool used. This will be a standard tool for the demonstrator and one either adapted from a standard or specially developed, according to need, for the advanced demonstrator and the prototype; some optimization may be undertaken for the final product. Cases can arise in which it is desirable, or necessary, to rewrite in a procedural language a system written orginally in declarative form; this can be so when there are serious demands on performance, for example when there are severe limits on response time, as when controlling a real-time process.

(4) Validation methods. The demonstrator and prototype are validated by an expert or a group of experts; the advanced demonstrator and the final product by a group of users.

(5) The operational environment. It is not practical to take into account at the demonstrator or prototype stage the constraints imposed here, but they are taken into account in the advanced demonstrator stage and the final product developed in the light of the observations made in that stage.

3.4 CHOOSING THE TOOLS

Developing an expert system is a lengthy task that requires skill, for which one must have adequate tools, both software – such as languages, programming environments and other tools developed specially for this work – and hardware. One way of going about the task, clearly, is to write the whole system in one of the standard programming languages. We have already expressd our reservations about this, but will discuss the approach briefly, in particular the choice of language to adopt, in Section 3.4.1 below.

The method most commonly adopted is to use one of the specially developed software tools to help with one or more of the various subtasks of the project: acquiring and formalizing the knowledge and the reasoning mechanisms, building the user interface and so on. We review the main types now available in Section 3.4.3 below and give some criteria for the choice in Section 3.4.4.

Finally, for this question of tools, developments in technology have made it possible to build machines specially adapted to the nature of AI work; we discuss this aspect briefly in Section 3.5.

3.4.1 Languages for AI

Because the characteristic features of AI systems are symbol manipulation, formal reasoning, recursion and similar activities, few present-day programming languages are well adapted to these systems and in particular to expert systems. However, two languages which include such features largely dominate AI work today:

(1) Lisp, designed in the USA in the 1950s at MIT; there are many dialects, the most commonly used being Interlisp and Maclisp.
(2) Prolog, designed in Marseilles in 1972 and taken up in Edinburgh; again there are many dialects, mutually incompatible.

Lisp [Winston and Horn, 1981; Queinnec, 1980, 1984; Farreny, 1984] is a list-processing language, well adapted to symbol manipulation. It has benefited from the large amount of use made of it over the last 25 years, which has resulted in there now being a very rich programming environment for the language, including editors, graphical presentations and other programming aids. The present trend is towards the adoption of a standard version, Common Lisp.

Prolog [Roussel, 1975; Colmerauer *et al.*, 1983; Giannesini, *et al.*, 1985] is a logic language based on first-order predicate calculus; being newer than Lisp it does not have such highly developed programming environments.

There are strong partisans for each of these languages and the arguments can get very heated. This seems to us pointless and misplaced: neither language is completely satisfactory. Thus Prolog is based entirely on strict logical reasoning, and introducing any form of approximate reasoning is difficult; Lisp on the contrary is well adapted to heuristic methods. It would seem sensible therefore to design software systems in which the two languages were integrated in such a way that advantage could be taken of the logic features of one (Prolog) and the functional features of the other (Lisp). Many such systems have in fact been designed [Dincbas, 1985], and have been used for writing expert systems; for example, Poplog: SDL and University of Sussex; LM-Prolog: University of Uppsala [Kahn, 1981 and Carlson and Kahn, 1983]; Loglisp: University of Syracuse [Robinson and Sibert, 1982]; Lovlisp: University of Paris VIII [Greussay, 1983]; Lislog: CNET [Bourgault *et al.*, 1982].

This route should lead to languages that combine the advantages of logical reasoning with those of heuristic search methods.

Lisp and Prolog are not the only AI languages. An important class, which we met in Chapter 1, is that of *object-oriented languages*, with which knowledge can be represented and manipulated in the form of hierarchical structures. Such languages are much used in AI work; as we shall see, they have been used in connection with certain development tools.

However, several of the classical programming languages – Pascal, PL-1, even Fortran and Basic or indeed Cobol – have been used for expert systems, often for the sake of easy and efficient interfacing with existing applications or of portability of the final system, and this has been done even if a prototype has been developed in a more flexible and convenient language. The language C is becoming increasingly important here because of its very good integration into the UNIX environment that has become the standard for many AI workstations. Finally, expert systems in Ada are beginning to appear; there is likely to be a bright future for this language for expert systems in industrial and military applications, because of its real-time capabilities.

3.4.2 Development tools for expert systems

Software tools are available that will relieve the expert system builder of the task of writing certain modules of the system and also will greatly ease the process of getting the system into operation; the builder is better advised to use one of these tools rather than write an entire new inference engine from the beginning, with all its operational environment.

Several dozen such tools have been developed, varying according to their complexity (the range of services provided), their position in the spectrum running from laboratory model to industrial product, and the target machine – from dedicated workstation to large central mainframe, with microcomputer somewhere in between. They can be put into two main classes, as follows.

First, empty systems, or 'shells': many of these were derived from existing expert systems by removing the knowledge base, the best known being Emycin – Empty or Essential Mycin [van Melle, 1980]. Others are Kas, from Prospector; Expert, from Casnet [Weiss and Kulikowski, 1979]; TG-1 [Cognitech, 1985a]; S1 [AIR, 1985]. These systems comprise an inference engine, to which all that has to be added is the knowledge base relevant to the particular application, and a set of software tools of greater or lesser elaborateness for handling the various stages of development of an expert system of the type required – for diagnosis, for example. We should note that the Prolog language itself contains an elementary inference engine that operates in backward chaining on a set of clauses.

Secondly, there are very high-level languages or other software systems, designed specially for knowledge-engineering applications but capable of being used in other fields. Some of these are based on knowledge representation by production rules, using propositional or predicate calculus: for example OPS-5 [Forgy and McDermott, 1977]; Rosie [Fain *et al.*, 1981]; Expert, Kes [Spang, 1985]; Prism, Sage, Tango [Cordier and Rousset, 1984]; Snark [Lauriére and Vialatte, 1985] and others.

The effectiveness of this second class of tools depends on the particular technique used. Thus OPS-5 can handle several thousand rules easily (cf. Xcon and Xsel already mentioned), deriving its power from a rules compiler that generates a graph which is then used to propagate new facts through the system as they appear. Others use more complex forms of representation, in particular the 'blackboard' model which enables knowledge of variable granularity to be represented: for example, Hearsay-III and AGE [Nii and Aiello, 1979]. And finally, a few combine several different representations, including some based on hierarchical objects: for example, Loops [Bobrow and Stefik, 1983]; Kee [Kehler and Clemenson, 1984]; Sr1+ [AIR, 1985]; RLL [Greiner and Lenat, 1980]; Knowledge Craft, MI4, and TG-2 (described in Section 3.4.3).

Many tools are offered for running on microcomputers such as IBM PC and compatibles, Apple Macintosh; for example, M1 [Spang, 1985]; MVP Forth [AIR, 1985]; Expert-Ease [Spang, 1985]; OPS-5, Nexpert [Spang, 1985]. These can be put into three categories, as follows.

(1) 'Inductive' tools, able to generate the rules of small-scale problems from a set of examples: for example, Expert Ease, TIMM, Rule Master.

(2) Relatively simple tools based on production rules and having limited functionality: for example Insight, Exsys. These are useful as a help to taking the first steps into expert system methods at little cost.

(3) Top-of-the range tools with performances approaching that of the most powerful computers: for example M1, OPS-5+ (the PC versions of S1 and OPS-5 respectively), Personal Consultant, Nexpert. With the continuing increase in power of microcomputers, in particular the 32-bit architecture and large memories, these tools will soon enable professional systems to be constructed with their help, although one cannot at the moment foresee their application to industrial-scale systems.

Thus a great variety of tools have been produced for helping to develop expert systems. However, none of these, nor any of the ready-made inference engines, will help with every application that arises and a choice has to be made according to the problem in hand, whether this concerns diagnosis, planning, advice or other activity; we give criteria for this choice in Section 3.4.4.

We now describe a few of these tools.

3.4.3 Software tools

3.4.3.1 Emycin and its derivatives

This was derived from the classic expert system Mycin, built for diagnosis of blood infections. It is therefore especially suitable for diagnosis-type systems in which the knowledge is represented as production rules:

> **if** ⟨condition⟩ **then** ⟨conclusion⟩(with likelihood/plausibility coefficient if available)

Approximate reasoning is conducted by propagating the likelihood coefficients as the rules are applied, using heuristic formulas based on conditional probabilities. The system works mainly by backward chaining: a particular goal is chosen and those rules applied whose conclusions contains this goal; this requires various subgoals to be established, and the process continues recursively. It is, however, possible to state explicitly that a rule is to be triggered by forward chaining. Emycin's reasoning is exhaustive and monotone, the latter in the sense of there being no backtracking.

Emycin includes two subsystems:

(1) A consultation-management system comprising:
  (a) an inference engine linking the rules and organizing the approximate reasoning;
  (b) software for processing the dialogue;
  (c) means for answering questions and explaining the reasoning.
(2) A system for helping in the acquisition and formalization of the knowledge comprising:
  (a) a syntax checker for the rules and a spelling checker;
  (b) a translator for the rules, from internal form to external clear language form;
  (c) some ability for induction on the rules, such as suggestions concerning incomplete or missing rules.

The progress of Mycin makes an interesting study. It became Emycin by removing the original medical knowledge base, which later became KS 300, an improved version, and finally the commercial product S1 marketed by Teknowledge and Framentec.

3.4.3.2 MI4

The family of tools MI2, MI3 and MI4 [Taillibert, 1985] produced by Electronique Serge Dassault enables Prolog to be used for writing expert systems. It provides an extension of Prolog to handle representations by oriented objects, on which is based a method for manipulating production rules. It allows descriptions of the type 'attribute – value' and includes mechanisms designed to ease the incorporation of special strategies for the problem being attacked, for example 'intelligent' back-tracking; such things are difficult to write in standard Prolog.

Because of these extensions an expert system can be written directly in the new language; but it is more convenient to use production rules. The syntax of the rules is not fixed but can be defined by the user, and in fact several different syntaxes can exist simultaneously.

MI4 has other characteristics that are well adapted to expert system building; these are:

(1) the possibility for remembering past states of the knowledge base and restoring these on demand;
(2) powerful mechanisms for aiding reference to the rules – tree structures, indexes, various attributes concerning the rules;
(3) a general method for evaluating the rules that allows strategies to be incorporated that are tailor-made for the problem in hand.

This MI4 environment has been developed for the IBM PC, using Prolog-VM.

3.4.3.3 TG-1 and TG-2

These were built by Cognitech who have used them to write most of their expert systems.

Knowledge representation uses two formalisms:

(1) production rules;
(2) tree structures of parameters, enabling inferences to be made by inheritance of properties.

The inference engine is oriented towards diagnostic-type systems and has these characteristics:

(1) it is based on propositional calculus, i.e. the rules contain no variables;
(2) approximate reasoning is achieved by strengthening or weakening hypotheses;
(3) forward and backward chaining can be mixed;
(4) operation can be in either closed or in open mode; in open mode TG-1 puts questions to the user in order to complete its facts base;
(5) explanations can be given either in the course of a session or at the end.

TG-1 also has software to help with knowledge acquisition and construction of a knowledge base, including the following:

(1) a full-page editor for rules and parameters;
(2) syntactic and semantic checking of the rules;
(3) a spelling checker;
(4) an archive manager;
(5) a test case generator, for use in setting up the knowledge base.

In addition, TG-1 offers the possibility of communicating with a video-disk reader and with other programs.

The architecture of TG-1 is such that it can be used either as a development tool in the usual sense of the term or in a run-time version that enables a knowledge base to be queried, on an IBM PC or an Apple Macintosh. It is available on all machines that support the INRIA language Le_Lisp [Chailloux, 1983].

TG-2, now in process of validation, has features that complement those of TG-1 and so enable it to attack problems of different types, in particular those of planning and of reasoning in a developing situation. Its formalism enables it to generalize the TG-1 concept of parameters to one of structured and hierarchical objects, and the inheritance properties can be made to apply selectively. Variables can be included in the rules, and rules of different types can be programmed as hierarchical objects. Thus the TG-2 inference engine is very flexible, for strategies for conflict resolution or for forward and backward chaining are easily expressed. Further, meta-rules can incorporated, that refer to lower-level rules.

3.4.3.4 AGE

AGE – Attempt to GEneralize – is the outcome of a series of activities at Stanford University concerning knowledge-based systems. It differs significantly from the usual development tools in that it does not presume in advance a fixed framework within which the development is to take place but allows the user to specify his own framework. It is thus a very advanced tool, intended to help a specialist to develop an expert system in the formalism of his choice.

AGE consists of four subsystems:

(1) a system for expressing the design;
(2) a set of editors for entering the knowledge and other information;
(3) an interpreter for testing the expert system, together with aids for implementation;
(4) a trace module to show the line of reasoning followed.

AGE is based on the blackboard model (cf. Section 1.2.2.4). The production rules that constitute the basic knowledge for the problem are grouped according to their nature so as to form the various knowledge sources; these are independent and communicate only through a common database, the blackboard, which at any instant holds all the hypotheses concerning the problem under consideration. The user has great freedom in choosing the design and structure of the blackboard to suit the particular needs of his problem, such as the reasoning strategy, the conditions under which the different knowledge sources can be called and so on. Further, each source can have its own form of representation.

There is no denying the power of such a tool, but it is not provided with the kind of programming environment that would make it both efficient and convenient in use. In fact, its complexity is such that it is really a tool for advanced AI specialists, which explains why, in spite of its power, it has been used in only very few applications.

3.4.3.5 Knowledge Craft

Offered as a commercial product by Carnegie Group Inc., Knowledge Craft arose out of work at Carnegie-Mellon University on SRL+ and OPS-5; it is a fairly complete tool that has been available on the Symbolics machine since April 1985.

Knowledge Craft is both a tool for constructing knowledge representation and an environment for developing expert systems using that representation; it offers several formalisms for representation:

(1) semantic networks, with inheritance properties defined by the users;
(2) frames (see p. 156), which include production rules;
(3) object-oriented languages.

The system combines a complete execution environment, which includes in particular a multiwindow graphical editor, with a frame management that is transparent to the user. The inference engine works by both forward and backward chaining.

3.4.3.6 ART

ART, Automated Reasoning Tool, was developed by Inference Corporation, Los Angeles [Clayton, 1985]. It provides:

(1) possibilities for hybrid representation, either production rules, structured objects or schemas;
(2) explicit representation of time as a variable, for handling evolving situations;
(3) a graphical package ARTIST for developing user interfaces involving menus selected by a mouse, and animation.

3.4.3.7 KRINE

KRINE [Ogawa, 1984] is a formalism for knowledge representation and use developed in Japan by the Nippon Telegraph and Telephone company (NTT) and intended for use on the Lisp-ELIS machine. Its power enables it to be used for systems that exploit complex expertise, such as aids to design of VLSI circuits.

KRINE uses hybrid knowledge representation, mainly object-oriented as is characteristic of 'Fifth Generation' tools:

(1) object orientation, based on use of frames;
(2) procedural, in terms of Lisp functions, the system being written in MacLisp;
(3) logic, using a Prolog interpreter;
(4) production rules.

3.4.4 Criteria for the choice of development tools

A point of fundamental importance that we have already mentioned is that there is no universal tool that will serve for developing expert systems in all possible fields: the existence of such a tool is made impossible by the variety of knowledge and of reasoning methods that are needed in the different fields. Further, the use of a tool, even if well adapted to the needs of a particular field, does not guarantee that all problems in that field can be solved with its aid nor that anyone who is an expert in the subject but not in AI can develop an expert system solely with its aid. There are still problems of conceptualization, of formalization of the knowledge base, of adaptation of the tool and so on that only the knowledge engineer can solve.

Any claim for universality must therefore be mistrusted. Thus although Emycin has been used to develop expert systems in fields as different as medicine (Mycin) and geology (Litho), the problems solved are all of the same type, that of 'fixed instant' or 'nonhistoric' diagnosis (cf. Section 1.3.1.1) in which a fixed set of hypotheses is given and the one chosen is that which best explains a given set of observed data. There is a fairly standard general procedure for solving such problems: the program acquires the data and facts needed for triggering the rules, leading first to a rough diagnosis which is then refined progressively.

However, there are other types of problem that do not fit this scenario and which require a different control structure: with problems of action planning or time-scheduling of interrelated tasks, for example, the method just indicated may give invalid results. With overdetermined problems (i.e. too many constraints) there is usually no solution and the program must relax one or more constraints, choosing these according to some given priority criteria, and look for a solution that is acceptable in the sense that it satisfies the constraints that have been retained. Not only are there differences in the control functions needed for the solution of problems of diagnostic and planning type respectively but also the formalisms used for expressing the assertions and the actions to be undertaken, respectively, are different.

The main considerations on which the choice of development tool should be based are the following:

(1) the type of knowledge representation that it allows, together with the control strategy, i.e. the nature of the inference engine;
(2) the quality of the interfaces offered to the system designer and to the user;
(3) the portability and the cost of the tool.

3.4.4.1 Knowledge representation

The first criterion to be applied concerns the expressive power of the formalism provided for knowledge representation, that is, the breadth of knowledge that can be understood and interpreted by the inference engine. There is always a compromise between a rich formalism that is difficult to master and a simple one that requires the designer to make many extensions and additions to meet new needs.

With variables or not?
Use of variables, implying of predicate calculus, is unavoidable in certain classes of problem, whilst in others the propositional calculus, with no variables, will suffice; the distinction was explained on page 29. If there

are a number of parameters to be manipulated but they all refer to the same object – such as physical measurements defining the symptoms of a single patient – then propositional logic can be used because only one patient is considered at a time. But if the parameters can take different values simultaneously, corresponding to different objects, then first-order predicate calculus has to be used. Suppose, for example, that we wish to express the rule that 'two people may know one another if they have worked for the same company at the same time', and that there is a facts base of biographical details of several hundred people to which this rule can be applied. The rule is expressed in first-order logic as:

for all persons x and all persons y such that there is a location L at which they have worked for intervals (t_1, t_2) and (u_1, u_2) respectively, where these intervals have a nonzero overlap, that is

either $(t_1 \leq u_1$ and $t_2 \geq u_1)$ or $(u_1 \leq t_1$ and $u_2 \geq t_1)$

persons x and y may know one another.

Four variables enter into this inference rule: the person, the place of work, the start of the period of working there and the end of the period; and these can be instantiated by many values obtained from the facts base. The 'unification' algorithm that finds all those occurrences that trigger the rule must be built into the inference engine.

Thus when choosing a development tool for an application that requires variables one must first ensure that these can be handled, and then look into the efficiency of the unification algorithm if there seems to be a risk of combinatorial explosion. If a particular application does not need variables, or if any variables needed are purely local (as would be the case with Emycin), then it would be best to choose one of the tools that uses propositional logic because of its greater computational efficiency and the simpler syntax it uses for expressing logical clauses.

Representing uncertainty

It may be necessary to be able to represent uncertain knowledge; this is often the case in some contexts, for example in medical diagnosis: 'If the patient has weak legs, high temperature and is aching then influenza is possible' is an uncertain rule. At present AI provides methods for representing two types of uncertain reasoning, corresponding to these situations:

(1) nothing more precise can be said about the value of a parameter than that it lies within some interval; this can be numerical, e.g. 'his age is between 27 and 31', or symbolic, e.g. 'I think it's green (0.7) but it could be blue (0.3)' (the numbers here being subjective indicators of strength of belief).

(2) the concepts being handled are themselves uncertain boundaries, such as 'young' or 'strong'. The problem in dealing with such cases is that of choosing some characteristic function that gives the closeness of the proposition to some 'preferred' value or values [Zadeh, 1979; Prade, 1983].

The method most commonly used in this second case is to give weights to the statements and combine these by means of formulas that either strengthen or weaken an inference according as it follows from a logical conjunction or disjunction.

A system that uses such a mechanism will usually be very flexible, for in the majority of cases it will find at least one solution, and possibly several that it can put in order of decreasing plausibility. The main difficulty is usually in assigning the coefficients that represent the strengths of belief that the human experts have in their stated conclusions, and this requires many tests and much iteration. These weights do not have any clearly defined formal meanings, and further are intended to represent frequencies noted by the human experts but which do not have any sound statistical basis.

Representing several formalisms simultaneously

In all fields there are different types of knowledge that are better represented by using different formalisms than by using one for all types. For example, an electrical circuit is represented most naturally by a diagram that shows the physical proximities of and interactions between its different components; whilst geological taxonomy such as putting rocks into classes, orders, families and genera is best represented by a tree structure of concepts or, as is done in Prospector, by a semantic network from which deductions can be drawn by an interpretive system.

Representing structured objects

We saw in Chapter 1 (cf. Section 1.2.2.4) that a style of programming currently popular is in terms of objects, possibly implemented in a manner that makes use of messages passed between the objects. The simplified form of this used in AI was strongly influenced by Minsky's paper on 'frames' [Minsky, 1975]; its features can be summarized as follows.

(1) The objects involved can be represented by lists of cases, called 'slots', that are filled after the problem has been analyzed.

(2) Properties of the objects are transmitted downwards from those at the top of the hierarchy to their descendants. The mechanism gives great flexibility because it can allow exceptions more easily than those mechanisms with strictly defined semantics such as first-order logic: thus 'Birds fly; ostriches are birds that do not fly'.

(3) Methods (procedures) can be shared by objects of the same class, that is by objects having similar behaviors.

(4) Procedures can be associated with some attributes, thus making it possible to mix declarative and procedural structures smoothly.

Meta-knowledge

In the sense that they can reason only at the level of their rules and not about these rules (which would involve *meta-knowledge*), expert systems are not very *deep*. Any meta-knowledge there may be is implicit in the system that the programmer has chosen; there is none at the level of consciousness.

Some programs that have a learning function have a meta-level of knowledge, as is necessary for reasoning at a level below that of the production rules; here is an example of a meta-rule:

If among the rules that I know there is a couple (R1, R2) of the form
R1: A & B $\Rightarrow$ X
R2: A & (NOT-B) $\Rightarrow$ X
then B is unnecessary in the rules and R1, R2 can be replaced by the single rule
R3: A $\Rightarrow$ X

There is of course no reason to stop at any one level of knowledge or meta-knowledge rather than any other; everything depends on the intentions for the future of the system.

One of the great strengths of the human mind is its ability to reason at different levels of abstraction, and to move freely between different levels in either direction. For example, in diagnosing failures the most superficial level is that of direct association of symptoms and possible causes, and this is often sufficient for a good diagnosis to be made; but in more complex cases there has to be recourse to a model that represents the physical processes that underlie this association between cause and effect. Human experts can integrate these two levels in their reasoning and this ability is often the source of their creativeness; the model may in fact be an instance of a much more general reasoning process that enables the expert to see analogies between different situations even though on the surface these appear very different.

We are still far from being able to represent such processes in our expert systems; however, we shall sometimes be led to construct multi-level expert systems in a very pragmatic way, provided that we can find a means for transferring information between these levels that is both efficient and powerful.

At present, whatever acts as a substitute for meta-knowledge is built into the inference engine for the purpose; with the steady trend towards a more declarative style of programming we can foresee the possibility of building the inference engines themselves in the form of rules or objects.

3.4.4.2 The control structure

After a syntax has been defined that can be understood by the inference engine, the next question concerns the type of reasoning that can be achieved. The main points to be considered here are the propagation of the inferences and the control of their proliferation. These cover the need to avoid a combinatorial explosion, to be able to examine different routes in parallel, to be able to retrace one's steps when a branch turns out to be unpromising and to know where to return to, to be able to delete the consequences of a decision when later considerations show this to have been taken in error, and other matters.

Forward or backward chaining?

Volumes have been written about these two fundamental strategies for an inference engine. Neither is superior to the other, they are merely better adapted to different types of problem.

If the main problem facing us is the attaining of a goal that can be stated precisely – such as 'put the King in check' or 'buy 10 000 shares' – then it is desirable to have a program that can find how to reach this goal, in other words what actions to undertake in the hope of succeeding: this implies using backward chaining. In contrast, if the program has to follow the progress of a number of actions in a changing situation without any possibility of intervening, so that it can only propagate the consequences so as to determine the new state of the system being modeled and perhaps take a decision, possibly initiate some new action, on the basis of this state, then forward chaining is the appropriate choice. Actually, many problems require forward chaining to be used in some stages of the reasoning and backward in others.

Open or closed mode?

Some systems are self-contained in the sense that they do not need to interact with the outside world: all the data concerning the problem (at least, all known data) are given at the start and there is no need to provide for any possible querying of a user. Such a system works in closed mode.

With problems in certain other fields, in contrast, interaction with the outside world is essential and the user interface is of fundamental importance. A conversational type of interaction from a terminal is necessary here, which can require sophisticated graphical provisions or giving the system an understanding of natural language, at least in the field of the problem. This latter can require some tolerance of faults, such as miskeying or misspelling.

Efficiency of the inference engine

Many systems based on production rules work by interpretation, and the consequential loss of efficiency in execution is not too serious provided that the number of rules is not very great and the propositional calculus is used. But if first-order logic is used and if the number of rules and facts becomes at all large the possibility of any rule being instantiated many times by different values of the same variable can lead to a combinatorial explosion, and this requires a study to be made of the efficiency of the unification algorithm.

The method most commonly adopted for improving efficiency is to compile the rules into a linked set and to allow the programmer to choose his own strategy for conflict resolution as described on p. 28. From the point of view of tool choice, the important thing is to have easy access to these different strategies.

Ability to explain reasoning

The ability to explain its own line of reasoning is one of the qualities most appreciated in an expert system. The explanation usually provided is a display of the rules used, either as they are used or at the end of some stage and then with an indication of their influence on the various conclusions reached. This requires the system to have some capacity for expression in natural language, and also for graphical expression so as to show the development of the tree of deductions and inferences.

It seems desirable that there should be the possibility of two levels of explanation, for the user and for the system designers. That for the user must be clear and concise with a piece of text or a diagram showing the links between the different stages of the reasoning and in particular giving the reasons for the program's choice of one hypothesis rather than another and the factors that contributed to this choice. That for the designers – the knowledge engineer and the field expert – will help in debugging the program; it can be much more complex and expressed in much denser form, for it is essential here to know exactly what is going on in the reasoning process and this can seldom be described concisely.

Nonmonotone reasoning

With the majority of problems so far attacked by expert systems it is assumed that there is no possibility of querying any of the data in the course of the process of solution. Thus the number of conclusions drawn – new facts derived – increases continually; hence the term 'monotone reasoning'.

However, the validity of a statement can change with time, for a variety of reasons. The situation can change as a result of some external influence: for example the replacement of a component presumed faulty in a system for diagnosing equipment failures, or in medical diagnosis the treatment given to a patient; or of the taking into account of a new data item that was not available previously and for which a default value has had to be taken – such as the temperature in a certain vessel in a chemical plant. In such situations information arriving at time t can show that what was estimated at time $t - 1$ was wrong and that therefore any conclusions drawn from that estimate must be reconsidered; so it must be made possible to retrieve such previous conclusions. Further, in the case of some problems the history of the changing values of one or more parameters must be preserved because the form of this variation may give important information concerning the development in time of the situation characterized by these parameters. There must therefore be an efficient system for managing the memory reserved for a possibly large volume of historical data.

The number of rules
The marketing brochures put out for some systems produced commercially give pride of place to the number of rules that the product can handle. This criterion is often fallacious; it would make sense only if:

(1) we knew how to define a 'standard production rule'; that is, some agreed mean size of rule, in terms of numbers of clauses, premises and conclusions, presence or absence of likelihood coefficients, and so on; and
(2) if we were considering, and comparing, only systems based purely on production rules; but as we saw in Chapter 1 this assumption is becoming invalid.

Consider a hybrid system consisting of both production rules and hierarchical objects. The objects can be characterized by a set of properties and represented by, for example, a taxonomy – such as chemical compounds grouped into lipids, proteins, glucosides, etc.; and the description of each category can be a representation of only the lowest level characteristic of that category. A large and complicated set of production rules giving explicitly the valid inferences concerning such things as molecular structure, toxicity and so on can with advantage be replaced by a few rules governing the inheritance of these properties; the expressive power of the structured object representation, and its syntax, is extremely difficult to quantify in terms of equivalent production rules. An illustration of this is that the demonstrator for the agricultural system Tom was developed with

Emycin and was therefore a pure production rule system; it needed some 200 rules to cover 20 diseases. The final system was developed with TG-1 and used both production rules and hierarchies of parameters with propagation of properties; it needs only 180 rules for over 60 diseases. It is not difficult to imagine the gains resulting from the new approach, in terms of reduced development time, memory demands, processing time in applications, maintenance and costs, and increased comprehensibility of the knowledge base.

3.4.4.3 Transferring the expertise and maintaining its consistency

The participation of a knowledge engineer is necessary to the development of an expert system, not only as a help to the field expert in expressing his knowledge but also because it is he who understands the IT tools that will best translate the expert's knowledge into formal terms and enable the system to be be brought quickly into an operational state. Advanced editors can help him in this work; and some means for helping to maintain the lexical, syntactic and semantic consistency of the system is essential.

Lexical aid can be provided by a generalized spelling checker which, when a term is not recognized by the system, may be able to suggest a similar term that is known. This is especially important when the expert uses uncommon scientific or technical terms, for which transcription errors are likely.

A syntax checker can examine the form of each new rule as it is entered, rejecting anything that for any reason cannot be used by the inference engine.

For the semantics there can be software that will detect similarities between different knowledge items, such similarities may be indicated by the system when suggesting a solution to the problem. Similarity between rules can be:

(1) one rule being a special case of the other; in the extreme, the two being identical;
(2) the two rules being in conflict – in the extreme, contradictory; the 'similarity' is then a matter of the premises being the same but the conclusions different.

The means employed for maintaining consistency must be able to detect any of these anomalies, not only in each new rule as it is entered but also when any existing rule is modified. Consider for example the following pair of rules that are not independent:

R1: **if** A **then** C (f1)
R2: **if** A & B **then** D (f2)

The meanings are

R1: if A is observed, then I believe C with likelihood coefficient f1
R2: if in addition I know B, then I believe D with likelihood f2

The existence of R1 must be known when R2 is entered, especially if the conclusion D is reached. Further, there may be other links between A, B, C and D than those expressed by these rules and the system must be able to detect these. In particular, if these other links reduce A & B to A a careful search must be made for a relation between C and D; the easiest type to detect would be one of specialization or exclusion, and in the case of the latter the contradiction mentioned above would be reached.

At the same time this software must give the system good powers of decision, meaning:

(1) ability to discriminate between possible conclusions;
(2) ability to reach a conclusion.

Because of the combinatorial explosion of the number of possible conclusions, it is very difficult to guarantee that criteria have been developed to cover all possibilities, even if the knowledge engineer has been very much on the alert in his dealings with the expert; nor is it easy to guarantee the same for the reaching of a conclusion, because the computation of the weights can become very complicated.

Experiments have been made recently with a tool of this type for examining the knowledge bases of systems written with the help of TG-1, already mentioned. This enables parameters to be classified according to their role in the reasoning – on entry, intermediate or in the goal – and whether or not they appear in the tree structures for the problem. The study of the rules enables sets of conditions to be found that would support the given conclusions, and so to generate illustrative cases. Applied to the knowledge for Tom this has shown:

(1) two of the rules were identical; their premises were syntactically different and their logical equivalence was masked by the existence of a semantic relation between two classes – this enabled the form to be simplified;
(2) two groups of diagnostics could not be sufficiently differentiated because of the lack of discriminating rules;
(3) there was a rule that could never be invoked because its premise would always be false;
(4) one rule was simply wrong, because of a confusion between two parameters with very similar names.

Such a check on the quality of the knowledge base would have been impossible to make without this IT tool; it is very likely that without it Tom would have lived with these hidden vices for a long time, until the day when some incident revealed their presence.

Few of today's commercial products can draw on this major body of experience which shows that the main cost of building an expert system is that of the testing and putting into operation of the knowledge base. The reader who has already developed a knowledge base will know how much effort is needed, for example, simply to find a set of parameter values that will cause the system to arrive at a given conclusion – a simple task which should be automated completely. This will be dealt with in Chapter 4, where tools for increasing the productivity of expert system development, and the quality of the product, are described; this activity could not be conducted on an industrial scale without such aids.

3.4.4.4 The interface with the user

Too many systems can be used only by professionals because the interface with the user is at too low a level. It should be possible for the human expert, who in the last stages of the development may wish to make minor changes himself, to be able to examine the knowledge base without having to know the internal forms and abbreviations used by the system; some software uses the simple but elegant idea of translating the internal form into 'quasi-natural' language and paraphrasing its meaning.

This ease of examining the knowledge base, and also a certain tolerance of miskeyings, should also be a feature of the interface with the final user. Here, data entry should be made easy, consisting for the most part of responding to questions put by the system. A few systems allow the user, if he wishes, to describe his problem in something like natural language; but this is still mainly in the laboratory stage because of the ambiguities in natural language and the many possible ways of stating the same thing. There are still very few programs that can analyze natural language, even in narrowly restricted semantic fields.

Many (human) applications, especially in diagnostics, conduct reasoning in terms of images – for recognizing a symptom or a fault, for example – or express results in image form – a circuit diagram for example, or an illustration to show how some difficult movement is performed. There are very few systems that can manipulate an image base, held for example on a videodisk.

One of the measures of the success of an expert system is its acceptance by the intended users. It must not only solve, or help to solve, problems that concern them but must be easy to use. The users for whom it has been written will usually have no skills in information science; the system must be such that they can learn how to use it in a few hours and can pick it up again almost immediately after a lapse of several days. In particular, they must not have to keep to some rigid command language syntax in order to read or modify a file: suitable text-processing facilities and a transparent file management system must relieve them of all such technical burdens.

3.4.4.5 Portability

One difficulty that has for a long time held up the integration of expert systems into industrial environments is that of enabling them to communicate with existing programs, often written in a variety of languages and running on a variety of machines. This difficulty is now gradually being overcome by the interfacing of AI languages such as Lisp and Prolog to other common programming languages; there is also some move towards standardization of the many dialects of Lisp so that in France the Le—Lisp version developed by INRIA is tending to become the standard and is available on Vax, DPS-8, Bull SPS-7 and SPS-9, Sun, Apollo, IBM PC and Apple Macintosh among other machines; whilst in the USA Common Lisp is becoming standard. Unfortunately the same cannot be said for Prolog: there are French, American, English and Hungarian Prologs, with far from compatible syntaxes and semantics.

A course often pursued in countries that are richly endowed with computing power – the USA for example – is to make a clear distinction between the development machine (a Lisp machine, for example) and the machine on which the final product will be run. Having a dedicated machine for several months or years can save a great deal of human time in the development stage, but much of this, even all, can be lost in the process of transferring the system to the final machine.

3.5 MACHINES FOR AI

The machines on which AI systems are being developed at present are very varied in type. They are as follows.

General purpose machines. For example, IBM, ICL, Bull and predominantly DEC (PDP-10, PDP 20, Vax), much AI software having been developed on these machines. Such software is now becoming available on microcomputers such as the IBM PC and Apple Macintosh.

Dedicated AI machines. These are usually referred to collectively as Lisp machines although the majority will also accept Prolog. These, as the name implies, have characteristics that are particularly well suited to AI work, as follows:

(1) Large-capacity random-access memories with elaborate management features that are transparent to the user, such as caches, virtual memory and built-in garbage collection.

(2) Tagged memories, meaning that each word is accompanied by a descriptor giving the type of the information that it contains. The Symbolics 3600 for example has a 32-bit word with a 4-bit descriptor.

(3) Central processors, mainly microprogrammed, for direct emulation of Lisp or Prolog instructions. This is an important contribution to efficiency.

(4) A fast bus for connections between the various processor and memory units. The Nubus, for example, used in the Lambda (LMI) and Texas Instruments Explorer machines, can handle up to 37.5 megabytes/s.

(5) Built-in stack management, contributing further to effficiency in handling recursion in languages like Lisp and Prolog.

(6) Extensive provisions for high-definition graphics such as bit-mapped screens of about 1000 × 1000 points, multiwindowing, control by mouse.

(7) Sophisticated interactive software, adding to the ease of use and to the productivity of the user.

Machines of this type are being offered by the American companies LMI and Symbolics and in Japan by Fujitsu and NTT, although at high cost. The French company AMAIA plans to announce a machine MAIA giving very high performance.

The Xerox machines are intermediate between general purpose and dedicated types; the 1100 Series AI workstations are a development of machines designed originally for office work, by addition of extra memory and, especially, new software.

Another machine we should mention is the PSI (Personal Sequential Inference) developed at ICOT in the Japanese 'Fifth Generation' project. This represents a first step towards efficient processing of symbolic information; it is unusual in being based on Prolog, in contrast to the majority that are Lisp-oriented – a notable exception being MAIA, the only machine microprogrammed for both languages. PSI has the advantage of a design approach that has integrated hardware and software; and has an operating system SIMPOS, written in a language ESP (an extension of Prolog), that is especially well-suited to AI.

These AI-oriented machines are certainly pleasant to use and efficient, but equally certainly they are not essential for developing expert systems.

One argument against them now is their cost, but developments in VLSI, in particular the arrival of such things as Lisp processors-on-a-chip, may make this questionable. The new TI Explorer is already exploiting such advances, and as an example we give a block diagram of its architecture in Figure 3.4, showing the fast bus (Nubus) and the microprogrammed symbol processor, with a processor of traditional type, actually the Motorola 68000, for disk management. The Explorer can be connected to a standard mainframe.

Work-stations. These are based on powerful microprocessors (initially 16-bit, now mostly 32-bit) with large real memories, efficiently managed virtual memories, powerful graphics (bit-mapped screens, multiwindow software, mouse), possibly coprocessors for arithmetic; altogether providing a very convenient and comprehensive programming environment. Competition is very fierce here, with most of the manufacturers taking part; this, together with the continual advances in the technology, means that the scene is changing all the time. It seems, however, that three hardware standards are appearing, all working under the UNIX operating system or one of its derivatives:

(1) Machines based on existing microprocessors, meaning in effect Motorola 68010, and 68020, the latter a true 32-bit processor. Examples are Sun, Apollo, Perq, Bull SPS-7 (derived from the CNET sm-90), Tektronix Series 4400, Hewlett Packard HP9000 Series 300 and the British company Whitechapel's MG-1 based on National Semiconductor's NS 32016 microprocessor.
(2) Digital Equipment's 'AI Workstation' based on the Microvax II.
(3) So-called RISC architecture machines – Reduced Instruction Set Computers – such as the recently introduced IBM PC RT (System 6150). RISC architecture embodies a new departure in central processor design: a much smaller set of basic instructions, many registers and an elaborate pipeline system for fast execution of these instructions. The idea itself is not new; it has already been used in some interesting machines such as Pyramid Technology's 98X and the Ridge Model 32, better known in France as the Bull SPS 9.

Actually, all present-day expert systems have been developed on machines of the classical von Neumann architecture, consequently their performance is relatively poor, only a few tens of thousands of logical inferences per second (Klips) against the several millions of instructions per second (Mips) of a medium-power computer. The reason is that this architecture is not well adapted to symbol processing: for real progress in non-numerical information processing we will have to wait for the new

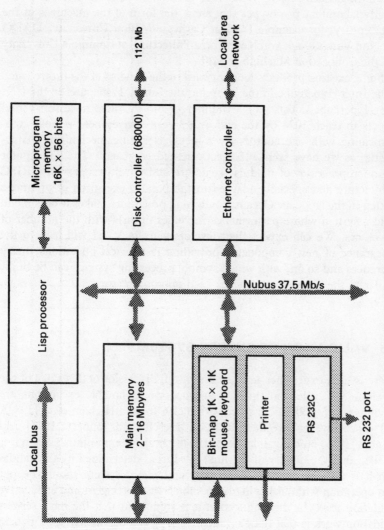

Figure 3.4 Block diagram for the Explorer machine

Microprogram memory 16K × 56 bits

112 Mb

Local area network

Disk controller (68000)

Ethernet controller

Lisp processor

Nubus 37.5 Mb/s

Main memory 2–16 Mbytes

Bit-map 1K × 1K mouse, keyboard

Printer

RS 232C

RS 232 port

Local bus

parallel architecture machines, such as data-flow machines, that are being developed in the 'Fifth Generation' projects. Much has yet to be done before these machines are commercial products, but nevertheless there are already laboratory prototypes that show the form of the machines of the 21st century, for example PSM at Carnegie-Mellon University, DADO and Non Von (i.e. not von Neumann architecture) at Columbia University and the Connection Machine at MIT.

Some existing products look forward to the systems of the future, such as the Intel Hypercube in the USA and the Inmos Transputer in the UK. The Hypercube consists of a number of 80286 microprocessors (Intel expects to reach 1024 by the end of a 3-year development period) communicating with one another by a message-passing mechanism characteristic, as we have seen, of object-oriented languages. The Transputer is a microprocessor of modular structure and novel design with a RISC architecture and specially adapted to the parallel execution of programs written in the language Occam; combining processors makes it possible to build a system whose performance increases linearly with the number of processors. We can expect that developments in VLSI will lead to the appearance of new components providing fast logical operations, fuzzy inferences and so on, with which symbol processing systems can be built, similar to the Texas Instrument's Lisp microprocessor.

3.6 VALIDATION OF EXPERT SYSTEMS

There is little experience to draw on for our discussion of this stage of the development cycle, and little theoretical work; notable exceptions are Gaschnig et al. [1983], Yu et al. [1979a, 1979b] and Hickam et al. [1983], and especially the excellent work of Fieschi and Joubert [1984] and Manuel [1985] on the validation of the medical system Sphinx. When it is recalled that the quality of the final product is determined by the validation it is difficult to understand why any expert system should be put into operation without having been subjected to stringent and exhaustive validation tests. In this connection it is significant that the most serious validation work is that done on medical systems such as Mycin, Oncocin and Sphinx – systems for which questions of personal responsibility are particularly acute.

That this is the position is undoubtedly a reflection of the youth of expert systems, and even more so of the fact that the responsibility for their ultimate use has not been given to those in the enterprise who are in charge of production. So long as this responsibility rests with the people concerned with strategy, long-term planning and research they will not be subjected to the constraints of deadlines, quality assurance, reliability and cost that bear on production, and there is no very evident reason to pursue the question of validation.

Of all the stages in the development cycle validation is without doubt, for those who have to undertake it, the least intellectually rewarding, the most restrictive, the most arduous and the most time-consuming; so the development team will find excellent reasons for devoting the minimum of effort to the task, clamining that it is unproductive and that effort would be better put into creating new rules than verifying old: after all, the expert himself has tested it with some typical cases, even some extreme cases, to see how it behaves, so why do we need anything more? And as a first estimate of the cost of a rigorous validation will look prohibitive there will be no difficulty in getting support for this attitude from whomever controls the budget; so in most cases the expert's quickly given approval will be taken as sufficient.

However, when the development team, conscious of its responsibilities, does decide to undertake an evaluation, it should:

(1) give the task of ensuring the quality of the product to someone other than the field expert, preferably the project leader;
(2) have the actual work done by a group other than the development team;
(3) make sure that the cost is provided for in the budget estimates on which the decision to go ahead with the system was based.

3.6.1 General principles

In general, validation of a product is a matter of checking that it meets the specification. Validation of an expert system differs significantly from that of other programs in that:

(1) As we have seen (page 146) its specification may be intended to change in an evolutionary manner, possibly quite considerably, in the course of development. Validation is therefore not a once-for-all check that the system meets a given specification.
(2) There is not usually any objective criterion for deciding whether or not a result obtained is the best possible. By definition an expert system manipulates imprecise knowledge and uncertain reasoning processes so as to arrive at conclusions that are neither optimal nor capable of strict proof. The only feasible course is to compare the performance of the system with that of a number of human experts, using real-life test

cases and having the comparison conducted by people who were not involved in the development.

Another fundamental difference is that the performance of an expert system depends very much on the quality of the users who supply it with information; that is, who answer the questions that it puts. The parameters taken into account by the system are by no means well defined and can themselves make demands on the user's perceptiveness and level of judgment: even the best informed system is deaf, blind and without any sense of smell. If the user is ignorant of the subject of the problem he can have difficulty in getting the precise sense of the question put by the system, or in describing the parameter that it is waiting for; and if he is more or less expert he can find it difficult to avoid inserting an idea of his own into this reply, with a risk of influencing the system's reasoning process.

In this connection a very interesting observation was made by INRA during the validation of the agricultural system Tom. Information was put into the system sometimes by agriculturalists, sometimes by agricultural technicians and sometimes by experts in vegetable pathology. When comparing the system's performance in these three circumstances the experimenters concluded that it was best when used by agriculturists who had no preconceived ideas about the problem in hand, while with the technicians who, although not experts in plant diseases, would quickly form an opinion concerning the sample given to them, Tom's reasoning was 'contaminated' by information that was biased subconsciously towards the implicit diagnosis. Actually Tom gave the correct diagnosis in all cases, but it suggested also, though with a lower likelihood coefficient, the diagnosis implied by the technician, this having been revealed in consultations with the experimenters. This observation is interesting from another point of view, in that it shows that the expert system's reasoning process is robust, meaning that it can arrive at the correct result in spite of having been given information that was partly erroneous.

It follows from these observations that a variable that it is important to control in the validation of an expert system is the interaction with the user – and this, as we shall see, is not without influence on the cost of the operation.

To end this discussion of general principles we must take another look at the philosophical aspect of comparing human and expert system performances in solving problems. There is always some risk of making too hasty a judgment on the relative abilities. If the comparison seems to favor the system it is salutary to recall that this knows only the subject of the problem and nothing else: it is presented only with problems in its narrow field; if outside this field, its performance deteriorates quickly and drastically. The human expert, on the other hand, has an infinitely broader store of knowledge which he must search for a subset that is relevant to the problem presented; it is this ability to search through the store of knowledge, to distinguish what is useful from what is not and to be aware of the limitations of one's knowledge that is likely to remain beyond the powers of an expert system for a long time.

A comparison may be unfairly unfavorable to the expert system, as was the case with the first trials of Mycin, which showed that the system found only 75% of the diagnoses reached by the group of human experts with which it was being compared. But then someone suggested comparing the performances of two independent groups of human experts, and it was found that the agreement between these was no better than that between Mycin and the testing group. Thus the test was in reality measuring not some absolute level of performance but the level of agreement between two diagnosing bodies.

3.6.2 The object of validation

We could decide to take simplification as far as possible and confine our validation to that of the knowledge base alone, paying no attention to the software tool that had been used to construct this. If we had bought this tool as a commercial product we should be entitled to assume that the price included a guarantee of quality; if we acquired it in some other way we should act as we should with any other piece of software – apply to whomever was responsible for its quality. This attitude, however, is equivalent to ignoring the possibility of interactions, often well hidden, between bugs in the software tool and bugs in the knowledge base; and proper validation of the system requires a complete knowledge of both.

But further, it can be equally disastrous to take into account only these two central components. We have already explained how the performance of an expert system can vary significantly according to the quality of its users, and this should make us aware of something that is overlooked in most of even the little that has been done on this question of validation: that what is being evaluated is not just the knowledge base, nor just the functional unit consisting of this combined with the inference engine (what we called the expert subsystem in the introductory chapter), not even the interaction of this with the user, but the complete, global system including all these certainly, but also all the other components on which the performance depends – operational environment, user support, staff training, documentation, maintenance and so on. The analogy is with the performance of a country's team in the Olympics: this of course depends on the quality of the members but also on the whole accompanying infrastructure and logistics. It is a platitude to say that the value of an expert system cannot exceed that of its weakest component: one that is excellent from the scientific point of view can be almost useless in practice because of its poor response time, the performance of another can deteriorate badly when used by anyone with less skill than the development team, whilst a third can become unusable after a few months because the maintenance has not kept up with changes.

3.6.3 Stages in the validation

This global attitude to validation must not lose sight of the need to assess the contribution of each component to the performance of the whole system; further, the process must be conducted in successive stages with each stage confined to measuring the performance of a single subsystem and excluding any subsystem that has been validated in a previous stage.

A general framwork for the procedure is suggested in the diagram of Figure 3.5; this can of course be modified to suit particular cases and particularly the stage in the development cycle that is to be validated. If the full validation is left to the final stage of putting the system into operation, many changes may have to be made that could have been made more easily if the demonstrator had been validated. At that stage, in fact, the main aim is to validate the expert subsystem; while at later stages the interactions with the operational environment, with the general information system and with the end users will be taken into account.

3.6.4 Typical progress of a validation

Apart from a few minor variants this goes as follows:

(1) Define the aims.
(2) Lay down strategy.
(3) Construct a set of test cases.
(4) Obtain the results given by the system and by a group of human evaluators, including expert and nonexpert users, for these test cases.
(5) Make a statistical analysis of the agreement between the two sets of results.
(6) Make a qualitative analysis of the most important differences.
(7) Put all this into a report on the validation: this report will be an

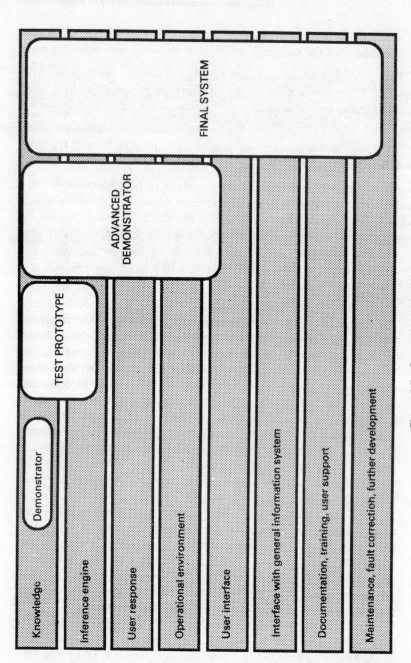

Knowledge

Inference engine

User response

Operational environment

User interface

Interface with general information system

Documentation, training, user support

Maintenance, fault correction, further development

Demonstrator

TEST PROTOTYPE

ADVANCED DEMONSTRATOR

FINAL SYSTEM

Figure 3.5　Stages in the validation

essential document on which to base the decision whether or not to continue with the project.

This procedure is clearly based on what is done in the experimental sciences. Whilst there may be no difficulty in grasping the principle, actually putting in into practice is not without some difficulties which we consider in the following paragraphs.

3.6.4.1 Defining the aims

This is a matter of defining precisely what is to be understood by the 'quality' of an expert system, and therefore of stating the criteria by which this is to be judged. This consideration of criteria of quality should be made in parallel with that of the aims of the system itself and be taken into account when drawing up the specifications of the demonstrator, the prototype and the advanced demonstrator. In the various stages of the development cycle interest will center on some or all of the following factors:

(1) The degree of correctness of the system's conclusion – was its advice good or not? Assuming that some standard of correctness is available, this would seem to be unambiguous. However, how does one rate the 'correctness' when the system gives the 'right' answer but also others that are less 'right', as often happens when the conclusion is reached by a process of manipulating likelihood coefficients and accepting all conclusions for which the final likelihood exceeds some threshold value decided arbitrarily by the knowledge engineer? The question becomes much more difficult when there is one very seriously wrong answer among the 'less right' – as for example the suggestion of a dangerous operation by an expert system used for controlling a nuclear reactor.

　　Thus the criterion must be supplemented by some concept of 'criticality' and one of the aims of the validation must be to ensure that the system *always* gives a response that is 'reasonable' (not merely 'not wrong'), even if this is not optimal. It will be clear that in order to apply such an amplified criterion it will not usually be sufficient to have some standard against which to assess the 'correctness', but that the judgment of a human expert will also have to be involved.

(2) The precision of the system's conclusions. For example, a system for diagnosing failures in electromechanical equipment may be excellent at showing which circuit or plugged-in component is faulty but very poor at identifying a failed contact-breaker or fuse; and a medical system may suggest the correct treatment but give the wrong prescrip-

tion details. Precision is not always so easy to evaluate as these examples might suggest. How, for example, are likelihood coefficients to be interpreted, which are often given by an expert system along with its conclusions? What meaning should be given to these when the human evaluators would not naturally express themselves in these terms?

(3) The sensitivity, that is, the extent to which the correctness and/or precision of the conclusions are affected by the correctness and/or precision of the input information. What is the effect, for example, of the system being given a wrong answer to one or more of the questions it puts to the user? A good system must be able to reason in an information environment that is incomplete or imperfect, just as can human experts.

(4) The correctness and precision of any intermediate conclusions, especially if the system is to be used for training.

(5) The precisions and economy with which the reasoning is carried out. The number of steps needed to reach the conclusion, the amount of data demanded as compared with what a human expert would require, the relevance of the data demanded and the order in which the items are called for are all factors that bear upon the acceptability of the system.

(6) The response time, meaning the total time taken by the system in giving its conclusion, including that taken up in acquiring the data it needs, which could include, for example, that required for activating and releasing some piece of equipment or accessing some measuring instruments. A well-designed system will often save significant amounts of time by optimizing the process of finding the information required. This is so for the Rufus system for diagnosing breakdowns in the RER trains, which plans the operations to be performed in such a way as to minimize the distance to be walked along the 300 metres length of the train; or [Barrielle, 1985] a system for identifying faults in printed circuits, which takes more time over the actual calculation than would a classical program but requires far fewer tests to be made: a test takes tens of minutes, but the calculation time for each test only seconds. As we shall see later, a proper assessment here cannot be got from a paper study but requires actual work with the system in real time.

(7) Robustness: resilience under variations in such factors as the environment and the quality of the users.

In addition to these basic criteria there are more qualitative aspects on which it would often be important to lay stress, such as the general acceptability of the system by the users, the ease with which it can be understood and its use learned, its impact on the users' knowledge, the quality of the explanations that it gives, and so on.

Finally, there are certain side effects to be considered; these cannot be included in the statement of the aims of the system but constitute secondary benefits flowing from its use. Thus a study of the effects of the regular use of the medical system Oncocin [Kent *et al.*, 1983] showed that the quality of the users' clinical observations had improved; and we have noted that nonexpert users of Tom showed a similar improvement in their observations of plant disease symptoms.

3.6.4.2 Validation strategy

The choice here will follow directly from the definition of the aims of the validation and constraints within which it has to be carried out. The main factors are:

(1) The criteria applied: quantitative or qualitative?
(2) The standard of reference: an objective fact or something representing a consensus opinion of a group of experts?
(3) Conduct of the study: theoretically with paper studies or actual work with real situations?

In every case the problem arises of standardization of the conditions under which the experiments are made. We consider this at the end.

Quantitative or qualitative criteria?
We have seen that the validation procedure can pursue two types of aim, either separately or together:

(1) Quantifiable, such as correctness, precision, robustness and response time, for which the main difficulties lie in the choice of units of measurement and standardization of conditions. Programs that collect and process the relevant data can certainly be of benefit here.
(2) Qualitative, such as acceptability and ease of learning and of understanding, for which the main difficulties lie in the availability of observations and the interpretation of the results. Whilst in the case of (1) above the protocol can be largely automated this is not so in this case, either for the observations or for their interpretation. Possible methods are loosely structured interviews with users, either individually or in groups, unbiased questionnaires and observations *in situ*: and these can consume large amounts of very highly qualified manpower – psychologists, sociologists and ergonomists. This last ex-

plains why validations of this type are so rare; they can be undertaken only by organizations that have available the human resources of the right types and with the necessary ability.

Objective fact or consensus opinion?

We need to distinguish between cases where the reference standard is an objective, unequivocal fact, as is usual for deterministic systems such as those of diagnosing failures, planning activities or managing financial portfolios, and those where it is a consensus of expert opinion, as is often the case in medical systems. In the first case the performance is measured by a level of agreement with (or difference from) reality, in the second with (or from) an opinion; although in some cases the standard can be an opinion at the start and later be accepted as reality, as for example can happen with risk evaluation. Validation of consensus-based systems has to be a continuous activity, and the cases must be followed over very long periods. As the example of risk evaluation shows, it may not be an easy matter to arrive at a statement of 'reality', and in some cases it may even be found necessary to give up the idea.

Getting a consensus of opinion may seem at first sight to be a simpler task. But apart from the fact that many opinions must be obtained if the consensus is to have any value, and the supply of available experts in the particular field may not be plentiful, there are several problems:

(1) Concerning the conditions under which the opinions are obtained: ideally the experts should not know one another, should not communicate with one another, and should all treat the same case at the same time. This is difficult, even impossible, to arrange in practice.
(2) Concerning the span of opinions: who decides whether or not the experts are agreeing among themselves?
(3) Concerning robustness: how would the result vary if sought at different times and in different places?

Paper studies or work *in situ*?

Ideally the conditions under which the evaluation is performed should be the same as those under which the system is normally used for live work; and therefore a validation should be performed on the bench, so to speak, and in real time on real or correctly simulated cases, whenever possible.

However, this can put a heavy load on the enterprise: validating a system for diagnosing breakdowns, for example, could involve taking a train or an aeroplane out of service; but as we have seen, this is the only way in which real-time events can be taken into account in the evaluation.

There are cases in which this approach is simply not possible, and in which a paper study has to suffice, with all the bias that this can involve. This will be so when the data needed for the solution, or the objective results against which the system's answers can be judged, will not become available for a long time, as for example when the problem is one of interpreting data that relate to some phenomenon that is evolving with a long time scale, or of long-term forecasting. Use of historical data may be justifiable in such cases.

Finally, if the expert system is embedded in an environment containing many numerically oriented programs, as for example on board a space satellite, the concept of a 'real' case may not make sense; more classical methods of validation must then be used, testing the program under all those conditions that are known to be likely to cause errors.

Standardizing the conditions

Since the validation consists of comparing the performance of the system with that of the group of evaluators it is clearly important to ensure that it is carried out under conditions that favor neither.

A first principle to be respected is the independence of the different groups involved – designers, users, evaluators – together with the use of a different team for the evaluation from the design team; and there must be no communication between these groups. In particular, the evaluators should not even know that they are validating an automatic system, and each should submit his own conclusions without knowing those of any of the others.

The second principle is that of equality of access to information: the system and the human evaluators must have the same information, provided by the same means. Thus there must be some arrangement such as represented in Figure 3.6, in which the information needed is provided to the system and to the evaluators along identical channels by a human 'information source' who alone is in contact with the complete situation and interprets the responses according to his own criteria.

This ensures that the system and the evaluators work with the same information of the problem and eliminates any bias due to the reliability of observations or qualification of facts, especially when the information relates to such subjective impressions as the shade of a color, the nature of a smell or the loudness of a noise. Failing any possibility of standardizing the vocabulary, we are here trusting to the internal consistency of the 'information source'.

It is easier to ensure this semantic consistency and identity of information supplied if this information is obtained from files rather than from a physical system running in real time, provided that all that is needed is there but only what is explicitly asked for in any request is given.

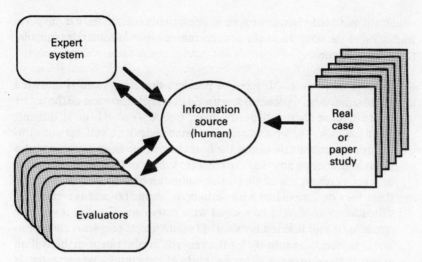

Figure 3.6   Standardizing the validation conditions

The intervention of the 'information source' becomes clear when the work is conducted with a real or simulated case because then he alone can ensure that the experts do not have access to any implicit information, which could not be taken into account by the system being validated. It is well known that as soon as a human expert becomes aware of a problem to be solved he will take in a great amount of data of which he will use only a tiny fraction: that forms the facts base. The unused knowledge is apparently forgotten, but the expert can recall it when faced with a difficult problem. This calling on reserves of information is usually a subconscious process; the arrangement we are recommending forces the expert to formulate an explicit request for specific information. A further benefit is that it enables the use of new rules to be made clear and rules to be deleted when it is seen that they are never used by the evaluators.

In this method of conducting the validation the system is isolated from the conditions of real use; but it is only after the relative performance of the system and the human experts has been established in this way that the impact of those conditions can be assessed, for example by observing the effect of changing or doing away with the 'information source', and giving the evaluators direct access to the system and the data.

3.6.4.3 Constructing a set of test cases

What is wanted here is a number of samples that will represent the problems that the system is intended to solve. They can be real or simulated situations on the one hand or paper problems constructed for the purpose, according to the style decided upon; and three types of constraint must be taken into account.

(1) Representativeness. All types of problem that the system is intended to solve must be represented, with no overrepresentation of the easier ones (because they will be the most frequent) or the most difficult (because they will be the only important ones). It will be useful to include a few cases that lie at the boundary of the field, but there is no point in including any that are outside. It may sometimes be desirable to overrepresent cases that arise only rarely in real life, because these may be asssociated with serious consequences and therefore the validation here should be treated with extra care. Finally, it scarcely needs to be said that the tests should relate to real problems and not to 'toy' problems thought up by the experts. It often happens that if an expert is asked to quote a case he thinks of something that corresponds not to a real-life situation but to something that he hopes to prove: there is a great temptation to use an expert system as a simulator; that is, to answer 'what if . . . ?' types of question.

(2) Size of the sample. To be meaningful, the test should be made on 40–60 cases for each type of problem, which implies a rather large set. Thus several hundreds of cases will be needed for the validation of a system intended to find the reasons for a dozen or so manufacturing faults.

(3) Cost and organization. This is certainly not the least important consideration. We have already raised the possibility of systems that have been designed for diagnosing equipment failures needing, for their validation, massive machinery to be taken out of service and technical teams to create breakdowns. In other fields account must be taken of the fragility of the object chosen for the validation, or of its change of properties with time; this is very much the case when living material is involved: a diseased tomato plant has quite a different appearance three days after is has been lifted. Finally, some situations are evanescent or unrepeatable and in the nature of things can be used only once; for example, the many cases in which the test destroys the object tested, or in continuous-flow fabrication where defective material is scrapped immediately the defect is identified.

The cost of setting up the files to be used in the validation can also be considerable. These must contain a very large amount of information, presented in a uniform style and be equally usable by the expert system and the evaluators. In this connection it will often be found necessary to take from the archives records that were not made for this purpose, to reorganize and reformat these and then, observing that they do not give all the information needed, go over them again to ensure that they meet the specifications for the test cases.

All this shows that validation will be one of the major items in the project's budget and a task most often lying on the critical path.

3.6.4.4 Statistical analysis of the results

The information collected during the validation can usually be summarized in a set of double-entry tables like those of Figure 3.7. The statistical analysis consists, at minimum, in computing the similarities and differences between the results given by the different classes of evaluators:

(1) between one expert (or expert group) and another;
(2) between experts and nonexperts;
(3) between the expert system and the experts;
(4) between the expert system and the nonexperts;

and for each style of evaluation adopted:

(1) with or without 'information source';
(2) with different 'information sources';

and all of the preceding for each evaluation criterion applied.

The question of comparing the responses of the system with those of the human evaluators is presented differently according to whether there are known solutions to the problems at the time of their presentation. There is no difficulty if there are; if not, a majority rule decision has to be established on what is the most likely solution, so that this can be reduced to the first case. Majority rule has the simple disadvantage that it is better to be wrong with the rest of the world than right on one's own; it can be refined here by giving different weights to the views of different experts if their reputations and experiences differ.

In each field the system can be assessed as satisfactorily validated if its mean success rate, within an agreed margin of error, reaches an agreed threshold; or simply if it exceeds that of the human evaluators.

3.6.4.5 Qualitative analysis of the results

The qualitative analysis of results is a matter of trying to relate any important differences between the results given by the expert system and by the human evaluators to certain nonquantifiable factors assessed during the validation, such as the acceptability and comprehensibility of the system and the presence or absence of side effects.

In the attempt to assess the significance and find the causes of these

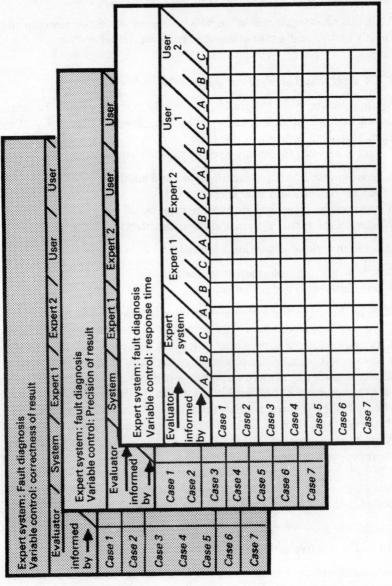

Figure 3.7　Records of observations

differences another team of experts should, if possible, be asked to look at each case about which there can be any argument; failing a different team, that employed in the validation will have to be used. Manuel [1985] suggests that the study team should classify the contentious cases as follows:

> level of difficulty
> system's conclusions identical with their own
> > acceptable
> > incomplete
> > unacceptable

and that they should give reasons; for example, why is the solution acceptable/incomplete/unacceptable?

The effect of this analysis on the quality of the final product will be greater, the more it is able to bring hidden defects to light and, especially, to suggest remedies for these.

3.6.4.6 Reporting the validation

It is the responsibility of the project leader to write the validation report. It is good practice to circulate a first draft to all those who took part in the exercise, for comment; and also to the development team to give them the opportunity:

(1) to suggest corrections and improvements to the system, in view of the defects noted;
(2) to assess the further effort that would be needed to overcome the reservations expressed. Some could need only minor modifications, others the incorporation of further information such as extra rules, or a restructuring of the knowledge base, whilst yet others could require some basic technical choice to be reconsidered, such as the way in which the knowledge was represented.

3.7 DOCUMENTATION OF AN EXPERT SYSTEM

3.7.1 For what and for whom?

Proper documentation of an expert system is essential for its quality and for ensuring that it is used over any significant period of time. Further, the documentation is of value to everyone who is in any way concerned with the system; its main uses are these.

ES—M

(1) To help bring about agreement among experts. Except in very few cases several, perhaps many, experts will have been invited to contribute their knowledge to the system, either individually or as a group; so each must be given the opportunity to support or criticize what others have contributed. It is well known that experts who are in close touch with one another, friends possibly, can disagree radically over the writing of a diagnostic rule because although they have the same objective they are starting with slightly different premises.

(2) To ease the problems of maintenance of the system by a different knowledge engineer from the one who was involved in the development This need can arise, for example, when the development engineer leaves the enterprise. The engineer who takes over the responsibility for maintenance will find all the information he needs in the documentation, including the reasons for the choices made for representing the knowledge and structuring the knowledge base.

(3) To help spread the expertise, and the understanding of this. The methodology of the expert system, with its hidden use of knowledge manipulation, may well represent a major advance over traditional IT, but perfect understanding of knowledge bases is still lacking and much explanation, at all levels, is still needed.

(4) To ensure that any likely legal complications are covered – and if possible, avoided. The question of assigning responsibility in a case in which the use of an expert system is involved has not yet come before the courts but is sure to do so one day. Of all those likely to be at risk in such a case the most exposed are clearly the expert, who may have been wrong, the knowledge engineer, who may have misinterpreted what the expert told him, and the actual user of the system, who may have misused it. It is therefore important to have a document that shows the various forms that the information has taken, from its initial expression by the expert through to its presentation as advice to the user; and it must show exactly what transformations were made at each stage, justify any simplifications or other changes, give the limits within which the rules can be applied and show what was done to minimize any errors in interpretation. It must also state who held responsibility at each stage, showing collective responsibility whenever this was the case, as for example in the validation exercise.

3.7.2 What should be put in the documentation?

We have already indicated, for each stage in the development, the various documents that should be produced. To summarize:

(1) A general description of the application for which the system is to be built, amplified in the course of the impact study. This provides a record of the motivation for the project and the reasons that led to the various decisions being taken.
(2) The various specifications drawn up for the successive stages from the demonstrator to the putting into service of the final system.
(3) The documents relating to validation and signing-off, for both intermediate and final stages; a description of the test material, with comments, should be included here.
(4) Documents relating to use and maintenance of the system, in particular the relevant manuals and reports of incidents, corrections made and any transfers of the system to a different environment.

We have also emphasized the importance of documenting the various components of the system, that is, the various parameters, rules and objects that it comprises. It would be useful also to preserve the records of sessions with the expert(s), ensuring that these have been approved by the expert(s) and by the knowledge engineer.

In addition to these very specific documents a high-level account should be written, giving the following:

(1) The field covered by the system, with its boundaries. An expert system, like a human being, never stops learning; but the field over which it can be applied at any moment must be clearly defined so that any extensions can be properly managed. Some of the limits may result from objectives set by the enterprise, others may represent the limitations of the experts' knowledge and yet others those of the reasoning powers of the combination of inference engine, method of knowledge representation and knowledge base. Any of these limits may change as time passes and these changes, together with the current state of the system, should recorded explicitly.
(2) The major choices made for structuring the knowledge and the reasoning process.
(3) The different sources of expertise: names of the experts consulted and relevant professional details, accounts of the roles they played. Where possible, literature references relevant to any knowledge items used.
(4) The history of the development of the knowledge base. It can happen that certain anomalous behavior of the system, due to some incorrect rule or rules, can be explained only after a study of the previous states of the knowledge base. Similarly, transfer to another environment can result in mistranslation of rules that can be detected only if a standard of reference is available.

3.8 MANAGEMENT OF THE PROJECT, SCHEDULING, COSTING

3.8.1 The project team

This, as we have seen, consists of the project leader, the field expert(s) and the knowledge engineer; their roles were defined in the first part of this chapter.

In addition to the tasks traditionally associated with his role, the project leader has two major responsibilities:

(1) Quality assurance, brought about by:
  (a) ensuring that the development is constructed along the lines laid down;
  (b) devising and organizing the validation exercise;
  (c) ensuring that the full documentation is produced.
(2) Ensuring the acceptance of the system by the user environment:
  (a) in the impact study, ensuring that the views of the intended users are sought and taken into account;
  (b) during the development, by keeping the intended users fully informed of all that is being achieved;
  (c) during testing and evaluation, involving them in the activities; and afterwards in the reviews;
  (d) when the system is brought into service, providing a users' manual and organizing training.

If any people not belonging to the project team need to be associated with the development, as can happen, for example, when the project requires the cooperation of other services, it is important that responsibilities and interfaces are clearly defined right at the start; in particular the formalities for internal correspondence and assignment and signing-off of subtasks must be made perfectly explicit. This need, however, should be avoided if possible in the case of the first expert system because of the extra complications it can give rise to.

3.8.2 The sponsor group

Outside the development activity, it is often useful to form a sponsor group for the project, with membership drawn from the eventual users, other services having an interest in the use of the system and the general management. In particular, the following should be included:

(1) the 'official' sponsor – as explained in Section 2.4.3, the project would benefit from the active support of a senior member of the enterprise;
(2) the head of the information services;
(3) the 'collaborators' in the impact study those proposed projects were not chosen but who could benefit from being kept informed of the development under way.

This group would have the special duty of:

(1) articulating the view taken by the enterprise, as a body, of the new technology;
(2) spreading general awareness of expert systems through the enterprise.

It should meet after each important stage in the project has been completed and should receive all the reports of evaluation of the system.

3.8.3 Scheduling

Figures 3.8–3.10 suggest schedules for the demonstrator, advanced demonstrator and prototype respectively for an expert system of modest complexity (static diagnosis); it is assumed that the development team has the experience of producing at least one previous system of the same type, uses proven methods and tools and is working in an environment of sound scientific and technical competence. The different tasks are located in the diagrams so as to show who is responsible for each, and the times given are means of observations made on several dozens of real systems developed by Cognitech.

We have preferred not to give a corresponding schedule for a final product because we feel that we do not have the experience necessary. As a study of the three diagrams will show, the full development from impact study to going into service will cover at least three years, from which it follows that the most higly developed systems in France are even now scarcely in their final stage. Further, it is not clear that there is a 'typical' schedule in this case, because the tasks to be completed, and the times needed, will depend very much on the environment – whether or not the system has to be integrated into some real-time activity (including even some mobile system), interfaced to a database, to a videodisk, to a voice-command system, and so on. Such tasks belong more to traditional IT then to AI and can involve very heavy costs in time and money; they can, however, be planned more precisely because the problems they present are more clear-cut.

The present indications are that when the aim is to put system into the

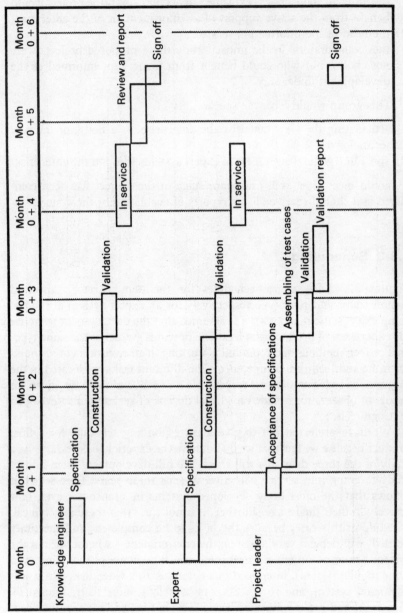

Figure 3.8 Schedule for development of a demonstrator

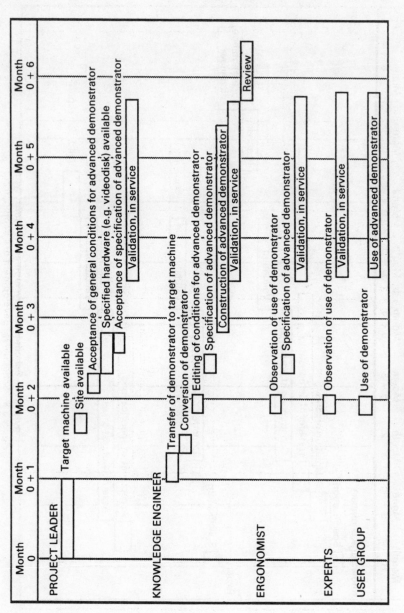

Figure 3.9   Schedule for development of an advanced demonstrator

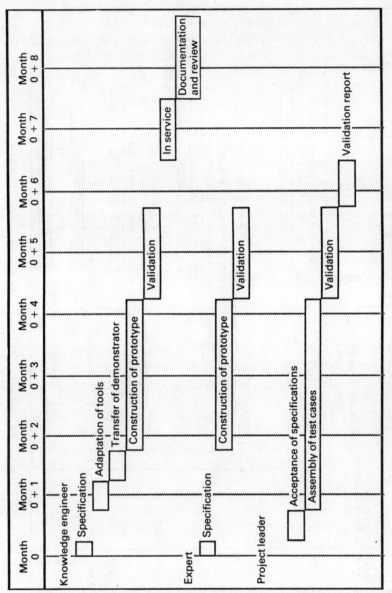

Figure 3.10   Schedule for development of a prototype

hands of a large number of users the effort needed in bringing it into service is at least twice that needed for the first three stages together. Against this, many systems will need much less than this, simply because they will never be used outside a very small circle, mostly of users very close to the development team or even the team members themselves. In such a case the prototype constitutes the final stage in the development.

The timings shown in the diagrams seem to contradict any assertion that an expert system can be developed quickly. Actually, these fairly long times take account of various types of delay, often outside the control of the project team, that were observed in these developments: for example, delays in getting approval for plans and specifications submitted, or of budgets for the successive stages. Such delays can double the time needed for the development alone; so although no more than 18 months might be needed to bring a system to the point where all that is needed is the decision to go into service, the actual time taken is more likely to be three years.

3.8.4 Costs

To cost an expert system completely the following must be taken into account.

(1) The human resources employed: experts, knowledge engineers, project leader, sponsoring group, etc. In some cases costs of lost services must be added, such as that of the experts involved in the project thus being unavailable for other work.

(2) The cost of any hardware or software bought or hired for the project, whether for the system itself or for any necessary interfaces. Under this heading the costs involved in an advanced demonstrator can be several times those of a test prototype: the cost of producing a video-disk, for example, is far from trivial.

(3) All consumables, including, in particular, machine time, which in AI work can be considerable: for example, when variables have to be processed, or nonmonotone logic used, or, failing anything better, progress has to be made by trial and error.

(4) Costs associated with the validation. As we have already indicated, the exercise can require expensive industrial equipment to be taken temporarily out of service; and production staff may be deflected from their normal work because of their involvement in the tests.

(5) Costs of the documentation.

In 1986 these costs totaled several million dollars for a system designed for a large population of users. The main possibilities for reducing such costs lie in the putting of effort into staff training and quality assurance.

To give a complete picture, the costs of use and of maintenance should be added to these development costs. These can vary widely, according to:

(1) the appropriateness of the technical choices made at the start of the project, in particular of the software tools because of the effect these can have on the ease of use and of maintenance;
(2) the strictness with which the laid-down methodology has been adhered to in the development: here again, the importance of the documentation is clear.

4

Industrial development of expert system skills

We have now reached the end of a journey that has taken us from the basic ideas about expert systems, through the process of choosing an application for the first attempt at building a system and ending with putting this into service. In the course of this journey we have, let us hope, steadily become more firmly convinced of the importance of the expert system technique, its value for our enterprise and finally of its feasibility; but at the same time we have become aware of the many difficulties along the way and the traps that line the route – and properly skeptical of the naive view, 'it's easy, it won't cost much and it will give a fine return'. In short, our attitude to expert systems has perhaps acquired something of that 'divine detachedness' in which Ignatius Loyola saw the beginnings of wisdom, and we are now able to look on them as just another addition to the armory of technical weapons from which we select the one best suited to attack the problem we are faced with.

We are now intellectually equipped, therefore, to embark on another stage of the journey: to change the status of the expert system technique from an exclusive possession of a small group of specialists to something fully integrated into the culture of the enterprise, so changing technical mastery to industrial mastery. A single joiner with good tools does not constitute a furniture industry, and a single knowledge engineer with his inference engines cannot incorporate these new techniques into all the production processes of his enterprise: there is an immense gap in organization, methods and investment between the craftsman's workshop – which can produce masterpieces – and the factory – whose purpose is to produce goods in the quantity and of the quality that our society calls for. In this last chapter we try to show how this gap may be bridged, using some actual experiences of expert system application; we beg the reader's indulgence if our accounts seem few and incomplete: published evidence of the use of expert systems in real-life situations is rare, but evidence of the acquisition of industrial mastery of the technique is rarer still.

4.1 SOME ADVANCED FRENCH EXAMPLES

4.1.1 The National Institute for Research in Agronomy (INRA)

We have already seen (Section 1.1.1) that INRA is one of the world leaders in investment in expert systems. The Institute's studies of the impact of these systems, and its first evaluations of Tom, have shown that they can be of special value:

(1) for exploiting the Institute's special expertise – we have seen how this has been done in the case of vegetable pathology; similar systems could be developed for animal pathology, for agricultural development, soil treatment, and so on.
(2) for preserving and making available the Institute's knowledge: too often knowledge acquired at great cost vanishes with its creators;
(3) for planning research – the compiling of knowledge bases will reveal gaps to be filled by new research.

These reasons convinced the Institute that is must build expert system methods into its technical fabric; it chose to do this by:

(1) training eight members of its staff as knowledge engineers;
(2) acquiring tools for expert system development that were specially suited to its own needs;
(3) developing operational systems and putting these into service.

This was started in October 1984, with the aim of making INRA completely self-sufficient in the design, construction and application of expert systems. In May 1986 the Institute had built up a team of fully trained knowledge engineers, had its own tools for development and use of diagnostic expert systems that supported all its developments and gave a commercial return by being licensed to a software house that specialized in AI, and was in the process of bringing into service 25 systems for French agricultural producers. Licenses are now being negotiated for the use of these systems throughout the world.

INRA's policy for expert systems provides a good example of what we have called industrial mastery. It comprises an awareness, at the highest levels, of their strategic importance, the acceptance of this importance by the entire institute – management, administration, professionals and supporting staff – and the determination to turn the available resources to good account as quickly as possible.

4.1.2 The European Space Agency (ESA)

In 1984 ESA initiated a group of activities, some internal and some contracted out, aimed at giving it some command of AI techniques, in particular of knowledge base systems; some of their systems are described in Section 1.3.3.3.

ESA's objectives in this were threefold:

(1) To acquire a familiarity with AI tools and techniques and to establish an adequate level of knowledge and expertise at the center of the Agency.
(2) To assess the potential importance of these techniques in certain specified fields of the Agency's activities.
(3) To be able to judge proposals made by contractors concerning expert systems.

Its activities in this context therefore progressed along two parallel tracks:

(1) Fundamental work, based on a study of the literature, attendance at conferences and study contracts with industry.
(2) Building a model of an expert system, using its own staff.

Two AI studies were commissioned by one of ESA'S establishments, ESTEC, one in the Mathematical Support Division and the other in the Information and Signal Processing Division; both were started at the beginning of 1985 and were to run for about a year.They were as follows:

(1) 'Expert systems in space projects'. This was conducted by two consortia in parallel, each comprising one member experienced in space technology and the other in AI: British Aerospace and SDL, Electronique Serge Dassault and Cognitech [ESA, 1986]. The aims of the study were:
   (a) to inform the potential users in ESA – by writing an introductory text and giving lectures and seminars;
   (b) to review current applications of expert systems;
   (c) to identify the possible fields of application in ESA;
   (d) to suggest a particular application concerning one of ESA's terrestrial activities and draw up a specification for the software.

This study was to be followed by the development of prototype systems.

(2) 'Expert systems for satellite management'. The consortium here was of European companies (Laben, CRI and MBB/ERNO) and the aims were:

(a) to study the feasibility of using expert systems in this field, bearing in mind the technology available;
(b) to specify what would be needed for the design, development and validation of a system for this use and to detail the consequential complications on board the satellite;
(c) to produce a first model of the system;
(d) to give the lines for future research.

Various activities were embarked on within ESTEC at the same time. The first thing that had to be done was to install Lisp and Prolog in the computers; there was then the problem, as with all new techniques, of knowing where to start, and ESTEC decided to learn on the job, so to speak, by developing a model for an expert system to help the orbit and attitude control subsystem (AOCMS) for the Giotto space probe. This was a natural choice, because several members of the team had worked in the Giotto project.

Using the Operations Manual for Giotto the engineers developed an expert system that, working with the satellite simulator, could do the following:

(1) analyze a problem arising in AOCMS, given information telemetered from the satellite;
(2) suggest to the operator a solution, in the form of commands to be telemetered to the satellite:
(3) on demand, explain its reasoning, at various levels: answering 'how?' and 'why?' questions and displaying the facts and rules used in reaching the conclusion.

ESA's intention is to continue its AI activities along the following complementary lines.

Software. Testing tools for developing expert systems and possibly acquiring one that is particularly well-suited to ESA needs, offering, especially, efficient representation of knowledge, flexibility, speed and facilities for linking to an external environment; a software development environment for AI applications, into which several languages – Lisp, Prolog, Pascal, Fortran, C and others – are integrated.

Hardware. Evaluation of AI machines and assessing their advantages in developing complex applications.

Training. Educating many more of its staff in the use of AI languages and other tools; organizing seminars for those running other services and projects.

Technical studies. Completing the specification of one of the expert systems sketched in one of the contracts mentioned above, building a prototype and then an operational system.

The Giotto system. Extending the model to other functions, connecting it to the real-time simulator so as to test it in approximately real-life conditions.

Other AI studies. Natural language processing, for possible improvements in the man–machine dialogue; state of the art in other AI fields.

ESA's strategy for AI is typical of the big purchasing agencies: to equip itself with the competence to identify potential applications, specify its needs, evaluate proposals put forward by its contractors and check the quality of the products they deliver. It implements this strategy by conducting experiments, either internally in its own establishments or externally with contractors, on real problems, and wherever possible takes these as far as true operational use, as well as using as a training program.

4.1.3 The Atomic Energy Commission (CEA)

The CEA found it necessary to equip itself with the most advanced skills in IT, and in particular in AI systems, for two inescapable reasons that, it is now agreed, will become only stronger with time:

(1) developments in communications, for example by satellite telemetry and optical fiber transmission, that require vast masses of information to be made comprehensible and usable;
(2) the development of civil and military programs that require scientific computation of ever-increasing complexity – a particular example being the simulation of fluid flow in heat exchangers; and the ability to design and build physical systems of increasing complexity but also of increasing reliability.

There is also something of a competitive element. The CEA and its associates have a unique mastery of skills in the nuclear sector and look to using AI techniques wherever these will help to maintain its leading position; they are also anxious to maintain this sector's status of excellence with respect to the other high technology sectors.

The process by which the CEA arrived at its present choice of strategies and tactics started almost ten years ago, conducted for some time with rather a low profile until it acquired official recognition. The initial impetus came from the need to manage complex nuclear plants, of which the Super-Phenix power station is an example. In 1973–75 the idea arose of a system for detecting and diagnosing faults in the reactor core, but adequate AI tools for building such a system were not available at the time. It was therefore decided both to route all the signals provided by the measuring equipment to one place for storage and later processing, and to put effort into studying and developing algorithms for signal processing and pattern recognition. It was through the influence of these last two techniques that AI became established in the CEA.

The first operational AI tools in the CEA were demonstrated in 1982–83. In mid-83 the management of the Commission's Institut de Recherche Technologique et de Développement Industriel (IRDI), recognizing the strategic importance of AI, decided that its technical possibilities should be developed and gave responsibility for this to a member of the management. Top-level meetings were held in May 1984 and May 1985, informed as a result of coordinated meetings of experts and working groups; a structure for AI development and exploitation was laid down and a training program launched.

In parallel with this, the management of the Institut de Protection et de Sûreté Nucléaire, (the body that oversees the safety of nuclear installations in France) alive to the possibilities of incidents and accidents at nuclear installations, set up a Centre Technique de Crise and decided to build a diagnostic expert system to help in taking decisions in crisis situations.

The CEA's AI undertakings relate to both the civil and the military sectors and are predominantly directed to two applications, robotics and production engineering. The following have been put into action:

(1) an ambitious program of staff training, involving several hundred people in all categories and all grades from top management downwards;
(2) development of basic software tools, specially suited to CEA needs;
(3) investment in hardware;
(4) launching of a major research and development program CRISTAL;
(5) a policy of active technical and industrial cooperation with other organizations;
(6) involvement of industrial subsidiaries of the CEA: CISI-Télématique, Informatique Internationale, GIXI, Graphael.

The funds allocated are planned to grow at a high rate, of the order of 30–50% annually until 1990, by which time the CEA should have acquired complete industrial mastery of AI.

4.1.4 Compagnie des Machines Bull

Bull takes the view that AI can no longer be separated from classical IT and that it must be thoroughly integrated into the company's products and made available to all its customers. With this in mind the company began to invest in AI at the end of the 1970s; the first formal declaration of its interest was the creation of a research team so designated in 1982, and this was followed in 1983 by the establishment of the European Center for Computer Research (ECRC) in Munich, dedicated to AI methods, by Bull (France), ICL (Britain) and Siemens (Germany) in collaboration. There are now some 80 people at ECRC.

Recently Bull has decided to set up machinery to ensure that commercial value is gained from the results of ECRC research in the form of products that exploit AI methods. It set up a committee to study and report on this, which has just finished its work. Some actions have already been started, including the setting up of an organization for producing basic tools for use throughout the whole of the Bull group; this center is also participating in internal AI applications being developed in various parts of the group.

A training program has been started, with the ambitious aims not only of training designers and users of AI products but also of endowing Bull's entire body of engineers with the AI culture considered indispensible in future information scientists. Further, the commercial arrangements are beginning to be decided.

Bull's product strategy is clearly to offer as complete as possible a set of AI tools on all its machine ranges. As well as its own products, here it will evaluate and recommend those of other bodies with whom it has entered into agreements, in France and other countries. It has also a policy of collaborating with companies that specialize in AI work, for example in cooperative projects and in particular projects in the ESPRIT framework.

4.2 ROUTES TO ACQUIRING SKILLS

The four cases we have just sketched briefly serve to highlight some constant features of the process of mastering the use of AI in industry.

(1) The main route is through training, and it is noticeable that most enterprises faced with the need to acquire these skills will prefer to train, perhaps, retrain, their existing staff rather than recruit specialists from outside: undoubtedly this will often be due to budget restrictions but there may be other explanations.

(a) Employers are not always convinced of the value of recruiting an AI specialist on whom considerable effort will have to be expended in familiarizing him in the activities of the enterprise before he can become useful. The cost of training a staff member seems much less in comparison, and the return greater.

(b) The qualification of the few knowledge engineers on the market seldom seem high enough to overcome this doubt.

(c) AI is often seen as a means for remotivating talented staff who are running out of drive in their present field: thus operational research teams are often the breeding grounds for the future knowledge engineers. We discuss later the features of an effective AI training program aimed at producing this industrial skill.

(2) The second method is through acquiring specialized hardware equipment and software tools. We shall explain why we feel that the tools now available are inadequate for the task and that effort should be directed to methods rather than tools.

(3) The third method is that of technology transfer, as occurs in cooperative scientific and industrial projects such as those of the ESPRIT program or, more rarely in France, in collaboration with a software house that specializes in AI.

4.2.1 Training the staff

4.2.1.1 The trainers' qualifications

The speed with which acceptance of expert systems spreads through the enterprise depends crucially on the availability of qualified people at every stage of the development cycle; and there must be enough to form a critical mass, for otherwise the technique will remain an elitist and peripheral activity. Several different skills must be represented, and must cooperate.

AI experts These guarantee the up-to-dateness of the special knowledge and its relevance to the enterprise's needs. They advise on the main lines that should be followed and on the resources that should be committed; they carry out research concerning future activities and help the production teams with the more difficult problems; and finally they form the interface between the enterprise and the scientific community. They themselves will be scientists of repute with at least ten years' research experience in their field, often in the USA. There are perhaps a few dozen such people in France, and the number is scarcely growing. The main problem for this population is its own training, as we shall see later.

Project leaders These, as we have seen, are responsible for identifying the needs, choosing the methods of solution, managing the resources, ensuring the quality of the products and preparing for the incorporation of the expert systems into their intended working environment. They have an important influence on the spread of AI in the enterprise. They will be recruited from among the laboratory staff and given a training that is essentially methodological – methods for impact study, for specification, construction, validation and documentation of expert systems and for project management. This training will take on average a year and will be completed with the construction of the first expert system.

Knowledge engineers These can be recruited from outside the enterprise, say young graduates who have had some basic AI training; alternatively, from those of the professional staff of the enterprise who have taken an interest in the subject, provided they can be given the necessary training. In both cases the training given should cover the complementary aspects of the psychological demands of the profession and the techniques of knowledge acquisition. These fundamental aspects are almost completely neglected in present university courses. The complete training of a graduate engineer takes a full year whilst six months, also full time, is needed for the additional training of a young graduate with some AI qualification.

Collaborators These (see Sections 2.3.1 and 2.4.2) are key people in the identification of potential applications; they are also the actual users of whatever system is produced and the final arbiters of its fate. They will form the audience for induction courses and seminars organized by the above three groups, the aim of which is to create an environment in which the new techniques can flourish; and this is achieved more effectively by converting the multitude than by relying on the presence of a small and remote elite.

Technical marketing staff These have the rather indefinite task of finding a commercial outlet for the new technology when it has been incorporated into the enterprise's products. They are clearly of key importance for the future of expert systems and the penetration of these into the market will depend on their perceptiveness, the strength of their conviction and their ability to convince others. It must be said that nothing is being done to educate the most talented marketing staff to this responsibility, expect by a few computer manufacturers who are beginning to make their sales forces aware of the position.

4.2.1.2 Existing provisions for training

We have seen that AI research has made it possible to carry the formalism of information science into new fields of human activity, such as perception and reasoning; and this applies to the whole of AI, not just to expert systems which constitute only one part among many. Further, new methods and concepts have been developed within AI that should be incorporated into other disciplines, and therefore the teaching of AI is of great importance not only from the scientific point of view but also from that of economics, when one considers the future needs for knowledge engineers and specialized research workers in this field.

In spite of this, AI teaching in France – and in the whole of Europe, essentially – for a long time amounted to no more than a few short introductory courses, often optional, given in the final year of a first degree course or a diploma in information science. In these very unfavorable conditions there was a great danger of failing to reach the large critical mass of specialists needed to ensure the ability to undertake leading-edge research, and also to disseminate the new ideas in industry and to create powerful AI products.

Fortunately, however, the situation is now changing rapidly. Special courses for AI tranining are being established in many universities and in the engineering schools where they can be taken as options. The training involves lectures and projects and occupies at least 500 hours; at present there are about 70 students per year, to which must be added about 200 who have taken an introductory course at university level.

There is an important research element in this training. In an advanced subject like AI it is essential to combine practical work with study of fundamental principles; the research element is important not only for academic activities but also for advanced applications in industry.

Three different levels of AI training can be distinguished, corresponding to three very different objectives.

General culture for information scientists

AI relies strongly on the hardware and software provided by IT, and conversely its methods are having a growing influence on software development. It seems essential that all training in IT should include some familiarization with AI, at two levels:

(1) Elementary – introduction to AI and its applications; elements of formal logic; problem solving; Lisp and Prolog.
(2) Advanced – further methods for problem solving; generation of action plans; knowledge representation; reasoning; applications: expert systems, computer vision, language understanding; machine learning.

Specialization in AI

The objective here is to produce the top level specialists in industry and research; a firm foundation in basic information science and technology must be assumed, covering information theory, formal logic, formal algebra, theory of algorithms and of formal languages, programming, systems analysis, communications and networks, databases and system architecture.

There is a particularly strong demand for such specialists in industry, to fill positions such as project leaders and knowledge engineers. The training must cover both basic and applied aspects of AI; it will be given over a relatively long period and must fit smoothly into the practical activities of the enterprise.

So far the universities have become only partially aware of the need for such training; the few courses available are offered by commercial companies that specialize in AI.

Multidisciplinary training

AI is essentially a multidisciplinary subject and can have influences in a great variety of fields. It is therefore valuable to stress this aspect in academic teaching of AI by including courses in linguistics, formal logic, cognitive sciences and neurosciences among others, and reciprocally to teach the rudiments of AI to linguists, psychologists, biologists and others, as is already done in some American universities where a more flexible attitude to the curriculum is taken.

4.2.2 Tools and equipment

4.2.2.1 Shortcomings in intellectual equipment

It is legitimate to put effort into finding the best possible hardware and software tools for the knowledge engineers but too much concentration on this risks relegating to a lower level the investment in intellectual equipment – that is, in basic methods. Our review in Chapter 3 of the hardware and software commercially available shows very clearly that the market is overflowing with excellent tools for building and using knowledge bases, among which can be found tools to meet almost any need that arises. In comparison with these lush pastures the methodology landscape looks dry and barren.

AI is in the curious situation of an industry that wishes to employ the most sophisticated production methods but is able neither to build the necessary production plants nor to manage the production process or to control the quality of its products. In such a situation the most able knowledge engineer, equipped with the most powerful tools, is no more than a manual worker and it is easy to imagine the polite skepticism with which his proposals are received by trained production engineers: how could one ever consider putting on the market a pseudo-product made in conditions so far removed from proper industrial practice? Or trust the safety of an aircraft full of passengers to an expert system for navigation that had not had the same rigorous validation as the rest of the onboard software? At present we do not know how to define and control expert system quality and this acts as a brake on AI's progress towards inclusion in the industrial skills. If the situation is to be improved then priority must first be given to establishing proper standards for each stage in the production of an expert system – design, construction, bringing into use and maintenance.

4.2.2.2 The Knowledge Engineering Workshop (KEW)

The tools should be the physical embodiment of the methods and standards that guarantee the quality of the final product. Their role is to ease the tasks of those who have to put these methods and standards into practice – project leaders, knowledge engineers, experts, users of the working system. But it has to be admitted that the tools available on the market today give only limited help to only one of these groups – the knowledge engineers – and at only one stage of the production process, that of coding the knowledge (cf. Figure 4.1).

This shows the importance and urgency of a project that we have called the Knowledge Engineering Workshop (KEW), an integrated set of tools for supporting industrial production of an expert system. It would have the following features:

(1) All stages in the development, construction and use of an expert system would be catered for, not merely the knowledge coding.
(2) Productivity of the development process and quality and reliability of the product would be taken into account in the agreed methods by applying the standards of design, development, documentation, etc. Existing tools are oriented only towards performance criteria such as response time or knowledge base capacity.
(3) Attention would be given to management problems concerning the production and use of a large number of expert systems by a single enterprise, in contrast to the usual assumption of only a single system.
(4) Problems of communication between expert systems and other, existing, information systems would be considered, in contrast to the usual assumption of isolated systems written in distinct languages and running on dedicated machines.
(5) The useful lifetime of an expert system would be considered; this (almost) by definition is much longer than that of the team that

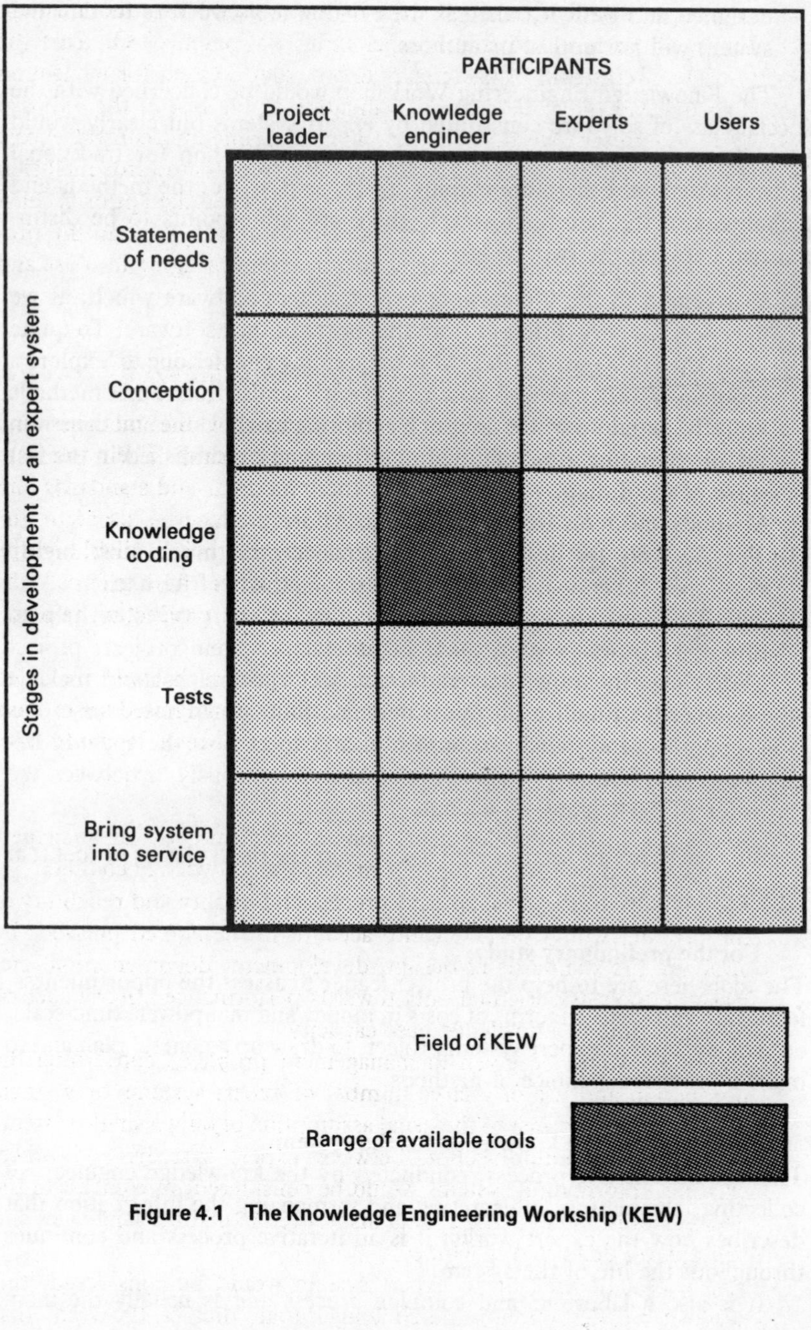

Figure 4.1   The Knowledge Engineering Workship (KEW)

designed and built it, whereas the existing tools work as though the system will not outlast its authors.

The Knowledge Engineering Workshop would be concerned with the special class of software constituted by expert systems but clearly would have the same objectives as a corresponding Workshop for traditional software; it should therefore employ, so far as possible, the methods and techniques of the latter. However, there are some points to be distinguished between the two:

(1) It is geared to the life cycle of expert system software which, as we have seen, is very different from that of traditional software. To quote Beau Sheil of Xerox PARC, AI programming enables one to 'explore a problem in order to find how to solve it', whilst traditional methods limit the extent to which any such exploring can be done and constrain the programmer to remain within a framework established in the last stage of the design.
(2) Methods and tools that are special to AI are used.
(3) The AI tools for design and maintenance need much more highly developed functions, possibly using the methods of AI itself.
(4) The KEW is concerned with providing different types of help to different classes of participant in an expert system project: project leader, expert, knowledge engineer, user. This help should make it possible to capitalize on the experience built up in the course of a succession of system developments, and to exploit the synergy between a number of systems developed simultaneously or between the different participants in a single development.

We conclude this section with a review of the main classes of tool that should be incorporated into the KEW.

For the preliminary study
The tools here are to help the project leader to assess the opportuneness, feasibility and scale (in terms of costs in money and manpower, time-scale, etc.) of a proposed expert system project, to draw up a general plan and to make a provisional choice of methods.

For acquiring the knowledge for the system
This acquisition is a process, conducted by the knowledge engineer, of collecting, elucidating, interpreting and formalizing the information that describes how the expert works; it is an iterative process and continues throughout the life of the system.

It is also a laborious and complex process and is usually the main bottleneck in the construction of the system; there is therefore a strong reason to have effective tools and methods, as follows, to structure and help the process:

(1) Help in defining, structuring and processing the vocabulary. The expert will use a special vocabulary for describing his field, which the knowledge engineer must learn, and whose semantics must be fixed and defined – otherwise maintenance of the system may become impossible, especially after several years when the original development team has been dispersed. Lack of a standard nomenclature may make constructing a glossary of special terms difficult; a tool is needed for generating the vocabulary, giving synonyms, abbreviations, plurals, word classification, generalizations of terms and so on, and checking for consistency.

(2) Help in documenting cases. Published papers in any field of expertise seldom give much information on how the expert used his knowledge. The knowledge engineer must investigate this 'expertise in action' in the course of interviews with the expert, in which he will usually start by asking the expert to explain how he dealt with some actual cases, choosing ones that are simple and yet typical of the reasoning used. This is an essential activity, for a human expert often forgets to mention quantities he has taken into account, and steps he has used, in his reasoning, because they are so obvious to him. These case studies must be documented and made accessible to the system with the help of editing and documentation software.

(3) Help in conducting interviews. There are many different methods of conducting interviews, aimed at extracting different kinds of information; there could be different tools for the different methods.

(4) A tool for defining, structuring, editing and processing parameters. As the study progresses the knowledge engineer will have to define sets of objects or parameters and give them a structure, such as a hierarchy and inheritance properties. Means for giving easy access to these parameters and structures, and allowing rapid changes to be made, would be of help here.

For representing knowledge and checking inferences
The knowledge engineer could be helped to choose from among the methods for knowledge representation and the inference engines available in the KEW, or to specify possible modifications to these.

For building and managing the knowledge base
(1) Modeling. As we have seen, the tasks of acquiring the knowledge and

putting it to use are not really separate; it is often necessary to implement a subset of the rules before even the general structure of the complete task has been defined. If a preliminary set of rules is obtained, these should be implemented quickly with the help of a modeling tool that will both ease this process and show up the major errors in the rules and any lack of realism in the program's requests for information.

(2) Capture and documentation of rules, for use by the expert. Once the first approach has been corrected and the first rules rewritten, the expert will have a better idea of what is expected of him and will usually be happy to enter rules himself provided he is given suitable means. The tool provided should check for consistency in use of terms, in particular.

(3) Editing, for use by the knowledge engineer. The knowledge engineer has to construct both the form and the logic of the rules at the same time. He would be helped in this by editors, including graphical, specially adapted to this work and enabling him to visualize the rules, renumber them, access their content in various ways, etc.

(4) Analysis and correction of the knowledge base, to ensure completeness and consistency. This comprises:
   (a) analysis and correction of the syntax of the rules;
   (b) analysis and correction of the semantics of the rules – use of this tool with a given set of rules and/or rules that can be inferred from these would enable any inconsistencies to be detected and would suggest any consequential changes;
   (c) checking for completeness – if the set contained the rule $a \Rightarrow b$ the system would ask the expert if there was also a rule for the case when a was found to be false.

(5) Analysis of the knowledge base.
   (a) detection of redundancies – the knowledge engineer would be alerted with a message of the kind: 'Rule 172, $a \& b \& c \Rightarrow d$ is triggered whenever Rule 58, $a \& b \Rightarrow c$ is triggered';
   (b) discrimination between parameters – it should be possible to identify rules that make it possible to discriminate between two parameters, and conversely to display any pair of parameters that cannot be distinguished by any rule.

(6) Tuning the knowledge base.
   (a) Tuning likelihood coefficients. Uncertain reasoning dominates in many fields. We have seen that the method now most used for handling this is based on likelihood coefficients, which are combined by means of formulas that strengthen or weaken a likelihood accordingly as it follows from a logical conjunction or disjunction respectively. Assigning these coefficients requires

much work of iterative testing and refinement by the expert and can reduce his productivity seriously. A tool specially designed to help with this work would be very valuable.

(b) Checking for robustness. Testing for robustness of the system's conclusions against small variations in the likelihood coefficients should be automated.

(7) Translation of the knowledge base. A special tool for this would help when the formalism for knowledge representation has to be changed.

For testing and validation

(1) Automatic assembly of a set of test cases. As soon as this becomes possible, the project leader should join with the expert and the knowledge engineer in assembling a set of cases with which to validate the model, the prototype and the final product. We have seen that this task often lies on the critical path and is one of the commonest causes of slippage in the timetable.

(2) Similarly, specially designed tools should be developed for analyzing and applying the results of the tests, in particular for assessing the agreement between the system and the human experts.

For bringing the system into service

Various standard IT tools and techniques are used in going from the prototype to the final operational system. These can be usefully complemented by special tools as follows:

(1) Compilers for the rule premises. Logical variables in the rules of a system based on predicate logic necessitate the use of some method of pattern matching, a computationally very costly process on which the inference engine can spend 90% of its time and therefore one to be optimized before the system is put into service. Advantage can be taken of any redundancies in the premises in this optimization. Specialized cross-compilers for improving performance by compiling the knowledge base and inference engine into a procedural system.

For measurements on the system

Measurements include the speed of the program in logical inferences per second (LIPS), memory occupied by the program and the working space needed when running, response times for the test cases and comparisons with human experts.

For communication within and between projects

Exploitation of synergies can be helped by the availability of adequate tools for communication. There are many aspects of this, among which the following may be mentioned:

(1) Communication between different bodies of expertise with the aim of:
    (a) combining the skills of several experts working in the same field;
    (b) combining skills from different fields;
    (c) combining the knowledge contents of several systems and of several different knowledge representations.
(2) Communication between the various people working on a single project. A comprehensive message system should be implemented, to generate and dispatch messages either as required by the participants or automatically when some specified situation is detected by the system.
(3) Communication between different projects. It is useful to be able to detect similarities, as for example in formal specifications, between different projects under development at the same time.

For project management
Throughout the project the leader needs to have available tools for planning and sizing. Such tools have a basis of classical software but for expert system projects there should be additions that allow the subject's special expertise and experience to be incorporated.

This concludes what we wish to say about the tools provided by the Workshop; we do not aim to give an exhaustive catalog but rather to indicate how much there is to be done before the right conditions for industrial production of expert systems can be established. The present state of the techniques is such that developing these systems consumes large amounts of scarce, highly qualified human resources; and that for various reasons, including initial choices of unsuitable applications, low productivity of the work and uncertain quality of the product, there is not an adequate return on the investment. All these restrain the penetration of expert systems into industry, even though a growing number of people in authority are convinced of their value. Only a determined effort in design and development methods and tool production will overcome these barriers.

4.2.3 Technology transfer

Industrial cooperation is not practiced to any great extent but can provide a route to building industrial skills in AI by bringing about fruitful associations between small organizations and companies that specialize in the field with the big industrial groups. Such associations are often welcomed by the big purchasing organizations such as defense departments and international agencies, and by international research and development projects such as ESPRIT; as well as increasing the large companies' skills in AI, they encourage the development of industrial attitudes in these small specialized companies, many of which, as we have seen, have been born in universities.

The big companies, and especially the Americans, have understood very well the strategic importance of such collaborations and the most advanced among them have taken this to its logical conclusion by participating on a large scale in the best of such companies. Thus General Motors and Elf Aquitaine have invested capital in Teknowledge; Boeing, Ford, Digital Equipment and Texas Instruments in the Carnegie Group; Wang and Xerox in Kurzweil; and others. It is estimated that a total of 60–80 million dollars has been invested in this way by the big American companies, the average investment being 3 million. When to this are added the investments of risk capital, about 120 M$ for 1985 and of public funds, 1000 M$ for AI alone from the SDI program, it becomes clear that industrial activity in AI is well under way in the USA.

CONCLUSION

Year 1 of AI

At the end of this short survey of AI's first expeditions into that *terra incognita* that is still for it the industrial world, it is pertinent to consider what chance it has of establishing itself there and founding colonies . . . .

Adapting an elegant image from Emmanuel Levinas, I can say that Artificial Intelligence will have one or other of two contradictory futures:

– either that of Ulysses, who after his wanderings beset with perils and mirages returned, penitent, to his home and the lovely Penelope whom he had left several thousand lines earlier.
– or of the tribe of Abraham, who, leaving with his followers his native land, had forbidden that his descendents should ever be shown the road back; the road ahead was to lead them to the Promised Land.

Thank you for your attention.

These poetic words concluded an address entitled 'How artificial intelligence is to come to industry', given by one of the authors of this book in June 1984 to a meeting of the Amicale des Élèves de l'École des Mines de Paris. They were the expression (discreetly veiled in metaphor) of the great uncertainty that was felt at the time about the future of AI as an economic activity. Then, the return of Ulysses to his home was felt to be the most likely fate and the idea of the Promised Land was raised only to be dismissed.

Two years, later, when we end this book, all doubts are dispelled: the most optimistic forecasts have had to be revised – upwards. In France, capital has been found for establishing ten specialist companies, and work to keep them in existence. In America, commercial companies have been founded and General Motors has just put into service an expert system for diagnosing ignition faults, to be used by its 10 000 dealers. And there is no longer any need to appeal to mythology to help us foretell the future: Ulysses and Abraham no longer speak to us: the Promised Land is here, under our feet, and strangely earthy. The fruits are no more luscious than before, nor does milk flow in rivers. To reap we must first sow.

If there is one way in which AI has made decisive progress in the last two years it is this: it has moved, without any trauma, from the mythical world to the world of realities. Freed from the ideological straitjacket in which it had been confined since the start, it can now behave as any other economic activity.

The first manifestation of this is the need for *hard work*. The fruits of AI are not wild berries, to be found by good luck and picked from the trees without effort. As in every other industry, success depends on a number of fixed factors: sensible choice, quantity and quality of resources committed, excellence of the technology employed, rigor of the methods. This is the source of the ideas that underlie our discussion throughout the book:

(1) An expert system project should be assessed as any other investment, systematically and in competition with other proposed projects, for its strategic and economic opportuneness, for its usefulness either as a product or as an aid to production, for its technical and human feasibility and for its chances of gaining acceptance by its users or in the marketplace.

(2) An expert system is something that is easy to understand but difficult to produce. The sophisticated techniques needed in the creation of an operational system can only be deployed by highly qualified people, not easily recruited or trained.

(3) For a given technology it is the methods used that make the difference between a laboratory prototype and an industrial product. Technology now having reached the level that industry needs, efforts and investments should be concentrated on methodology.

(4) It is inevitable that very many large enterprises will be forced, sooner or later, to integrate expert systems into their technological stock-in-trade. The acquisition of the necessary mastery of AI by our major economic undertakings is one of the main challenges of the next few years.

Abbreviations, references and further reading

ABBREVIATIONS USED

AAAI-82	*Proc. of the 2nd National (American) Conference on Artificial Intelligence*, Pittsburgh, Pennsylvania, 1982
AAAI-80	*1st*, Stanford, California
ADI	Agence de l'Informatique
AFCET	Association Française de Cybernétique et d'Etudes Techniques
AIR	*Artificial Intelligence Report*
ARC	Association pour la Recherche Cognitive
CAO	Conception Assisteé par Ordinateur
ECAI	European Conference on Artificial Intelligence
IEEE	Institute for Electrical and Electronical Engineers
Trans PAMI	*IEEE Transactions on Pattern Analysis and Machine Intelligence*
IJCAI-85	*Proc. 9th International Joint Conference on Artificial Intelligence*, Los Angeles, USA, 1985
IJCAI-83	*8th*, Karlsruhe, Germany, 1983
IJCAI-81	*7th*, Vancouver, Canada, 1981
IJCAI-79	*6th*, Tokyo, Japan, 1979
IJCAI-77	*5th*, MIT, Cambridge, Mass, USA, 1977
IJCAI-75	*4th*, Tbilissi, USSR, 1975
INRIA	Institut National de Recherche en Informatique et en Automatique
TSI	*Technique et Science Informatiques*

REFERENCES

AIR (1984). *The Artificial Intelligence Report*, vol. 1, no. 3.
AIR (1985). *The Artificial Intelligence Report*, vol. 2, no. 8.

Albert, P. and Billon, J.P. (1984). Report on the SPEC project, *Journées d'études sur les systèmes-experts*, Avignon.

Aldridge (1984). AIRID: an application of the KAS/Prospector expert system builder to airplane identification, SPIE, *Applications of Artificial Intelligence* **485**.

Allen, E.M. (1982). *YAPS: Yet Another Production System*, University of Maryland, CS TR-1146.

Ancelin, J. et al. (1985). *Couplage d'un système-expert et d'une simulation pour l'étude du pilotage d'un processus*, Actes du Congrès Cognitiva, Paris.

Ayel, M., Laurent, J.P. and Soutif, M. (1984). CESSOL, un système-expert pour définir des campagnes de reconnaissance géotechnique du sol, *4ème congrès AFCET de reconnaissance des formes et Intelligence Artificielle*, Paris.

Barrielle, E. (1985). *Applications des techniques de l'Intelligence Artificielle au diagnostic des défauts des circuits imprimés*, PhD thesis, Ecole Nationale Supérieure des Télécommunications, Paris.

Barstow, D. (1979). *Knowledge-based program construction*, New York, Elsevier.

Bennett, J.S. and Engelmore, R. (1979). SACON: a knowledge-based consultant for structural analysis, *IJCAI-79*, 47–49.

Bennett, J.S. and Hollander, C.R. (1981). DART, an expert system for computer fault diagnosis, *IJCAI-81*.

Bétaille, H., Massotte, A.M. and Maury, M. (1984). REINART, système-expert appliqué au rein artificiel, *Journées d'études sur les systèmes-experts*, Avignon.

Blancard, D., Bonnet, A. and Coleno, A. (1985). Tom, un système-expert en maladies des tomates, PHM, *Revue Horticole* **261**.

Bobrow, D. and Winograd, T. (1977). KRL, another perspective, *Cognitive Science* **3**, 29–42.

Bobrow, D. and Stefik, M. (1983). *The LOOPS manual*, Xerox PARC, Palo Alto.

Bonissone P.P. and Johnson, H.E. (1983). *Expert system for diesel electric locomotive repair*, Knowledge-based systems report, General Electric Co.

Bonnet, A. (1985). *Artificial Intelligence – Promise and Performance*, London, Prentice Hall.

Bonnet, A., Harry, J. and Ganascia, J.G. (1982). LITHO, un système-expert inférant la géologie du sous-sol, *TSI* **1**, no. 5, 393–402.

Bourgault, S., Dincbas, M. and Feuerstein, D. (1982). LISLOG: programmation en logique en environment LISP. *Actes du séminaire sur la programmation en logique*, 32–48, Perros-Guirec.

Boy, G.A. (1983). Le système MESSAGE: un premier pas vers l'analyse assistée par ordinateur des interactions Homme/Machine, *Le travail humain* **46**, no. 2.

Boy, G.A. (1985). *HORSES (Human Orbital Refueling System Expert System). System Modeling and Design Report 2: HORSES Knowledge Acquisition*, NASA Ames Research Center, ONERA/CERT/DERA.

Brown, M. *et al.* (1983). *PALLADIO: an exploratory environment for circuit design computer*.

Buchanan, B. and Feigenbaum, E. (1978). Dendral and Meta-Dendral, their applications dimension, *Artificial Intelligence* **II**, 5–24.

Callero, M., Waterman, D.A. and Kipps, J.R. (1984). *TATR, a prototype expert system for tactical air targeting*, Report R-3096-ARPA, Rand Corp.

Carbonell, N. Fohr, D. and Haton, J.P. (1986). APHODEX, design and implementation of an acoustic-phonetic decoding expert system, *Proc. Int. Conf. Acoustics, Speech and Signal Processing*, Tokyo.

Carlson, M. and Kahn, K.M. (1983). *LM-Prolog user manual – UPMAIL*, Uppsala University, Sweden.

Chailloux, J. (1983). *Le-Lisp de l'INRIA, manuel de référence*.

Champigneux, G. (1984). *CECILIA, a computer environment for fault analysis and design assistance at Avions Marcel Dassault Breguet Aviation*, ECAI, Pise.

Champigneux, G. (1985). MARIA, manœuvres aériennes réalisées par l'intelligence artificielle, *Journées Science et Défense*, Toulouse.

Chassery, J.M. and Garbay, C. (1984). An iterative segmentation method based on a contextual color and shape criterion, *IEEE Trans. PAMI*, **6**, 794–800.

Clayton, B. (1985). *Inference art programming primer*, Inference Corporation, Los Angeles.

Clayton, J. *et al.* (1981). *SEQ–sequence analysis system*, Report HPP-81-3, Computer Science Dept, Stanford University.

Cognitech (1985*a*). *TG-1 Manuel de Référence*, Version 1.1.

Cognitech (1985*b*). *Rufus. Bilan de la réalisation d'un démonstrateur de système-expert d'aide à la maintenance des trains pour la RATP.*

Cognitech (1985*c*). *Pénélope. Bilan de la réalisation d'un démonstrateur de système-expert de planification de chantiers de bâtiments pour Dumez-Bâtiment.*

Cognitech and ESD (1985). *Application des systèmes-experts aux projets spatiaux*, Report ESTEC/6028/84/NL/JS.

Cohen, P. (1983). *A report on FOLIO, an expert assistant for portfolio Managers*, Stanford University, Heuristic Programming Project, Stanford.

Colmerauer, A., Kanoui, H. and Van Caneghem, M. (1983). Prolog, bases théoriques et développements actuels, *TSI*, **2** no. 4, 271–311.

Cordier, M.O. and Rousset, M.C. (1984). TANGO: moteur d'inférences pour un système-expert avec variables, *4ème Congrès AFCET de reconnaissance des formes et intelligence artificielle*, Paris.

Descotte, Y. and Latombe, J.C. (1981). GARI: a problem solver that plans how to machine mechanical parts. *IJCAI-81*, 766–72.

Dickey, F.J. and Toussaint, A.L. (1984). *ECESIS: an application of expert systems to manned space stations*, IEEE.

Dietrich, E.S. and Immamura M.S. (1983). An expert system concept for autonomous spacecraft energy management, in *18th IECEC, Intersociety Energy Convention*, 2288–93.

Dincbas, M. (1985). Les langages combinant LISP et PROLOG, *Génie Logiciel* **1.2**, 25–8.

Dubois, D. and Prade, H. (1982). A class of fuzzy measures based on triangular norms. A general framework for the combination of uncertain information, *Int. J. General Systems* **8**, no. 1, 43–61.

Dubois, D. and Prade, H. (1985). *Théorie des possibilités, application à la représentation des connaissances en informatique*, Paris, Masson.

Duda, R., Gaschnig, J. and Hart, P. (1979). Model design in the PROSPECTOR consultant system for mineral exploration, in *Expert system in the micro-electronic age*, D. Michie (ed.), Edinburgh, Edinburgh University Press.

Dufresne, P. (1984). *Contribution algorithmique à l'inférence par règles de production*. Doctoral thesis, Paul-Sabatier University, Toulouse.

Electronics (1985). AI tools automate software translation, in *Electronics*, 23 September.

Engelmore, R. (1979). Structure and function of the Crysalis system, *IJCAI-79*, 250–256.

Erman, L.D., London, P.E. and Fickas, S.F. (1981). The design and example use of HEARSAY III, *IJCAI-81*, 409–15.

ESA (1986). *Etude de l'application des systèmes-experts aux projects spatiaux*, final study report, ESD and Cognitech, contract ESTEC 6028/84/NL/JS, January 1986.

Fagan, L. M. (1980). *VM: representing time-dependent relations in a clinical setting*, Ph.D dissertation, Heuristic Programming Project, Stanford University.

Fain, J., Hayes-Roth, F., Sowizral, H. and Waterman D. (1981). *Programming examples in ROSIE*, Rand Corporation, Technical Report, N-1646-ARPA.

Feigenbaum, E.A., Buchanan, B.G. and Lederberg J. (1971). On generality and problem solving: a case study using the DENDRAL program. In *Machine intelligence*, Vol. 6, 165–90. Meltzer and Michie (eds.), New York, Wiley.

Fieschi, M. (1981). *Aide à la décision en médecine: le système SPHINX, application au diagnostic d'une douleur épigastrique*, PhD thesis, Marseilles.

Fieschi, M. and Joubert, M. (1984). *Some reflections on the evaluation of expert systems in medicine*, Working paper, MIT, Cambridge, Ma.

Forgy, C. (1981). *OPS 5 user's manual*. Carnegie-Mellon University Technical Report CMU-CS-81-135.

Forgy, C. and McDermott, J. (1977). OPS, a domain-independent production system language, *IJCAI-77*, 933–939.

Fox, M. (1981). *The intelligent management system, an overview*. Carnegie-Mellon University Report CMU-RI-TR-81-4.

Garrido, C., Mortensen, U.K. and Mondot, T. (1985). Artificial intelligence – a space tool of the future? *ESA Bulletin* no. 42.

Gaschnig, J., Klahr, P., Pople, H., Shortliffe, E. and Terry, A. (1983). Evaluation of expert systems: issues and case studies, in *Building expert systems*, F. Hayes-Roth, D. Waterman (eds), Reading, Ma, Addison-Wesley.

Gascuel, O. (1981), *Un système-expert dans le domaine médical*, doctoral thesis, University of Paris VI.

Gelernter, H. *et al.* (1984). Realization of a large expert problem-solving system. SYNCHEM 2, case study. *Proc. 1st conference on artificial intelligence applications*, Denver. December.

Genesereth, M.R. (1984). *An overview of M.R.S. for AI experts*, Report HPP 82-27, Stanford University.

Georgeff, M.P. and Firsheim, O. (1985). Expert system for space automation, *IEEE Control Systems Magazine*, November.

Ghallab, M. (1980). Near optimal decision trees for matching patterns in inference planning systems, *2nd Int. Meeting on AI*, Leningrad.

Giannesini, F., Kanoui, H., Pasero, R. and Van Caneghem, M. (1985). *PROLOG*, Paris, InterEditions.

Golden, M. and Siemens, R.W. (1985). An expert system for automated satellite anomaly resolution. *Computer in aerospace Vth conference* AIAA/NASA/IEEE, October.

Green, C. (1976). The design of the PSI program synthesis system. *Proc. of the Second International Conference on Software Engineering*, 4–18.

Greiner, R. and Lenat, D. (1980). A representation language, in *AAAI-80*, 165–9.

Greussay, P. (1983). LOVLISP: une extension de VLISP vers PROLOG *Actes du Séminaire Programmation en Logique*, 111–21, Perros-Guirec.

Haton, J.P. (1985). Intelligence artificielle en compréhension de la parole: état des recherches et comparaison avec la vision par ordinateur, *TSI* 4, no. 3.

Haton, J.P. and Haton, M.C. (1985). Application de l'intelligence artificielle dans l'enseignement des langues. *Colloque GREDIL sur l'enseignement des langues*, Québec, Canada.

Haton, J.P., Méhu, B. and Vesoul, P. (1986). Les systèmes-experts pour les applications spatiales: science fiction ou ouverture vers de nouveaux systèmes intelligents?, *Journées d'Avignon*, ADI, April.

Hickam, D., Shortliffe, E and Jacobs, C. (1983). A blinded evaluation of computer-based cancer chemotherapy treatment advice, *Clinical Research* 31, 2.

Hollander, C.R., Iwasaki, Y., Courteille, J.M. and Fabre, M. (1983). *Trends and Applications Conference*. Washington.

Imamura, M.S., Moser, R., Aichele, D. and Lanier R. (1983). Automation concepts for large space power systems, in *18th IECEC, Intersociety Energy Convention*, 2295–302.

IN.PRO.BAT (1986). *Le bâtiment et l'intelligence artificielle*, supplément au plan construction-actualité, no. 23.

Kahn, K. (1981). *UNIFORM: a language based upon unification which unifies (much of) Lisp, Prolog, and Act 1 – UPMAIL*. Uppsala University, Sweden.

Kay, A. and Goldberg, A. (1977). Personal dynamic media, *Computer* 10, 31–410.

Kehler, T.P. and Clemenson, C.D. (1984). An application system for expert systems, *Systems and Software*, 212–24.

Kent *et al.* (1983). The impact on quality of data management of a computer-based consultant program, *Medical Decision Making* 3, 362.

Kessaci, A. and Vesoul, P. 1984. *Etude et réalisation du système SEAGOS (système-expert d'Aide à la Gestion Opérationnelle des Satellites)*, Rapport de Stage de Spécialisation Automatique Avancée Robotique et Systèmes, ENSAE, July.

Kowalski, R. and Sergot, M. (1985). Computer representation of the law, *IJCAI-85*, 1269–70.

Kulikowski, C. and Weiss, S. (1982). Representation of expert knowledge for consultation: the CASNET and EXPERT projects in *Artificial Intelligence in Medicine*, P. Szolovits (ed.), Boulder, Westview Press.

Lakin, W.L. and Miles, J.A.H. (1984). IKBS in multi-sensor data fusion *First Conference on applications of artificial intelligence*, Denver.

Lamboulle, M., Haton, J.P. and Muller, J.F. (1985). EXSYLA: un système-expert pour l'interprétation de spectres de masse en spectroscopie laser, *Journées Internationales d'Avignon*.

Laurent, J.P. (1984). La structure de contrôle dans les systèmes-experts *TSI* 3 no. 3.

Laurière, J.L. (1982). Représentation et utilisation des connaissances, *TSI* 1, no. 1, 2.

Laurière, J.L. and Vialatte, M. (1985). *Manuel d'utilisation de SNARK*, University of Paris, 6.

Lehmann, M. *et al.* (1984). *SICONFEX, ein Expertensystem für die Konfigurierung von Betriebssystemen*, Document Siemens AG, Münich, FRG.

Le Pape, C. and Sauve, B. (1985). SOJA: un système d'ordonnancement journalier d'atelier, *5'emes Journées Internationales systèmes-experts et Applications*, Avignon.

Lesser, V.R. *et al.* (1975). Organization of the HEARSAY II speech understanding system. *IEEE Trans. ASSP* 23, No. 1, 11–23.

Levesque, H., (1983). Système-Expert en paye et gestion du personnel. University of Paris VI.

Levine, M.D. and Nazif, A. (1982). An experimental rule-based system for testing low level segmentation strategies in *Multicomputers and image processing*, New York, Academic Press.

McDermott, J. and Forgy, C. (1978). Production system conflict resolution strategies, in *Pattern-directed inference systems*, Waterman and Hayes-Roth (eds), New York, Academic Press.

McDermott, J. (1980). R1: an expert in the computer system domain, *AAAI-80* 269–71.

McDermott, J. (1984). R1 revisited; four years in the trenches, *AI Magazine* 5, no. 3, 21–32.

Manuel, C. (1985). *Validation du système-expert SPHINX dans son application à la thérapeutique du diabète*. PhD thesis, Marseilles.

Mariot, P., Haton, J.P. and Drouin, P. (1986). Un système-expert avec moteur cumulatif à variables: applications au calcul des doses d'insuline chez le diabétique. *6èmes Journées internationales systèmes-experts et applications*, Avignon.

Martin, N., Friedland, P., King, J. and Stefik, M. (1977). Knowledge-based management for experiment planning in molecular genetics, *IJCAI-77*, 882–7.

Martin Larsen, P. (1981). Industrial applications of fuzzy logic control, in *Fuzzy reasoning and its applications*, Mandani and Gaines (eds), New York, Academic Press.

Maruyama, F. *et al.* (1984). PROLOG-based expert system for logic design, *Proc. Inf. Corp. On Fifth Generation Computer Systems*, Tokyo.

Masui, S., McDermott, J. and Sobel A. (1983). Decision-making in time-critical situations, *IJCAI-83*, 233–5.

Matsuyama, T. and Hwang, V. (1985). Sigma: a framework for image understanding Integration of bottom-up and top-down analyses, *IJCAI-85*, 908–15.

Michalski, R.S. and Larson, J.B. (1978). *Selection of most representative training examples and incremental generation of VL1 hypotheses: the underlying methodology and the description of programs ESEL, and AQ11*, Report 867, Computer Science Dept., University of Illinois, Urbana.

Minsky, M. (1975). A framework for representing knowledge, in *The psychology of computer vision*, Winston (ed.), New York, McGraw-Hill.

Mitra, S.K. and Parker, J.M. (1984). An expert system for identifying defects, stones and cord in glass, *Proc. ECAI-84* Amsterdam, North-Holland.

Mittal, S. and Chandrasekaran, B. (1980). Conceptual representation of patient data bases, *Journal Medical Systems* **4**, no. 2.

Moore, R.L. *et al.* (1984). A real-time expert system for process control, *Journées Internationales sur les systèmes-experts*, Avignon.

Moses, J. (1967). *A Macsyma primer*, Mathlab Memo 2, MIT Computer Science Lab.

Nachtsheim, P. and Gevarter, W.B. (1985). *A knowledge-based system for scheduling of airborne astronomical observations*, NASA Ames Research Center, CA.

Nagao, M. (1984). *Strategies for human-like image understanding systems*, Actes du Congrès Cognitive, Paris.

Nagao, M. and Matsuyama, T. (1980). *A structural analysis of complex aerial photographs*, Plenum Press.

Nazif, A.M. and Levine, M.D. (1984). Low level image segmentation: an expert system, *IEEE Trans. PAMI* **6**, 555–77.

Nelson, W.R. (1982). REACTOR: an expert system for diagnosis and treatment of nuclear reactor accidents, *AAAI-82*.

Nii, H.P. and Aiello, N. (1979). AGE (Attempt to GEneralize): a knowledge-based program for building knowledge-based programs, *IJCAI-79*.

Nii, H.P., Feigenbaum, E.A., Anton, J.J. and Rockmore, A.J. (1982). Signal to symbol transformation: HASP/SIAP case study, *AI Magazine* **3**, no. 2, 23–35.

Nilsson, N. (1980). *Principles of artificial intelligence*, Palo Alto, Tioga.

Ogawa, Y. (1984). Knowledge representation and inference environment: KRINE, an approach to intergration of Frame, Prolog and Graphics, *Proc. Int. Conf. on Fifth Generation Computers*, Tokyo.

Papert, S. (1980). *Mindstorms, children, computers and powerful ideas*, New York, Basic Books.

Pauker, S., Gorry, A., Kassirer, J. and Schwartz, W. (1976). Towards the simulation of clinical cognition. Taking a present illness by computer, *Am. J. Medicine* **60**, 981–96.

Polit, S. (1985). R1 and beyond, AI technology transfer at DEC, *AI Magazine* **5.4**, 76–9.

Pople, H. (1982). Heuristic methods for imposing structure on ill structured problems; the structuring of medical diagnostics in *Artificial intelligence in medicine*, Szolovits (ed.), Boulder, Westview Press.

Prade, H. (1983). A synthetic view of approximate reasoning techniques, *IJCAI-83*, 130–6.

Queinnec, C. (1980). *Langage d'un autre type: LISP*, Paris, Eyrolles.

Queinnec, C. (1984). *LISP, mode d'emploi*, Paris, Eyrolles.

Rajagopalan, R. (1984). *Qualitative modeling in the turbojet engine domain*, Report T-139, Dept of Electrical Engineering, Univ. of Illinois.

Reboh, R. (1981). *Knowledge engineering techniques and tools in the prospector environment*, Tech. Note 243, Artificial Intelligence Center, SRI International, Menlo Park, CA. June.

Rice, J.P. (1984). MXA-A framework for the development of blackboard systems.

Proc. Third Seminar on Applications of MI to defense systems, RSRE, UK.

Robert, R.B. and Goldstein, I.P. (1977). *The FRL primer*, MIT AI Lab. Memo 408.

Robinson, J.A. and Sibert, E.E. (1982). LOGLISP: an alternative to Prolog, *Machine Intelligence* 10, 399–419.

Rogers, J.-L. and Barthelemy, J.-F. M. (1985). An expert system for choosing the best combination of options in a general-purpose program for automated design synthesis, *International Computers in Engineering Conference and Exhibition*, Boston, Ma.

Roussel, P. (1975). *Prolog, Manuel de référence et d'utilisation*, Groupe d'Intelligence Artificielle, UER de Luminy, Aix-Marseilles University.

Sauers, R. and Walsh R. (1983). On the requirements of future expert systems, *IJCAI-83*.

Saulais, J. (1986). Personal Communication.

Scarl, E.A., Jamielson, J.R. and Delaune, C.I. (1984). A fault detection and isolation method applied to liquid oxygen loading for space shuttle, *IJCAI-85*, 414–16.

Schank, R. and Abelson R. (1977). *Scripts, plans, goals and understanding. An inquiry into human knowledge structures.* Hillsdale, New Jersey, Lawrence Erlbaum Associates.

Selfridge, O. (1959). Pandemonium, a paradigm for learning. *Symposium on Mechanization of Thought Processes*, National Physical Laboratory, Teddington, UK.

Shafer, C. (1976). *A mathematical theory of evidence.* Princeton University Press.

Shortliffe, E.H. (1976). *Computer-based medical consultations: MYCIN*, New York, Elsevier.

Spang (1985). *The Spang Robinson report, vol. 1.1.* Palo Alto, California, Spang Robinson.

Stammers, R.A. (1983). *SUS language manual*, SPL International, Abingdon, UK.

Taillibert, P. (1985). MI3, outils de représentations et d'exploitation de la connaissance. Description et exemple d'utilisation. *5èmes Journées Internationales systèmes-experts et applications*, Avignon.

Thorndyke, P.W. (1981). AUTOPILOT, a distributed planner for air fleet control, *IJCAI-81*.

Van Melle, W. (1980). *A domain-independent system that aids in constructing knowledge-based consultation programs.* PhD Dissertation, Stanford Univ. Computer Science Department, STAN-CS-80-820.

Vere, S.A. (1983a). Planning in time. Windows and durations for activities and goals, *IEEE Trans. PAMI* 5, no. 3 246–67.

Vere, S.A. (1983b). Planning spacecraft activities with a domain independent planner, *AIAA Computers in Aerospace Conference*, Hartford, Connecticut, October.

Vesonder, G.T. *et al.* (1983). ACE: an expert system for telephone cable maintenance, *IJCA-83*.

Vialatte, M. (1985). Description et application du moteur d'inférences SNARK,

doctoral thesis, University of Paris, 6.
Vignard, P. (1985). *CRIQUET, un outil de base pour construire des systèmes-experts*, Research report INRIA 380.

Weiss, S. and Kulikowski, C. (1979). EXPERT: a system for developing consultation models. *IJCAI-79*, pp. 942–7.
Winston, P. and Horn, B. (1981). *LISP*, Reading, Ma., Addison Wesley.
Wipke, W.T. *et al.* (1978). Simulation and evaluation of chemical synthesis–SECS, *Artificial Intelligence* 11, 173–93.
Wright, J.M. and Fox, M.S. (1983). *SRL 1/5 user manual*, The Robotics Institute, Carnegie-Mellon University.

Yu, V. *et al.* (1979a). Evaluating the performance of a computer-based consultant, *Comput. Prog. Biomed.* 9, 95–102.
Yu, V.L., Fagan, L.M. *et al.* (1979b). Antimicrobial selection by a computer: a blinded evaluation by infectious disease experts, *J. Am. Med. Assoc.*, 241–12, 1279–82.

Zadeh, L. (1979). A theory of approximate reasoning. In *Machine intelligence* vol. 9, 149–94, Hayes, Michie and Mikuch (eds), New York, Wiley.

OTHER BOOKS ON AI

Addis, T.R., (1985). *Designing Knowledge-Based Systems*, London, Kogan Page.
Alty, J.L., and Coombs, M.J., (1985). *Expert Systems – Concepts and Examples*, Chichester, Wiley.
Aubert, J.P. (1985). *Pratiquez l'intelligence artificielle*, Paris, Eyrolles.
Benchimol, G., Levine, P. and Pompol, J.C. (1986), *Systèmes-experts dans l'entreprise*. Paris, Hermès.
Boden, Margaret (1977). *Artificial Intelligence and Natural Man*, Brighton, Harvester Press.
Bonnet, A. (1984). *L'intelligence artificielle – Promesses et réalités*, Paris, Inter-Editions.
Bonnet, A., (1985). *Artificial Intelligence – Promise and Performance*, London, Prentice Hall.
Bundy, A., (1983). *The Computer Modelling of Mathematical Reasoning*, London and New York, Academic Press.
Chouraqui, E. (1986). *Intelligence artificielle – Modélisation des connaissance et des raisonnements*, Paris, Hermès.
Ernst, C. (1985). *Introduction aux systèmes-experts de gestion*, Paris, Eyrolles.
Gondran, M. (1984). *Introduction aux systèmes-experts*, Paris, Eyrolles.
Griffiths, M. (1986). *Techniques algorithmiques pour l'intelligence artificielle*, Paris, Hermès.
James, M. (1986). *Introduction à l'intelligence artificielle sur micro-ordinateurs*, Paris, Eyrolles.
Krutch, J. (1984). *Expériences d'intelligence artificielle en Basic*, Paris, Eyrolles.

Latombe, J.C. and Lux, A. (1986). *Intelligence artificielle – Concepts et applications*, Paris, Hermès.
Laurière, J.L. (1986). *Intelligence artificielle: résolution de problèmes par l'homme et la machine*, Paris, Eyrolles.
Partridge, D. (1986). *Artificial Intelligence – applications in the future of software engineering*, Chichester, Ellis Horwood.
Pitrat, J. (1985). *Textes, ordinateur et compréhension*, Paris, Eyrolles.
Regg, V. (1986). *Eléments d'introduction des systèmes-experts en CAO*, Paris, Hermès.
Winston, P.H., (1984). *Artificial Intelligence*, Reading, Mass., Addison-Wesley.
Yoshiaki Shirai and Jun-Ichi Tsujii (1982). *Artificial Intelligence – Concepts, Techniques and Applications*, New York, Wiley.

BOOKS ON AI LANGUAGES

Chailloux, J. (1984). *Le—Lisp de l'INRIA, manuel de référence*.
Clocksin, W.F. and Mellish, C.S. (1985). *Programmer en Prolog*, Paris, Eyrolles.
Farreny, H. (1984). *Le langage LISP*, Paris, Masson.
Giannesini, F., Kanoui, H., Pasero, R. and Van Caneghem, M. (1985), *PROLOG*, Paris, InterEditions.
Queinnec, C. (1982). *Langage d'un autre type: LISP*, Paris, Eyrolles.
Queinnec, C. (1984). *LISP, Mode d'emploi*, Paris, Eyrolles.
Wertz, H. (1985). *Initiation à LISP*, Paris, Masson.
Winston, P. and Horn, W. (1984), *Lisp* (2nd ed.), Reading, Ma, Addison-Wesley.

JOURNALS

AI Magazine (quarterly), AAAI, 445 Burgess Drive, Menlo Park, California 94025-3496, USA.
Artificial Intelligence (9 issues a year), North-Holland, PO Box 211, 1000 AE Amsterdam, Netherlands.
Artificial Intelligence in Engineering (quarterly), Computational Mechanics Publication, Ashurst Lodge, Ashurst, Southampton SO4 2AA, UK.
Computational Intelligence, Distribution P-88, National Research Council of Canada, Ottawa, Canada K1A OR6.
Data and Knowledge Engineering, North-Holland, PO Box 211, 1000 AE Amsterdam, Netherlands.
Expert Systems (quarterly) KIRI, Computer Services Corp, Sumitomo Building, 2-6-1 Nishi Shinjuku, Tokyo 160-91, Japan.
Expert Systems (quarterly), Learned Information Ltd, Besselsleigh Road, Abingdon, Oxford, OX13 6LG, UK.
Expert Systems: Research & Applications, JAI Press Inc., 36 Sherwood Place, PO Box 1678, Greenwich, Connecticut 06836-1678, USA.

Expert Systems User (10 issues a year), Cromwell House, 20 Bride Lane, London EC4 3DX, UK.

IEEE Expert (quarterly) 10667 Los Vaguenos Circle, Los Alamitos, California 90720-2578, USA.

Journal of Automated Reasoning (quarterly), Kluwer Academic Publishers Group, PO Box 322,3300 AH, Dordrecht, Netherlands.

Machine Learning (quarterly), Kluwer Academic Publishers Group, PO Box 322, 3300 AH Dordrecht, Netherlands.

NEWSLETTERS

AI Financial Report (16 issues a year), Sendico Corp., 1422 North 44th Street suite 208, Phoenix, Arizona 85008, USA.

AI Trends Newsletter (monthly), DM Data Inc, 6900 Comelback Road, suite 1000, Scotlstade, Arizona 85251, USA.

Applied Artificial Intelligence Report (monthly), ICS Research Institute, PO Box 1308-EP, Fort Lee, New Jersey 07024, USA.

Artificial Intelligence Abstracts (monthly), EIC/Intelligence, 48 West 38th, New York 10018, USA.

Artificial Intelligence Markets (monthly), AIM Publications Inc., PO Box 156, Natict, MA, D 1760, USA.

Artificial Intelligence and Super Computers (25 issues a year), Posha Publications, 1401 Wilson Boulevard, suite 910, Arlington, Virginia 22209, USA.

Expert Systems Strategies (monthly), Cahners Publishing Co, PO Box 59, New Town Branch, Boston, Massachussetts 02258, USA.

IMPAK (monthly), Impak, PO Box 59, New Town Branch, Boston, Massachussetts 02258, USA.

La lettre de l'Intelligence Artificielle (11 issues a year), 43 rue de la Victoire, 75009 Paris, France.

Lettre Intelligence Artificielle et Formation, CESTA, INRP, 1 rue Descartes, Paris, France.

Machine Intelligence News, Oyez IBC Ltd, 3rd Floor, Bath House, 56 Holborn Viaduct, London EC1A 2FX, UK.

The Spang Robinson Report (monthly), 3600 West Bayshore road, Palo Alto, California 94303, USA.

STUDIES

Arthur D. Little Inc., Acorn Park, Cambridge, Massachusetts 02140, USA. Brattle Research Corp.
• *Artificial intelligence computers and software – the technology and market trends*, 1984.

- *artificial intelligence and Fifth Generation computer technologies – the technology and commercial prospects.*

Business Communications Co. Inc., 9 Viaduct Road, Stamford, Connecticut 06906, USA.

- *Artificial intelligence, current and future commercialization,* 1985.

Cognitech

- *Les systèmes-experts – produits existants et besoins à venir,* 1985, étude effectuée pour le compte de la DAII.

DM Data, Inc., 69000 E. Camelback Road, suite 700, Scottsdale, Arizona 85251, USA.

- *The emerging artificial intelligence industry, 1983.*
- *AI Trends '84.*
- *AI Trends '85.*

FIND/SVP, 500 Fifth Avenue, New York, NY 10110, USA.

- *Artificial intelligence: a market assessment.*

Frost & Sullivan, Inc., 106 Fulton Street, New York, NY 10038, USA.

- *The expert systems market in Europe,* 1985.

IDC, 12 av. Georges V, 75008 Paris, France.

- *Artificial intelligence: techniques, tools and applications,* 1985.

IRD – International Resource Development Inc., 30 High Street, Norwalt, Connecticut 06851, USA.

- *Artificial intelligence,* Report no. 552, 1983.

LINK, 215 Park Avenue South, New York, NY 10003, USA.

- *Artificial intelligence: issues and opportunities for the information industry,* 1985.

Mackintosh International, Mackintosh Consultants France, 2 rue de Vienne, 75008 Paris, France.

- *The commercial potential of knowledge-based expert systems,* 1985.

OVUM, 44 Russell Square, London WCIB 45P, UK.

- Johnson, T.: *The commercial applications of expert systems technology,* 1984.
- Hewett, J. and Sasson, R.: *Expert systems 86,* 2 volumes. Vol. 1: *USA and Canada* (March, 1986). Vol. 2: *UK, France, GDR and Italy* (October 1986).

SLAI Technical Publications, PO Box 590, Madison, Georgia 30650, USA.

- Miller, R.K.: *Computers for artificial intelligence – a technology assessment and forecast,* (1986).
- Walker, T.C. and Miller R.K.: *Expert systems 86 – an assessment of technology and applications,* (1986).
- *Artificial intelligence: a new tool for industry and business* (see Technical Insights Inc.).
- *The 1984 inventory of expert systems* (1984).
- Miller, R.K.: *Artificial intelligence applications for manufacturing* (1984).
- *AI profiles.*

STRATEGIC Inc.; 10121 Miller Avenue, PO Box 21501, Cupertino, California 95015-2150, USA.

- *Expert systems and natural language: case studies, issues, market & supplies,* (1985).

Technical Insights Inc., PO Box 1304, Fort Lee, New Jersey 07024, USA.

- *Artificial intelligence – a new tool for industry and business,* (2nd ed, 1984), 2 vols.

CATALOGS

Bundy, A. (ed.): *Catalogue of artificial intelligence tools*, Berlin, Springer-Verlag (1984).

The international directory of artificial intelligence companies, 1984, Artificial Intelligence Software srl, Casella Postale 198, I-45100 Roviga, Italy.

Index